CAREER
CHANGE

CAREER CHANGE

EVERYTHING YOU NEED TO KNOW TO MEET NEW
CHALLENGES AND TAKE CONTROL OF YOUR CAREER

DR. DAVID P. HELFAND

Printed on recyclable paper

VGM Career Horizons
a division of *NTC Publishing Group*
Lincolnwood, Illinois USA

DEDICATION

To those of you undertaking a career change—may you be a success and find one that you'll enjoy.

Library of Congress Cataloging-in-Publication Data

Helfand, David P.
 Career change : everything you need to know to meet new challenges
and take control of your career / David P. Helfand.
  p. cm.
 Includes bibliographical references.
 ISBN 0-8442-4274-8
 1. Career changes. 2. Vocational guidance. I. Title.
HF5384.H44 1995
650.14—dc20   94-20724
                                                   CIP

Published by VGM Career Horizons, a division of NTC Publishing Group
4255 West Touhy Avenue
Lincolnwood (Chicago), Illinois 60646-1975, U.S.A.
© 1995 by David P. Helfand. All rights reserved.
No part of this book may be reproduced, stored in a retrieval system,
or transmitted in any form or by any means,
electronic, mechanical, photocopying, recording or otherwise,
without the prior permission of NTC Publishing Group.
Manufactured in the United States of America.

4 5 6 7 8 9 0 VP 9 8 7 6 5 4 3 2 1

CONTENTS

Part II

The Job Search: Strategies for Dealing with Challenges

Part III

Strategies for Groups with Special Challenges in the Workplace

ACKNOWLEDGMENTS

To my family and friends, thank you for your patience, understanding, and support throughout the years and especially during the period of writing this book.

To my colleagues at Northeastern Illinois University and throughout the career counseling field, thank you for sharing your knowledge, feedback, and insights during the course of this project.

To my clients, from whom I've learned much, thank you for the opportunity of working with you in your quest to finding a satisfying career.

Thanks to the staff at NTC Publishing Group: Sarah Kennedy, VGM Editor, for providing overall guidance to the development of this book through her sense of professionalism, talent, and skill; Amy Yu, Designer, for adding her creative touch to the final "look" of the book; and to Anne Knudsen, Executive Editor, for her overall support from the beginning to the end of this project. And thanks to Paula Dempsey, Copy Editor, for transforming my many pages of transcript into a finely tuned finished product.

And finally, thanks to the Committee on Organized Research at Northeastern Illinois University, whose grant helped to make this project possible.

PREFACE

If you are considering, have just decided to make, or are in the midst of a career change, this book is for you. It's designed to help you better understand the challenges of changing careers and offers strategies for dealing with them. Much of this book will also benefit job seekers within the same field.

You might be wondering how this book differs from other career-related publications. This book pulls together in one volume strategies for facing all of the major challenges of changing one's career.

This book includes the following features:

- A Work Values Satisfaction Self-Assessment to help you decide whether it's time to consider a career change

- An Entrepreneurial Personal Characteristics Self-Assessment to help you judge your potential success in starting a business

- Strategies for overcoming your fears of change, failure, and success, as well as perfectionism and procrastination

- Practical steps to help you increase your self-esteem and thus expand your opportunities

- An in-depth case study reviewing the assessment and testing process to help you identify relevant career options

- Guidance in interpreting your Strong Interest Inventory and Myers-Briggs Type Indicator if you're among the millions who have taken or will take them in the near future

- Ideas for dealing with the practical challenges of career change: the need for education, training, experience, time, and money

- Strategies for dealing with the competitive job market of the 1990s and beyond

- Suggestions for groups with special challenges in the workplace, including women, minorities, people over 40, people with disabilities, dual-career couples and single parents, ex-military personnel, and mid-level managers

- Steps to take if you're considering pursuing professional career counseling

In addition to discussing the major challenges of and strategies for the career change, we profile ten career changers. We will refer to their real-life experiences periodically throughout the book. We asked the ten career changers if they had any advice to pass along to potential career changers reading this book. Here's what they had to say:

- **Larry:** "Don't stop developing yourself; look for opportunities to grow; have a plan in place."

- **Victoria:** "Just go ahead and try it. If you don't find out, you are always going to wonder—should I have done that?"

- **Mac:** "You may not be able to control your age in *years,* but you can control your *attitude,* one of thinking and feeling younger. If so, you'll have the energy, know-how, and intelligence to make that change, just like anyone else. It's just one more life adjustment. You've made many previously."

- **Martha:** "Look forward; be determined; do your best."

- **Allen:** "Never let age be a factor. It's a figment of one's imagination. You could make it a benefit or a hindrance—it's up to you. You have a direction, a purpose, you know exactly what you want, and you're mature."

- **Patricia:** "Go for it—believe that everything will be okay (with careful planning, of course). You're expanding, moving, going on to new things."

- **Ed:** "Don't give up on your dream—Life is too short. If you're confident and feel good about yourself, give it a try. Give it your best shot."

- **Zephree:** "Pursue your goals; don't be afraid; be true to yourself."

- **Vincent:** "There's a lot of pressure that comes with a career change. Having self-confidence and doing your research is important, so consult with others who are already doing what your intended career goal encompasses. Develop a well-thought-out plan (the entire change process may take a year, or more, to complete) and welcome the support of family and friends."

- **Sandra:** "Don't underestimate the positive influences that changing to a satisfying career can have on the overall quality of your life."

Remember that what all these people had in common was not being afraid of facing the possibility of failing. They felt secure enough with themselves to allow themselves to take the risk. In their minds, if they did fail, they would just pick themselves up and try again. We hope you'll find the information in this book to be practical and helpful in your quest for a satisfying career.

MEET OUR TEN CAREER CHANGES

W e experience change all our lives, yet we deal with it with varying degrees of success. Whether we're changing careers, getting a divorce, remarrying, mourning the death of a loved one, buying a home, getting that long-awaited promotion, moving to another city, watching our children leave home, being assigned to a new supervisor, returning to school to earn a degree, or experiencing any of the other possible life transitions, our ability to deal with change will have a profound impact on the course of our lives. Some of us will adjust well and others will find changes traumatic.

To set the stage for understanding the career change process, we will suggest a framework within which to view transitions in general and career transitions specifically. Researchers of adult transitions have shown that our life follows a sequence of stages. As our life cycles progress, we move through developmental and transitional periods, and each presents tasks to be mastered and problems to be solved. These developmental tasks pose a challenge that must be met and overcome if we are to move ahead to the next period of development and cope successfully with its demands.

Now let's meet the ten career changers whose real-life experiences will be used throughout the book to illustrate key concepts. They show the wide range of career change situations and strategies for tackling them. Perhaps one of them has a similar background to your own.

Larry

Larry, a 42-year-old Caucasian, had spent 20 years working as an environmental technician, in a variety of related positions that involved monitoring and overseeing heating, ventilation, and air conditioning equipment. At age 37, Larry became a senior training specialist for a major manufacturer of heating and cooling building controls. Thus, Larry went from a blue-collar to a white-collar job.

Larry's interest in the training field began as a result of his enrollment in a university career planning course. He saw it as an excellent way to take his mechanical skills and move them into a more people-oriented position with greater salary potential.

Larry's B.A., with an emphasis in training, was part of a nontraditional academic program in which he designed his own major. Larry and his wife have two sons and a daughter (ages 4, 8, and 6 at the time of Larry's career change).

Victoria

Victoria, a 44-year-old Caucasian, had earned a B.A. in sociology with a minor in journalism. During high school, Victoria was the editor of the student newspaper. She combined these two areas of interest by working as a diagnostic social worker for 15 years, which involved significant report writing.

After experiencing a layoff, Victoria returned to school for a certificate program in technical writing. She was spurred on by a TV commercial. Four years ago she became a technical editor for an auto parts franchise corporation.

Thus, Victoria's career change represented moving from the nonprofit area to a for-profit corporation. She believes that about 20 percent of corporations have a positive work environment.

Mac

Mac, a 59-year-old African-American, earned a B.A. in sociology and then worked for 10 years in the recreation departments of two major midwestern cities. He had earned two master's degrees, in counseling and educational administration and supervision, by the age of 34. Mac completed his Ph.D. in educational administration at the age of 36.

While completing his Ph.D., Mac began working in the field of market research, specifically related to the consumer needs of African-Americans. After working for someone else for about two years, Mac set out on his own to develop a market research business, which he owned and ran for 18 years.

Last year, because business was slow and Mac had some health problems, he decided to become a high school guidance counselor, something he had trained for some 25 years earlier. Mac and his wife have two grown children.

Martha

Martha was born in Cuba and came to the United States at the age of 10. She stayed with foster parents until her real parents followed four years later. At the age of 28, after seven years of teaching elementary school, Martha and her husband became the owners of a liquor store.

Soon thereafter, they added groceries and a small restaurant. Their business eventually became one of the most popular Hispanic restaurants and lounges in a major U.S. city. In addition, this year they opened a second restaurant, specializing in Mexican food.

Martha has a B.A. in foreign language secondary education, with a minor in psychology. She and her husband have a 17-year-old daughter and a 15-year-old son.

Allen

After earning a business degree with a minor in education, Allen, a 45-year-old African-American, taught elementary and secondary school for two years. He then switched back to a job more related to his business degree and became a budget analyst at a university for seven years.

At age 30, Allen returned to school for training to become a dentist, something he had been thinking about since he was 25. It turned out that his own family dentist from his childhood had had a big influence on him.

After four years of dental school, Allen became a dentist at the age of 34. He joined two established dentists in their practice. Four years later, at the age of 38, Allen opened his own dental practice. Allen and his wife have a 3-year-old child.

Patricia

With master's degrees in both music history and library science, Patricia, a 45-year-old Caucasian, spent eight years as a music librarian in the libraries of two major cities, as well as at a prestigious university. At the age of 35, she became a law librarian, which sparked an interest in becoming a lawyer.

With one year left in law school, Patricia gained a summer clerkship position pertaining to copyrights, trademarks, and patents for music and art professionals. Upon completing law school at age 40, she accepted a law firm position with a similar emphasis in the creative arts. Five years later, at the age of 45, Patricia set out on her own, opening a practice with a specialty in serving professionals in the creative arts.

Patricia is currently single, with no dependents, after being married twice.

Ed

Ed was born in Puerto Rico and came to the United States at the age of 5. Since the age of 12, Ed had wanted to become a police officer. This was influenced by his friendship with the police officer stationed at his school, whom he admired.

Ed earned his B.A. in criminal justice (with minors in sociology and foreign language). He also became involved in local politics as a college student. After experiencing some discrimination with regard to becoming a police officer, Ed took a job as a criminal law clerk at the age of 20 and began law school via a special program for minority students.

At the age of 26, Ed passed the police examination. After just two months in police training, Ed learned that he had finally passed the bar exam. Ed worked for five years as a police officer. Because of further discrimination and department politics, he decided, at age 31, to focus on a career in law with his own practice. Ed and his wife have no children.

Zephree

Zephree, a 42-year-old African-American, had an interest in law enforcement that dated back to high school. However, she was uncomfortable dealing with death and thus began to focus more on a career as a juvenile probation officer. During the past 13 years she has used her secretarial skills to gain employment in hospital and university settings, as well as a secretary position in a county pre-adult probation program. This allowed her to test out her career interest in probation work, and it confirmed her interest.

When she applied for yet another secretarial position, this time at a social service agency, Zephree was told she was overqualified. She was then offered the position of research assistant instead, working on a project investigating child abuse, so at age 39 she changed careers.

Zephree is also working toward finishing her B.A., via a credit-for-life-experience program, with an emphasis in criminal justice, continuing toward her goal of becoming a juvenile probation officer. She has one son from a previous marriage and has since remarried.

Vincent

Vincent, a 44-year-old Caucasian, changed careers at 39. After nine years in investment banking (a victim of a reorganization), he opened his own bookstore specializing in history and mystery.

Vincent has a B.A. in political science (with a minor in history) and an M.A. in history, as well as an MBA in finance. History was a favorite subject dating back to Vincent's childhood, and he became interested in mystery during his undergraduate college years. He appreciated being able to combine these two favorite interests into a specialty bookstore, as well as the chance to use the skills he acquired through his MBA program. Vincent is married and has a 9-year-old son.

Sandra

Sandra, a 34-year-old Asian-American, became a lawyer after earning a B.A. in political science and history and a law degree from a prestigious private university. Her interest in law began in high school, where she was active in student organizations.

After eight years as a practicing attorney, Sandra felt dissatisfied and became a writer/publisher of multicultural books for children. This career choice was much more in line with what Sandra saw as her mission, or purpose. Having attained what her friends and family members would consider a position of great status for a female Asian-American, Sandra felt some pressure not to follow through with her career change, which made letting go even more difficult. Sandra is married with no children.

Part I

Self-Assessment: The Basis of a Successful Career Change

CHAPTER 1

ADULT DEVELOPMENT AND HOW IT AFFECTS YOUR LIFE CHANGES

This chapter discusses three ways of viewing life transitions: age related, life stage related, and life events/transitions related. This will give us a context from which to view adult life transitions, including changing careers, and a better understanding of the role they play in our overall personal development. We'll also look at a definition of career change and a description of the various reasons why one might undertake a change of careers. This theoretical background will prepare us for the all-important groundwork of self-assessment.

Age-Focused Approaches

Studies of Men

In 1978, Dan Levinson set out to create a developmental perspective of adulthood in men, presenting the male life course as consisting of alternating stable and transition periods. With its career emphasis, much of Levinson's work also applies to women in the 1990s.

Levinson identified developmental periods occurring at approximately the same ages for the men he studied. Of course, individuals' ages vary for the onset and ending of these stable and transition periods, but no more than 5–6 years from the age span indicated. The pattern of developmental periods Levinson identified is shown in Figure 1.1

FIGURE 1.1

•••

Levinson's Research on Men's Life Patterns

Early Adult Transition (17–22):   Moving from pre- to early
                                   adulthood.

Entering the Adult World (22–28): First adult life structure.

Age 30 Transition (28–33):   Changing the first life structure.

Settling Down (33–40):   Second adult life structure.

Mid-Life Transition (40–45):   Moving from early to middle
                                   adulthood.

Entering Middle Adulthood (45–50): Building a new life structure.

According to Levinson, a central component in individuals' lives is their work. Through our work we are plugged into an occupational structure that will exert a heavy influence on the cultural, class, and social aspects of our lives. Occupation is the primary factor in determining income, prestige, and place in society. It places us in a particular socioeconomic level and strongly influences the options available to us, the choices we make, and our possibilities for advancement and satisfaction. Occupation becomes the medium for fulfilling our dreams and achieving our goals—or possibly the opposite, which can lead toward a growing alienation from self, work, and society.

Studies of Women

With a variety of possible combinations of how to pursue education, career, and family, women in the 1990s face many choices. In fact, because of the many alternative ways to approach these major life issues, women may experience more confusion and stress at these points in their lives than do men. Gail Sheehy described patterns in the lives of women (see Figure 1.2).

Age 30 Transition

For both men and women, the Age 30 Transition is a period of self-evaluation and assessment of career and marriage. It's an opportunity to work on flaws and create the basis for a better future. Men and women view this stage in their lives as one of growth and expansion. However, it's not necessarily a smooth transition. Both men and women experience difficulty at this time if things have not progressed as planned and hoped for.

FIGURE 1.2

Sheehy's Research on Women's Life Patterns

Caregiver: Marries during early 20s, no intention of going beyond domestic role.

Either/Or: Feels, in 20s, required to choose between love and children or work and accomplishment and thus can be one of two types:

- **Nurturer who Defers Achievement:** Postpones career efforts to marry and start a family; will pursue a career later.

- **Achiever who Defers Nurturing:** Postpones motherhood and often marriage, spends 6–7 years in career.

Integrator: Combines marriage, career, and motherhood.

Never Married: Pursues work on a permanent, full-time basis.

Transient: Wanders sexually, occupationally, and geographically.

Sheehy points out that some people experience an inside stirring during the Age 30 Transition, seeking greater independence. Yet those who choose not to marry or not to have children might have second thoughts at this time. Possibilities at the Age 30 Transition follow:

- Has already entered career, still single; wants change (career or getting married)

- Has already entered career, married, no children; wants children or career change

- Married, has children in school; wants to enter or reenter career

For some, the Age 30 Transition represents a time to move toward new choices or recommit to existing ones. People may question themselves about how well they're meeting goals and whether they're progressing toward their dream. If things are going well with job, family, and friends, then the transition will most likely be smooth. However, for most it is stressful. Self-evaluation can be painful if things haven't gone according to plan. Possible life adjustments during this period could be career related (getting/not getting a promotion, losing a job, or making a career change), family related (birth of children, children starting school, divorce, or caring for aging parents), or friends related (job change, move to another city, or just growing apart). Issues at the Age 30 Transition are summarized by the following questions:

- What have I done with my life so far in my career and with my family and friends?

- Have I progressed toward my dream (hopes and wishes in life)?

- How do I feel about it?

- What new directions might I choose?

Mid-Life Transition

During the period between the Age 30 and Mid-Life Transitions (Settling Down, 33–40), what becomes central for many men is the symbol of the "ladder," which represents advancement. This is hoped to lead to desired affirmation, independence, or seniority. However, the reality of today's job market reveals that many positions the "ladder" once led to are gone. In fact, some are worried about still having a job, much less climbing the corporate ladder. Therefore, desired goals may not be obtainable, and thus people experience frustration and dissatisfaction with their career situation.

In addition, with the onset of the Mid-Life Transition (40–45) comes another self-evaluation process. Some of the questions people might ask themselves include the following:

- What have I done with my life?

- How are my significant relationships (spouse/partner, children, friends) going? What am I getting from and what am I giving to these relationships?

- How is my career going?

- What is my role in the community?

- What do I really want for myself and those close to me?

At this point in life, men want to be able to express their true desires, interests, values, skills, and goals. However, the degree of success in the prior period could predict how well this transition goes. For some, this period is one of moderate to severe crisis. The focus shifts to the future. The Mid-Life Transition is a bridge between early adulthood and middle adulthood. (See Figure 1.3.)

FIGURE 1.3
....

Issues and Needs for Men at Mid-Life Transition

- Experience a time shift, realizing their own mortality
- Reassess the dream (recognizing that some aspects are illusory), marriage, and relations with others
- Choose to change jobs for greater challenge and satisfaction or decide to emphasize other areas of their lives to a greater extent, such as family or leisure
- Feel a need to give something back to society, to make some type of contribution, to help others in some way
- Desire to express more emotion

Possible external changes at this time include getting divorced, remarrying, sending children away to college, changing job/career, changing functioning level, losing or supporting a parent, and increasing social mobility. Internally, it is common to feel a shift in values, a desire to give something back to society, and a need to express more emotion.

Some men encounter obstacles to pursuing the goal of having a stronger sense of who they are and what they want. Anxiety, guilt, dependence, and animosities from earlier years keep them from examining the real issues at mid-life. This can result in emotional turmoil, despair, and a feeling of not knowing where to turn.

Sheehy viewed the mid-life passage for women as a crossroads, with many opportunities presenting themselves. Her research revealed women arriving at this point earlier, at about 35, than what men experienced (40–45) as reported by Levinson. During the early 1970s, when Sheehy's research took place, age 35 represented the average age that a mother sent her last child off to school, a divorced woman remarried, biological limitations come into sight, and a married woman reentered the work force. Even though 35 represents the age that many married women reentered the work force, very few homemakers were prepared to do so at the time Sheehy completed her research. However, even today, many women considering reentering the work force are confused about which path to take and how their family will fare as a result.

In addition, reentry after a long absence often presents an additional problem. The field that a woman originally entered (if she is still interested) might have advanced to the point where she now needs additional education to catch up and be competitive for jobs. If a career change is desired, further education or experience might be necessary as well.

Along with the increased possibilities for women at mid-life (see Figure 1.4) comes a feeling of last-chance urgency, similar to that of men at mid-life. The choices made at this time will depend, largely, on what path was followed earlier. Though initially hesitant, many women at their mid-life passage gather the necessary courage, perhaps with the help of personal or career counseling, and respond in an energized way.

FIGURE 1.4
••

Possibilities for Women at Mid-Life Transition

- The **Caregiver** could resume education or take a job.
- The **Deferred Achiever** could enter a career.
- The **Deferred Nurturer** could have children.
- The **Integrator** could decide to own a business.

"The Switch": Age 40

Sheehy asserts that at around the age of 40, the changes identified in Figure 1.5 occur. This can result in an interesting situation, sometimes causing a crisis for married couples.

As the wife expands into new pursuits, the husband often feels less needed. As a result, the wife sometimes feels guilty. The fact remains, however, that today more than ever, the wife needs to return to work out of financial necessity. So even if this is somewhat threatening for the husband, overall he's probably glad to see it happening.

If the couple is going to survive this difficult period intact, they'll need to renegotiate their relationship, readjust over a period of several years, and eventually reach a point where the relationship can continue in a healthy manner.

FIGURE 1.5

"The Switch": Age 40

Women	Men
• Increasing strength of opinion	• Increasing emotional vulnerability
• Increasing assertiveness	• Increasing emotional response
• Increasing independence, setting out to pursue education, career, or community involvement	• Reacting with envy to wife's new pursuits, which occur at an awkward time in his personal development

---

Life-Stage Focused Approaches

Life Stages and Related Developmental Tasks

Some theorists state that adults pass through developmentally sequenced stages, as illustrated in Figure 1.6. Erik Erikson studied the progression in ego (self) development. Each stage consists of a developmental problem/task. The resolution of that primary task determines future personal development, good or bad. Some of us move through these stages faster than others, and some become stuck at certain points and never move forward.

Let's look at an example. At mid-life, the central developmental task is a choice between generativity and stagnation. If you are dealing effectively with this task, you are able to shift focus from your own interests and concerns to the development and achievement of others, especially the next generation.

You may have chosen to be a mentor to a younger employee on the job, gaining satisfaction from helping someone by sharing your career knowledge and experience. As a healthy individual, at this stage you would accept responsibility for the generation to come. Those who do not often find life to be missing something.

FIGURE 1.6

Additional Research on Transitions

Erikson's Adult Stages		Gilligan's Central Issues for Women
Identity:	Who am I?	
		Attachment
Intimacy:	Can I be committed and close to others?	
		Caring
Generativity:	Can I nurture others?	
		Interdependency
Ego Integrity:	Am I satisfied with my life?	
Critical issue: Resolving each stage's primary developmental tasks		**Critical issue:** Renegotiating interdependency in important relationships

---

Stage Theory and Women

Erikson's research on life stages was based on men. Some stages might be applicable to women, but Carol Gilligan believed that the stage theory over-emphasized education, occupation, and achievement as one progressed through the various stages. She found that women have different central issues: attachment, caring, and interdependency. Her approach stated that renegotiating interdependence in important relationships is a critical issue for women's adult development. These relationships include a woman and her husband (partner, significant other), children, or friends, and the process is continuous. A woman at the Age 30 or Mid-Life Transition often experiences increasing aspirations for personal achievement and accomplishment and seeks greater independence and autonomy.

You may be feeling a need to renegotiate your interdependence in your important relationships. You may be desiring to reduce dependence on your husband, or significant other, as you shift away from a role that centered on providing nurturance and support. However, if married, this can be complicated by the fact that your husband, if also at mid-life, could be seeking greater intimacy and increased emotional contact. It's important that couples communicate effectively so that as they pass through these different stages they understand what the other is experiencing and can adjust their relationship appropriately.

Current Trends and an Additional Perspective

The age- and life-stage focused approaches to adult development are important for helping us to better understand our own personal development and the forces operating in our lives. Perhaps they became popular because we like predictability and may feel a need, at times, for a definition of "normality" to make sure we're within the range.

Yet it is also important to consider current trends, which make it difficult to plug people into particular stages. These trends include the following:

- More men and women are delaying marriage while pursuing further education and careers.

- When people do marry (delayed or not), they more frequently choose to delay having children or to not have children.

- The high divorce rate leaves many women as single parents who need to enter or reenter the work force, resulting in an increase of women working full time, perhaps when they didn't expect to.

- Because of different circumstances (such as losing jobs and getting divorced), many adults are returning to college to begin, complete, or extend their education.

To further emphasize how life events in today's society are difficult to tie to chronological ages and life stages, Nancy Schlossberg points out that one could be a grandparent at 40 or 80, newly divorced at 20 or 60, and a first-time parent at 20 or 40.

Rather than looking at someone as being 45 years old, it's more important to note that this person has college-age children, is recently divorced, and needs to find full-time work. The actual life experience, or event, is more significant than the person's age. We need to view life flexibly to incorporate this variety of individual experiences. The life event– or transition-focused approach attempts to accomplish this goal.

Life Event– or Transition-Focused Approaches

What Constitutes a Life Transition?

Changes in your roles, relationships, routines, and assumptions about yourself or the world constitute a major life transition. Descriptions of these aspects of significant life events/transitions, as defined by Schlossberg, follow:

Change in role: New set of responsibilities (job promotion, career change, new baby, etc.)

Change in relationship: Getting a new job means new co-workers; being a new parent puts one in contact with new people.

Change of routine: A new job requires some overtime, which affects one's routine; a new baby alters one's sleeping hours.

Assumptions about one's self or the world: Changed career; took on challenge and succeeded; recognized one's own strengths

A major transition involves all four changes identified here. One of less magnitude could involve one or two of these changes.

Similar transitions can affect people differently. How you handle your transition will depend on your self-esteem, confidence, attitude/outlook, coping ability, preparedness, and the degree of your ability to deal with change. For example, retirement is a major trauma for someone who is unprepared for and not good with change, but it is a minor adjustment for someone who is better prepared and more adept at dealing with change.

Most important, however, is to recognize that whether a transition is major or minor, it will still take time for a person to adjust. Major transitions for some people can take anywhere from six months to one year, and even up to two years, before passing through and moving on with one's life. A good example is divorce. For some, depending on the circumstances and the individuals involved, no more than six months might be required. For others, this is a major trauma requiring a few years to adjust to it. Yet even a positive, less disruptive transition (e.g., a promotion) requires a period of adjustment as well.

Phases of Life Transitions

No matter what transition you experience, William Bridges states that each begins with an ending. We have to let go of the old before beginning the new, no matter what the nature of the transition is. The second phase of a transition is the neutral zone. This is described as a time of confusion and emptiness, a period of needing to be alone, a time of inner reorientation, leading to greater self-understanding, renewal, confidence, and courage to move forward to the third phase: a new beginning. The new beginning involves adjusting to the change that has just occurred in one's life and thus successfully passing on and through the transition.

Types of Life Transitions

Researchers on the subject of transitions agree that events that change our lives come in a variety of shapes, sizes, and combinations. There are three basic types: elected, unelected, and nonevents. **Elected transitions** are transitions we expect and are up to us, that we have time to think and plan for. These could include graduating college, moving away from home, the first "real" job, getting married, having children, some career changes, and retiring.

Unelected transitions are unexpected and therefore test our coping skills. Examples could include a spouse of 30 years leaving, losing a job after a long tenure, or the unexpected death of a child. These terrible events shock us, leave us numb, and challenge our ability to adjust.

However, not all unelected transitions are negative. We can still be surprised by positive transitions, such as an unexpected job promotion or a surprise proposal of marriage. These transitions can also require adjustment of our roles, relationships, routines, and assumptions about ourselves or the world.

Nonevents, the third type of transition, are changes we thought would occur but do not, such as unsuccessful attempts to have children, a love relationship not developing as expected, or not getting a much-desired job promotion. Even though these do not occur, our expectation that they would leave us in a potentially difficult position, possibly just as difficult as an unelected transition. We did not elect for the change to not occur.

Coping with Endings

It's very difficult for many of us to move on, to let go of aspects of our past. Bridges suggests that we can accept transitions better by recognizing that letting go can be at best confusing; trying to understand the phases related to transitions; and developing skills to better negotiate our way through these phases. To accomplish this, we need to understand how one copes with endings. When breaking our connections with the familiar and approaching the unfamiliar, fear is a common response. Four key aspects of the ending experience are described in Figure 1.7, with related suggestions, using the example of losing one's job.

FIGURE 1.7

Phases of the Ending Experience: Suggestions for Coping

1. **Disengagement:** To break away from the context (activity/job, relationship/co-workers, setting/workplace, or role/job title) in which we have known ourselves.

   Suggestion: The process of change can begin when one recognizes and accepts that this change must be made, either by your choice (career change) or not by your choice (being fired). Therefore, move toward what you fear, rather than away from it. If you need help in doing so, get it.

2. **Disidentification:** By breaking old connections (with the job itself or with co-workers), we lose self-definition or a role that determined our behavior and made us more identifiable. The impact here is usually greater than we expect.

   Suggestion: At this time, it becomes important to attempt to be more open and flexible in how we think of ourselves so that we can move on through a transition toward a new self-identification.

3. **Disenchantment:** Once separated from the old situation, we seem to be floating between two worlds (former job and next job). We learn that the world is no longer the way we believed it to be.

   Disenchantment related to one's career occurs when an organization or individual betrays your trust, the perfect job turns out not to be so perfect, or when we lose a job and recognize our false sense of security.

   Suggestion: To really change you need to ascertain whether an important part of your old reality was only imagined (e.g., the "noble" boss or the "perfect" job). Recognize the disenchantment

   "continued"

---

as a minor or major signal of your need to look below the surface of what was thought to be true in order to bring your perception and reality together.

4. **Disorientation:** As a result of leaving the old reality (former job) behind, your sense of orientation is gone, resulting in the following:

    - Feelings of being lost, confused, and not quite knowing where you are
    - Feeling that life is breaking down and no longer going anywhere
    - Plans for the future being disrupted

    The disorientation aspect of the ending is meaningful but not enjoyable.

    Suggestion: The confusion and disruption are inevitable. Perhaps recognizing its part in the process can help you cope better as you enter the neutral zone, or "time out" period. This will lead to adjustment to the transition, with increased self-understanding, on your way to a new beginning.

For example, a person who gets fired needs to pass through disengagement, disidentification, disenchantment, and disorientation in order to complete the ending phase of the transition. The problem is not necessarily that the person does not want to give up the job or can't let go of that piece of his or her identity. The real problem is that before people can identify a new something, they need to deal with a period of nothing.

People in the midst of a transition seem to find a way to be alone and away from the many familiar distractions. Some people lack the initiative to find another job, because they don't want to take the chance of getting fired again. Bridges suggests that the neutral zone provides a way of viewing life that isn't always available otherwise.

For fired workers, this could be a good time to try to identify what they really want in terms of life goals in general and career goals specifically. They can view this as an opportunity to begin a new chapter in life. (Here's where self-esteem and a positive attitude pay off.) Perhaps they will even get a chance to regain old dreams, ideas, and interests.

The empty time (neutral zone) is important because we simply can't always leave one thing and go right into another. We need to take time out and give some thought to what we want for ourselves and the important people in our lives. As new ideas for the future emerge during the neutral zone phase, people begin to enter the third and final phase of the transition: making a new beginning. This phase involves an inner realignment and renewal of energy.

This inner realignment is more important than only an external shift (e.g., obtaining a new job). If the new beginning is consistent with a person's purpose and mission in life, it will help him or her overcome many obstacles. The shift may not be easy. For example, a change to a more desirable area of work might involve a cut in salary. This could affect one's affluence, requiring adjustments in life-style.

Adult Development Influences on Career Transition

Now that we have discussed adult transitions in general, it is worthwhile to discuss career transitions more specifically. Most principles presented for transitions in general are also applicable to career transitions. By understanding the different types of career transitions, you will be able to form a framework from which to create a plan for mastering career change and profiting from it.

The Twenties

Levinson's age-focused approach states that people in their twenties are busy making and testing tentative career choices. However, they're feeling pressure from two opposing needs: to experiment and explore and to begin settling down. This could be considered the entry stage of one's career. We make a first commitment to a job and become involved in developing the skills and the personal meaning that make up our career identity.

The Thirties

The thirties are a time for evaluating the validity of the choices we've made, including our career choices. This questioning of past decisions might reveal that we have actually ignored important needs, interests, and desires. At this time some people decide to make changes and new commitments, in their careers as well as in other areas of life.

If our experiences are similar to those of the men Levinson studied, then we will probably place more value on the quality of our lives at this time. What's becoming important is leading a more balanced life, becoming more family oriented, and developing our relationships. All or some of these goals might take priority over our careers.

Toward the end of the thirties, job satisfaction starts to become more important than climbing the corporate ladder or earning a higher salary. Feeling self-fulfilled, deriving challenge and independence from a career, and using valued skills become most important. This shift in values often leads to a career change if the job presents too great an obstacle to attaining new levels of job satisfaction. Even if we take no action during our thirties, there is often an imperceptible shift in the way we feel about our lives that could, very likely, lead to later changes.

The Forties

The forties is a period when career change becomes even more likely. Some experts believe that mid-life career change (particularly voluntary change) cannot be separated from the developmental issues of mid-life. Career change can be a strategy for coping with developmental issues that is either growth oriented or a step backward. If it offers us an opportunity to integrate more of our total personality into our life-style, then it stimulates growth and even helps us to better manage other mid-life developmental tasks. Yet other career changes represent a retreat, in the sense that we may not be true to ourselves in finding what we would identify as meaningful work involving our strongest interests, skills, values, and personality preferences.

Mid-life career change involves an attempt to find a better fit between our mid-life self-identity and a work environment that provides an opportunity to integrate our dreams and goals. Around the age of 40, people must deal with the disparity between what we are and what we dreamed of becoming. If our dreams have not been realized, then it could be a time to begin to come to terms with failure (including the accompanying feelings of loss and grief) and to decide on a new group of choices from which to rebuild our lives. For those who have experienced success in attaining their dreams and goals, mid-life becomes a time to consider the meaning and value of success and generally to sort things out in life.

Career Changing Is Not Just a Mid-Life Situation

Of the three approaches to describing adult development and related career transitions, perhaps the events-focused approach applies to most of us. Further support for viewing adult career changing from an events-focused approach comes from Richard Bolles, who analyzed a 1986 survey of 10 million job/career changers. He found that only 1 of 10 were at mid-life. This strongly suggests that career changing is not just a mid-life situation. When it becomes necessary, it must be dealt with, regardless of one's age or related life stage.

Career Change Defined

Sometimes the terms *career, occupation,* and *job* are used interchangeably, which can be confusing. In *Taking Charge of Your Career Direction,* Robert Lock clarifies these terms as follows:

Career	One's entire work history
Occupation	One's vocation, business, profession, or trade
Job	A position of employment within an organization (One can have a succession of jobs in the same occupation.)

The term *career* covers a working life that might include one occupation or several occupations in which one job or several jobs were held.

Therefore, in keeping with these definitions, this book should be titled *Occupation Change.* However, in common usage, the terms *career* and *occupation* are equivalent. Perhaps *career* is a more modern reference than is *occupation.* Therefore, most people who change occupations think of it as being a "career change."

Paula Robbins claimed that a true career change involves **a marked shift in jobs requiring new (primary) skills or knowledge or a totally different work environment, or both.** Therefore, one could experience a job change that is not a career change (consisting of similar skills and work environment) or a job change that can be classified as a career change (involving change in skills/knowledge applied or environment, or both). Thus, the term job change alone can be confusing. In one situation it could be a job change, and in another it could be a career change as well. (Not to mention that some might use the term *occupation.*)

Because career change can occur in varying degrees, how and if one gets classified as such should depend more on the purpose of the endeavor. The major focus of this book is to help readers learn about overcoming the challenges of changing careers. Therefore, I will adopt Robbins's career change definition.

Reasons for Job or Career Change

Reasons for career changes/transitions can be classified as being internal (motivation to change comes from within one's self and we have some degree of control over the situation) or external (the change has primarily to do with trends in society and other factors outside of ourselves, and we have little control).

Internal Reasons

These types of career transition reasons are related to developmental issues in one's life. As a result of dealing with these issues, one decides on new goals, desires to satisfy higher-level needs, or seeks new purposes and aspirations. A shift in personal values is often related to wanting more time with family, seeking activities involving different interests or skills, experiencing a changed financial situation, or deciding to no longer put up with excessive stress.

Other reasons for a career change are more directly tied to the work environment itself.

Following are seven areas of potential job satisfaction or dissatisfaction, with examples of job/career involvement:

1. **Company/organization:** Is the company highly regarded in its field? Is it growing? Are its policies satisfactory overall?

2. **Work environment:** Is it a safe, pleasant work setting? Are the hours, dress code, distance to work, and co-workers satisfactory?

3. **Supervisor relations:** Are you treated fairly, given deserved recognition and some degree of freedom? Are supervisors open to your suggestions?

4. **The job itself:** Is the work enjoyable, interesting? Are you using your preferred skills? Do you find your work to be challenging? Do you have an opportunity to be creative?

5. **Rewards/benefits:** Are you receiving an appropriate salary and related benefits (e.g., health insurance, vacation time)? Do you have a reasonable amount of job security?

6. **Professional growth opportunities:** Is there potential to increase your autonomy, possibilities for a leadership role, chance for advancement (in position and/or salary), or an opportunity to be more creative in your work?

7. **Personal development:** Do you identify with a sense of purpose in your work? Are you fulfilling, to some degree, your mission in life?

If you are currently dissatisfied with your career and contemplating change, one or more of these categories could be the source of dissatisfaction.

External Reasons

We have little or no control over external reasons for career change. External reasons can be categorized into four areas: societal trends, economic conditions, demographics, and technology. Any of these could have a negative impact on your current job, thus leading to the need for change. They are important factors to consider when seeking your next job or change in career.

Some current trends that impact the job market are listed here. As you read the list, consider which trends have impacted your career, and how.

1. **Societal trends:**

   The women's movement and growth of women's representation in the work force

   Hiring of older workers and changing retirement policies

   Emphasis on environmental awareness and action

   Health and fitness consciousness

   Use of leisure time (increased travel, cultural events, and related entertainment)

   Young adults staying single longer

   Those who do marry waiting longer to have children

2. **Economic conditions:**

   Growth of a global economy

   Government spending cutbacks

   Corporate restructuring

   Increased opportunities for small business

3. **Demographics:**

   Increased representation of minorities in the workplace

   Aging of the population

   Baby boomers having to care for both young children and older parents as they themselves are at mid-life

   Increased divorce rate

4. **Technology**

Rapid advancement in high-tech machinery and computers

Many of us are well aware of the tremendous negative impact that internal and external reasons, especially economic trends and technological advancements, can have on our job/career changing. Most of us have been touched in one way or another by these forces of change, and they have spurred some of us to pursue a job/career change.

If you have any doubt about the number of dissatisfied workers, consider the statistics that Bolles reports from a 1991 survey. They indicate that 39 million U.S. workers (one-third of the total) thought seriously about changing their jobs during the previous year. Sixteen million (14 percent of the total) actually did change jobs over a two-year period. That leaves 23 million workers who are probably still considering a job/career change. When you add the estimated 9–17 million unemployed people who are seriously looking for work, you have well over 30 million workers who are job seekers or career changers. The goal of this book is to help career changers overcome the challenges that face them, whether they want to change their job/career or have been forced to change.

Types of Job or Career Changes

Whether our career change is our choice (voluntary) or not our choice (involuntary), it can also be anticipated or unanticipated. When we know it's coming (anticipated) we have time to think about it and plan for it. However, when we're unaware that it's coming (unanticipated), it can leave us shocked, feeling helpless, and having far less time to think it over or plan. Figure 1.8 depicts the intersection of four possible types of job/career changes within the framework of Voluntary/Involuntary and Anticipated/Unanticipated.

The goal would be to move the situations in boxes 2, 3, and 4 toward the more favorable situation in box 1, the Voluntary/Anticipated box, where you have the most control over your job/career situation. This would mean that in order to be prepared for outcomes like plant closings, mergers, and large layoffs, you need to stay abreast of general conditions in society mentioned earlier and their relationship to your particular industry. These would include societal trends, economic conditions, demographics, and technology. In addition, you need to stay on top of the situation at your specific organization. What is its financial condition? Is it focused on keeping pace with the latest advancements in the field? Do you or other experts in the field see it as being susceptible to reorganization, merger, or buyout?

FIGURE 1.8

Types of Job or Career Changes

	Voluntary	Involuntary
Anticipated	Offered expected promotion (accepted)	Plant Closing (laid off)
Unanticipated	Change in management; offered voluntary separation (accepted)	Merger; middle managers fired (lose job)

Your research in these areas could generate information that would allow you to at least move the decision from Unanticipated to Anticipated, even if it's still Involuntary. You could then be in a position to better prepare and to consider changing sooner rather than later, when, most likely, there would be greater stress and pressure to be dealt with. In closing, when a career change is up to you (voluntary) it tends to not be too stressful, though it wouldn't be unusual to seek some counseling for help in understanding and managing fear.

CHAPTER 2

Not Your Choice: Layoffs, Firings, Voluntary Separations, and Related Dilemmas

Three major possible ways of losing your job include being laid off, fired, or requested to take voluntary separation. It's helpful for you to learn to recognize the warning signs of being laid off or fired, so you will be in a position to take action, if you decide to, before others do it for you (or to you). You will then need to be prepared to cope with the emotional turmoil of losing your job, if that becomes a reality. This involves taking care of yourself (coping with the emotions of job loss, diet, exercise, creating a routine, and self-esteem). In addition, this chapter identifies beginning steps you can take related to losing your job, searching for a new job, and financial concerns.

Warning Signs of Layoffs

There are numerous warning signs that can help clue you in to a possible layoff. Kathleen Riehle identifies the following:

- Economic conditions worsen; news of falling revenues or rising losses for your division, company, or industry

- Mergers produce redundant positions in the new, merged company

- Best employees leave with concern over financial trouble

- Long closed-door meetings; department manager or director called into a series of meetings

- Managed attrition, retaining current personnel for other tasks, or requests for new positions cancelled

- Pay cuts or revisions of vacation policy (either cancelling, deferring or giving short-term vacation without pay)

- Widespread early retirement, especially those with the highest salaries; layoffs may still follow

- A large contract/project is fulfilled, especially for smaller companies; additional ones are not forthcoming

If you're able to read the signs of a layoff ahead of time, you can help put yourself in a position to take action. Keep your network current, both in-house and on the outside. In-house information can be gained via the office grapevine and by communicating with the right people, those who are at the level where decisions are made.

Warning Signs of Being Fired

Times have changed: Being fired is not viewed as harshly as it once was. The impact of a changing economy has contributed to the fact that job loss is much more common today. At the same time, reasons for being fired could be personal, related to your job performance, or just a management decision, and these are more difficult to deal with. Consider being fired as a possibility if you are:

- Having difficulty with your supervisor (relationship deteriorating, possible angry encounters/confrontations)

- Assigned less important duties or projects, or some of your current responsibilities are delegated to others

- Past due for a raise or promotion and someone else gets it, or you are the only one at your level not to get a bonus

- Being avoided by your supervisor, co-workers, and subordinates

- Not receiving information and resources needed to get job done

- Not being personally productive

- Always being criticized by someone at a higher level

- Have had three consecutive poor job performance ratings

- Unable to set up a meeting to discuss your job dissatisfaction or future possibilities

If you decide to leave, follow the steps outlined in Chapter 3. If you decide to stay and end up losing your job, you will need to contend with the inevitable flood of emotions stemming from losing one's job.

●●●

Four of our ten profiled career changers had left prior positions not entirely by their choice. Both Ed and Patricia were more or less pushed out as a result of negative politics on the job.

Ed had experienced this as a police officer and decided to pursue his law degree. Patricia also decided to pursue a law degree after negative politics in a music librarian position that pushed her toward becoming a law librarian and eventually on to law school.

Both Victoria and Vincent were victims of downsizing. Victoria went from a social-work position in a nonprofit organization to a corporate position in technical writing. Vincent went from investment banking to opening his own specialty bookstore.

●●●

The Emotions of Losing Your Job

We have identified four types of career transitions:

- Anticipated, voluntary
- Unanticipated, voluntary
- Anticipated, involuntary
- Unanticipated, involuntary

The top two changes, which are more in our control, will be addressed in Chapter 3. These are the types of situations where we can decide to change or not.

However, being laid off or fired is not up to us or within our control and therefore stirs up strong emotions. Loretta Bradley identifies five stages of reaction you might experience as a result of losing your job:

Denial: Many respond with shock when told they're going to lose their job (especially if unanticipated). They think that it can't be true—it can't really be happening to them.

Anger: After the realization of losing one's job does set in, many become hostile and angry. After all, they're losing something valuable.

Bargaining: Some people try to bargain for more time on the job or to be given another chance. They promise to do better and make a last effort to work something out.

Depression: When one realizes the job is lost and faces the fact that it is happening, there could be a desire to be alone. Feeling sad is not unusual.

Acceptance: Although unhappy about what's happening, eventually one begins to accept it and starts to look for a new job. (This is easier when laid off than when fired.)

These stages are not applicable to everyone, but generally speaking you might identify with a number of these stages if not all of them. In fact, two additional stages (or emotional states) that could be added are *fear* and *shame.* Fear may occur between denial and anger and include concerns such as needs of family, paying bills, and the question of "will I ever work again?" You might also fear losing some of your identity and telling others about what has occurred. Shame may come after anger and prior to depression, which is largely due to the importance and authority we give to the opinions of others.

If one doesn't experience these stages of job loss as presented, it's more than likely that, in addition to shock, anger, depression, fear, and shame, a variety of other emotional responses may be experienced, including disbelief, disappointment, despair, hurt, sadness, betrayal, confusion, self-pity, and possibly even relief.

However, some people who lose their jobs do not necessarily respond as outlined here. Some people are able to let go of anger and unhappiness about having been fired and are often the ones who conduct the best job search. They generally end up with a better job than the one they left.

Taking Care of Yourself

Coping with the Emotions of Job Loss

The emotional impact of job loss can become a huge psychological burden, not to mention a financial one. As indicated earlier, the initial shock is usually followed by anger and grief. Sometimes depression can follow anger and grief. In response, one might tend to withdraw more and more, wanting to be alone. Counseling professionals suggest recognizing and accepting one's feelings and explaining to family or significant others what has happened, as soon as possible.

Talking it out with others can include, in addition to one's family or significant others, friends or personal confidants as well. In fact, joining a support group can be beneficial. To meet groups of people dealing with the same problems, contact places of worship (churches/synagogues), social service agencies, and local colleges. Check the phone book under headings such as Career Counseling or Vocational Guidance (or Counseling).

Seeking help is not a weakness, it is a sign of strength and an indication that you intend to improve your situation and are not wallowing in it. The purpose of this "talking it out" phase is to finish dealing with the past in order to prepare yourself to deal with the future. Letting go of anger is an important step in the process, and personal counseling can help achieve that. One's thoughts will shift from what has happened to what to do next.

Still Finding Yourself Thinking Negatively?

Try to take positive action through the steady, ongoing completion of small, meaningful goals. You'll be able to gain a new attitude and perspective, increase your self-satisfaction and self-esteem, and realize the power and control you do have in your life. Don't underestimate the importance of diet, exercise, a routine, and self-esteem in turning around negative thoughts.

Diet. During periods of unemployment, people can get depressed and neglect themselves. This may lead to skipping meals and possibly just taking anything from the refrigerator without considering its impact on your health. Many try to eat or starve away their problems. They also fail to exercise enough, which, in combination with a haphazard diet, could lead to health problems such as high blood pressure, heart attacks, arteriosclerosis, and even cancer. In addition, these bad habits can feed the depression and anxiety already happening, and even help make a person look and feel older.

If health reasons alone weren't enough to encourage someone to stay in shape, there's always the fact that there is a prejudice against overweight job seekers and workers. They could be viewed as lazy, less productive, and even a health risk, as unjustified as it might be.

A proper diet can truly impact someone in that they can be more mentally alert, increase their stamina, and thus deal most effectively with stress. Your diet should include vitamin-rich and high-fiber foods such as raw fruits and vegetables, bran, wheat, and other cereals. In addition, reduce your intake of foods that are high in saturated fats, salt, or refined sugar and stay away from alcohol and caffeine.

If you have difficulty properly adjusting your eating habits, be sure to add multiple vitamin and mineral supplements daily. The B-complex and C vitamins, especially, have an effect on our energy level, which gets depleted with excess stress and pressure. These dietary suggestions can help ward off the health risks mentioned earlier in this section and promote the possibility of having a successful job search as well.

Exercise.
It's a simple fact—people who exercise regularly have more energy. Try to maintain at least an every-other-day exercise program of about 30 minutes in length. The goal would be to engage in an aerobic exercise that raises the heartbeat and oxygenates the body: jogging, walking, rollerblading, biking, swimming, cross-country skiing, jumping rope, dance, or racquetball. If you have followed this type of program in the past, you know already the benefits as far as looking and feeling better.

Results of an effective exercise program, if done on a regular basis, could include improved physical appearance, increased mental sharpness, less anxiety and depression, a better ability to fall and stay asleep, and simply feeling better as a result of the brain releasing certain biochemicals that help to ward off depression and anxiety. All of this would lead to an improved mental attitude and thereby enhance positive job search outcomes.

Create a Routine.
Provide the necessary structure for yourself to accomplish what needs to get done in the areas of job searching (calls, correspondence, interviews, library research, etc.), family, and self. Through effective time management, you will experience greater control in your life as well as increased self-satisfaction as a result of accomplishing your goals.

Get organized about your job search and life. Create daily schedules of things to do. Keep a record of all contacts made and when follow-up correspondence or calls need to be done. Organization can go a long way in helping your job search be successful.

Be sure to schedule quality family time also. Your unemployment takes a toll on them as well as they try to be helpful to you and make sacrifices related to necessary cutting back of spending. In addition, you'll want to schedule relaxation (or quiet time) for yourself, probably on a daily basis, if possible. This can take on many forms: reading, listening to music, gardening, biking, watching television or a video, sewing, or any number of hobbies.

Self-Esteem.
How you feel about yourself is important, especially during challenging times such as losing your job. In difficult times it's important to do the things that help you, whatever they might be. Some could be part of the relaxation time just mentioned. Self-help books and tapes can also be useful. In addition, exercise has all-around positive results: mentally, emotionally,

and physically. All of this leads to feeling better about life in general and yourself, specifically.

One could view a period of unemployment as one of reevaluation and regeneration. Of course, that's easier said than done. However, numerous books take an upbeat, positive view of unemployment. Collectively, they advocate viewing this time, after losing one's job, as an opportunity—an opportunity to take a look at yourself, evaluate who you are and where you want to go, and then to proceed to pursue that goal. These are definitely positive perspectives and worth taking a look at.

Losing Your Current Job: Next Steps

Severance Negotiations

One good reason for handling your emotions well after losing your job is that very soon thereafter you may find yourself discussing and negotiating a severance package. Severance can be seen as a financial bridge to your next job. Take care of it as soon as possible because, as time passes, your employer might not care as much about being fair.

Because offering severance is optional for an employer, whatever they offer can be considered acceptable in that regard. However, with large corporate reductions of employees, the offering of severance has become a regular practice at many companies, whether or not it is part of an official policy.

Severance policies are commonly hidden from view. Many companies prefer to deal with each employee individually. There are several reasons why it's in the best interests of companies to deal fairly when it comes to severance.

- Impact on their reputation in the business field (i.e., information regarding poor treatment of employees can spread)

- Effect on their ability to attract high-quality employees in the future

- Morale of employees still working there

- Avoiding possible lawsuits and bad publicity

- The opportunity to relieve guilt they may feel for potentially messing up the employee's life

Many employees who have lost their jobs enter severance negotiations wondering what would be fair. Some companies use a formula based on a number of possible factors: age, position (title), current salary, and length of service. Of course, different companies give different weights to each, while others use additional, more standardized approaches.

However, certain averages do seem to exist. Usually, one year or less of employment will generate two weeks of severance pay. For longer-term employees, a standard could be one week, two weeks, or at best one month's pay for every year of service. Yet, for larger companies the maximum severance will usually be six month's pay regardless of how long an employee has served. Severance might be offered for a specific time period or until you find a job, whichever comes first.

If you're not satisfied with the length of severance package you receive, try negotiating for something better. Good reasons to point out could be a long tenure with the company and your contributions to the company (new business, saving money, etc.). Additional possible severance benefits include the following:

- **Nature and timing of payments** (lump sum or in installments)

- **Supportive counseling**

- **Medical coverage**

- **Outplacement counseling**

- **Office space and/or secretarial assistance**

- **Unused vacation time**

You can now see the importance of maintaining your calm upon losing your job, for much is at stake as you negotiate your way out (assuming you're fortunate enough to have had a position where this was possible in the first place). By being professional, you enhance the possibility of achieving a fair severance package. Keep in mind, if you feel you've been unfairly treated, that federal law entitles you to a reasonably fair treatment. Contact a lawyer if necessary.

Separation Statement/Letter of Reference

Developing a separation statement is important for presenting yourself to future employers. The separation statement described the truth as you see it, and casts you in as much of a positive manner as possible and with which your former employer can agree.

If you were laid off due to reasons related to organizational restructuring, this statement will be easier to prepare and probably easier for former managers to agree with. However, even if you've been fired for a personal reason, there may be a way to frame the reason so that it doesn't endanger your future employment and at the same time is one that management is willing to go along with. For example, perhaps some reorganization was going on when you were fired and can be worked into the statement as having an effect. There may be a payoff for management if you do succeed at gaining a new job, and that is a reduction of guilt, if it's there to begin with. Therefore, they may be willing to work with you on this.

A separation statement should begin with a positive statement and overview of contributions made on your previous job and follow with an explanation of reasons for leaving, which is as honest and positive as possible. Discuss the statement with your former supervisor. Help him or her to remember all of your accomplishments, and then explain your new career objective, in an attempt to build a longer-term perspective rather than focusing on recent problems. It's to your advantage to reach a point of agreement on the separation statement. Then when you do use it, it will be with the knowledge that the former supervisor agrees, in case the person is contacted about you by a potential employer.

Most reference requests are now channeled through human resources departments for legal reasons. This creates an even stronger reason to prepare a separation statement. Otherwise, potential future employers can have inadequate information. If the human resources department offers only limited information, your separation statement can fill in the holes.

Voluntary Separation

Voluntary separation is an outgrowth of the early retirement programs. Companies found themselves with an excess of middle managers who, most likely, would not move any further up the corporate ladder because of a lack of room, skills, experience, or motivation. At the same time, newer employees were arriving with stronger educational backgrounds and better skills. However, the companies knew that releasing older workers could lead to lawsuits and public relations problems. Early retirement programs were typically offered to workers 55 and over, with ten or more years of service. Incentives in the form of benefit packages were offered to employees who elected to leave voluntarily.

Around the early 1980s, voluntary separation was introduced against a backdrop of corporate reorganization, in which companies redefined the focus and nature of their business. More than an issue of too many middle managers, now it was a matter of whether an entire division remained in a company's plans for the future. Voluntary separation involves the company identifying an eligible group of employees, creating a package of severance benefits (usually not negotiable when presented to a group, as compared to an individual losing his or her job), and offering those eligible a time period in which to accept the offer. Therefore, the company decides who is eligible, and those individuals decide how to respond.

If you are offered a voluntary separation, it's important to learn as much as possible about the company's future plans and needs. Insight could be gained by talking with your supervisor. Do you have the skills and experience that could plug into its future plans? Obviously, initially the company didn't think so or you wouldn't be among the group offered voluntary separation. However, that doesn't mean it's not possible for you to persuade them otherwise. In order to do that, you need good information on which to base your argument. You might even simply ask your supervisor whether you should take the voluntary separation offer. Both verbal and nonverbal responses can be important clues for you. If you feel you have a realistic chance, then pursue it. If not, then it might be best to take the offer of voluntary separation and begin a job search campaign.

Financial Concerns

Unemployment Compensation

When you are laid off or fired, you are eligible for unemployment compensation. If you are laid off because your former company has financial problems, you are eligible for benefits. If you're fired, whether you are eligible depends on the reason. Your former employer would have to prove you were guilty of some form of misconduct to make you ineligible. This would include being caught stealing, sabotaging employer property, or assaulting co-workers, not necessarily personality conflicts or disagreements.

Unemployment compensation is difficult for hardworking individuals to accept: they don't want handouts. Remember that rather than charity, this is a government insurance program to which you have contributed through withholding from your paychecks. Keep in mind that its purpose is to help job seekers survive the period between jobs. This period could stretch from six months to a year, depending on such factors as your career objective, related skills and experience, how effectively you market yourself, and the state of the economy.

Find out what amount of unemployment compensation you're entitled to. In most states it's $200/week for someone with no dependents and up to $300/week with one or more dependents. You can continue to receive benefits in most states even if you obtain a part-time job, as long as it pays less than your total benefit amount. You may still be able to receive the difference between your part-time pay and your benefit amount. The number of weeks you're allowed benefits may be limited. Most states limit the number to around 26 weeks. However, there is the possibility of legislation extending this, so check with your local unemployment office for the most up-to-date information.

Develop an Accurate Budget

Identify your and your family's needs and list all expenses.

- What do you need to keep?

- What can be delayed? Talk with your creditors; you may be able to arrange some type of payment plan.

- What can be cut back (e.g., housing, food, utilities, or entertainment expenses)?

- If you were covered by a group medical insurance policy with your former employer, you can maintain coverage by paying your and your employer's share (COBRA).

If, after figuring all this out, you realize you can't survive 9–12 months on your current savings and/or unemployment, you may want to consider a home equity loan or other low-interest loans (e.g., from insurance policies) to help get you by.

CHAPTER 3

YOUR CHOICE: A QUESTION OF VALUES

This chapter presents a method for assessing your current level of job satisfaction in order to guide you in deciding whether to change or not to change. If you decide to make a change, it will be only the first of many important decisions. This chapter also guides you in the choices of finding a new position with the same employer, working for another employer, or starting your own business.

Defining "Good" Work

What is "good" work? C. Wright Mills considered this question more than 40 years ago. According to Mills, good work is

1. Concerned with the quality of a product and the skill that product requires. Rewards such as money, fame, status, and prestige come second to being able to do work one loves and can do well.

2. Owned by the workers. The relationship between the part and the whole is visible.

3. Challenging. It stretches workers as individuals and professionals.

4. Controllable. When workers can decide when to start and stop work, it influences not only work, but leisure time as well.

5. A source of self-development for workers, including techniques (skill).

6. Integrated with play. There should be some pleasures in our work.

7.   Companionable. It provides company for the many hours away from friends and family.

This is but one definition of good work. What else might you include? Mills developed this definition in 1951, but it still covers what most people would consider key elements of good work.

• •

Half of our ten profiled career changers changed careers by choice: Larry, Martha, Allen, Zephree, and Sandra. Larry left his environmental technician position to become a trainer for a related manufacturer. Martha left teaching to start a business with her husband that grew to be a popular Hispanic nightclub and restaurant. Allen left his budget analyst position to go to dental school and eventually own his own practice. Zephree left secretarial work to become a research assistant in a social service field. Sandra left the law profession to write and publish books for children.

Mac left his business to become a high-school counselor for two reasons: a health problem and a business slowdown. So, even though in one sense it was his choice, there were factors operating that brought him to that choice.

• •

However, many other factors affect how satisfied we are with a particular job. Individuals identify different types of factors as important, both in life in general and on the job. The factors an individual considers important are referred to as *values*.

Defining a Value

A value is anything to which one attributes worth, merit, or usefulness. More specifically, job or work values are the rewards, satisfactions, and desirable qualities one seeks in a career. You might ask, "How do I know if something I attach importance to is really a value?" If you can answer yes to the following seven criteria, then you can be certain that the importance you've attached to something is significant. According to Sidney Simon, Leland Howe, and Howard Kirschenbaum, you can consider something a value if you:

1. Chose it freely.

2. Chose it from a set of desirable alternatives.

3. Chose it after thoughtful consideration of the consequences of each possible alternative.

4. Prize, cherish, and feel proud of it.

5. Are able to discuss it freely and openly with others.

6. Invest your time, money, or other resources in it.

7. Act on it consistently for a considerable period of time and across a variety of situations.

The Importance of Values

A value is formed by continuously considering and deliberately choosing from alternatives, after careful consideration of the consequences of each. Once chosen, you will prize a value, noting its importance with respect and pride. After you've chosen a value, you will affirm it consistently over time by giving it your time, money, or energy.

Thinking about your values helps in your search to find purpose and meaning in your life and work. Setting priorities requires you to think more deeply about what is important in your life. Through identifying and evaluating your values, you can get to know yourself better. With every decision you make, no matter how small or large, you are making a statement about what matters to you.

How Values Develop

Many factors enter into the process of developing values, beginning in early childhood. Relationships play a key role, especially those with your parents, siblings, relatives, neighbors, friends, teachers, institutions, and other aspects of your community. Your cultural surroundings also influence your values. This includes newspapers, magazines, radio, television, film, music, art, and books. Values are related to needs. Your needs will usually determine what motivates you. In turn, what motivates you will influence what is important to you.

Figure 3.1 (on page 52) gives you a chance to assess your degree of satisfaction by ranking 80 work values on your current job, or the degree of importance you attach to these values if you are currently unemployed.

Very few people ever have a job that satisfies all aspects covered in this self-assessment to a high degree. However, a balance among the seven categories is desirable. Pay particular attention to the categories of work satisfaction values to which you give the highest importance ratings. These are the key values for you.

In addition, pay serious attention to the work value categories with percentage scores of 60 and below. Suggestions for what can be done to improve your situation at your current job are provided in the next section. Consider these carefully before deciding whether to change your career.

• •

Sandra was dissatisfied in her legal work. She felt her work could have a greater purpose (category G, Personal Development Goals), more of a sense of mission. Growing up as an Asian-American was difficult for her, as it is for other people of color. The books that Sandra writes and publishes feature minority children and describe their experiences growing up. Sandra hopes that minority children who read these books will feel a greater sense of pride in and enjoyment of their own experiences.

• •

If you are currently unemployed and completed your importance ratings for the 80 work values, this can now serve as a source for assessing possible upcoming career opportunities. Zero in on those values that you rated 4 or above (above-average to very important). Your goal is to try to find a job that satisfies those values that you identify as most important to you. If you don't achieve some level of satisfaction for a fair number of these work values, then you're more likely to be dissatisfied with your next position.

Seeking a Change with Your Present Employer

Even if you are dissatisfied with your present job and are thinking about seeking a new position with a different organization, the best opportunities might be with your present employer. Three advantages of seeking a change with your present employer are:

- You'll have access to people in the organization who can help you determine the needs of your present campaign.

- By knowing the needs of your company, you could possibly position yourself to help contribute in the most important areas.

- Organizations often prefer to promote from within. There is no need to train someone new, you are a known quantity, and it helps to build morale.

Finding a new position with your current employer will favorably affect your salary, pension plan, and other benefits. Some negatives of seeking a new position include starting over somewhere new, having to prove yourself, and a possible drop in salary or benefits. You'll find more information on this subject in Chapter 8.

Some problems with resigning without having found a new job are:

- Financial support while job searching

- Loss of health insurance

- The perception that smart people don't leave their jobs until they have new ones lined up

However, a benefit is that you can give your job search full-time attention, which can pay off in the end.

If you can stay on your job at least until you have a chance to do some research, it might help to reduce stress. It also puts you in a better decision-making position. However, there may be good reasons not to stay, such as the following:

- You can no longer tolerate the situation.

- Your dissatisfaction is causing significant performance problems, which could hurt you in the future by possibly getting you fired or leading to a poor reference while job searching.

- Your unhappiness is ruining the rest of your life.

Seeking Work Elsewhere

If you have exhausted all of your options to remedy the situation in your current position, seeking other employment is your next step. If you have a solid relationship with your supervisor, you might try to negotiate your way out gradually. It's somewhat risky, but under the proper conditions it produces good results. Possibilities include the following:

- Getting assigned a special project that allows you to spend time job searching.

- Helping to select and train your replacement, minimizing headaches for both you and your employer.

Because this is a small world and there's no sense in burning your bridges, we've provided some suggestions for going out gracefully:

- Finish up projects or leave them in a state that they can be easily passed on to others.

- Be discreet about how you use time for job search activities. Use breaks, lunch hours, personal time, and other nonwork hours.

- Play by the rules (e.g., do not make long-distance phone calls or use the copy machine to copy your resume).

- Give a month's notice, or at least enough time to complete major projects.

- Return anything that belongs to the office and leave the office in an orderly condition.

With increased downsizing and related layoffs, especially of middle managers, there is less room at the top of the ladder. You might have to redefine your career goals to be more realistic with today's job market. Only thorough research will reveal to what extent these trends will influence you in trying to reach your career goals. Perhaps upgrading your skills or learning new ones is necessary. Remember that most fields are highly competitive.

The following three points will get you started on a successful career path:

- **Identify** what it is you *most want to do,* your purpose or mission in life.

- **Develop** an *expertise,* become *the best* you can in the career you most want.

- **Learn** how to *effectively job search.*

Remember these strategies. We'll add to them later.

Starting Your Own Business: What Are Your Chances of Success?

Many "baby boomers" who sought to climb the corporate ladder didn't like what they encountered as they attempted to build their careers. Competition is fierce at the middle tier of most companies, and workers wanting to advance were frustrated. They learned from their employers what it takes to create and manage their own business and had the confidence to try it.

Why Start a Business?

People start their own business to have something to call their own, to have greater control over their career, and to create something from their own ideas. Here are some additional reasons:

- You can live and work where you choose.

- You will experience greater independence.

- You can avoid potential difficulties of working for others: difficult or incompetent supervisors, office politics, etc.

- You can control your own time. In the beginning you will work long hours, but at least you are the direct beneficiary of those efforts, rather than someone else.

- You have a greater likelihood of remaining vitally interested in your work.

- There is a better chance to make money as an entrepreneur than working for someone else.

- It is a source of self-satisfaction and pride to take your own ideas and establish a business.

How to Succeed in Starting Your Own Business

You need to be aware of the motivations underlying your decision to start a new business. Otherwise, you may be increasing the odds of failing. Reasons such as wanting to make a lot of money soon, being bored with your present job, wanting more free time, having a strong desire to escape from a difficult supervisor, or an unhappy social situation with fellow employees are *not* good reasons to start a business of your own. Entrepreneurship is a risky business with many emotional, mental and physical demands.

•••

To achieve greater independence, Sandra, in addition to writing multicultural children's books, decided to publish them as well. This was the only
way she knew to maintain editorial control. Her mission of writing cultur-
ally aware books for children was so central to who she was, that she was
willing to add to an already difficult transition the role of publisher in
order to maintain control over the content of her books.

•••

Some valid reasons for starting a business include life-style choices. For
example, you might want to choose the hours that you work, rather than
being stuck with a 9–5 routine. You will probably work more hours with a
new business, but at least it's up to you and for you. It allows you greater
freedom and control in your career. However, it's nothing to rush into. There
are no salary, benefits, office, or support system, unless you work on providing them yourself.

Figure 3.2 (on page 64) is an exercise designed to help you assess your potential to be a successful business owner. You will identify to what degree you
have attained each of 50 entrepreneurial personal characteristics.

What to Do about Weaknesses

It's unusual for anyone to score 90 percent or better in all eight categories,
but there should be a balance among the eight categories. Pay particular
attention to any category with an average attainment percentage score
(70–79%) or less, as well as any individual item rated 3 (average) or less.
These are areas that you need to improve in, to help enhance the possibility of
success if you plan to open your own business.

•••

Patricia found upon starting her legal practice that she was weak on
the administrative, day-to-day aspects of running an office. She hired
someone part-time to help with client billing and related matters.

•••

Some of your lower scoring characteristics will be more possible to improve in than others. It's important to ask yourself, and others who would

know, how much having an average (or lower) amount of a certain characteristic will affect your chances of success. If the responses are "somewhat to a lot," then you have four choices:

1. Try to acquire more of that characteristic through coursework, workshops, seminars, personal counseling, personal goal settings, etc.

2. Find a partner who possesses the qualities you do not have.

3. Use consultants as needed to shore up weak spots.

4. Decide that owning a business isn't the best choice for you and that working for someone else will fit you better.

The Sacrifices Required to Be Successful

Even if you are encouraged by your results on the Entrepreneurial Personal Characteristics Self-Assessment, you must also know that following such a path involves much personal sacrifice in the form of time, energy, money, family, and friends. It's not unusual for new business owners to work 12–14 hours a day, 7 days a week, taking little or no time off for vacation, as they attempt to get their business off the ground. This takes not only tremendous energy and vigor, but also the cooperation of those close to you. Quality family time will be cut down dramatically, as well as social time with friends. Here's where good communication helps out.

The biggest single reason for business failure is undercapitalization. As a beginning entrepreneur, you could go heavily into debt, experience cash-flow problems, and have creditors knocking at your door. Thus, it makes more sense to wait to start your business until you're at least moderately sure that you have enough funds to avoid setting yourself up for major financial distress.

Typically, in the first year, and perhaps in the second, you will be doing well if you break even. Even if you do make some profit with your new business, it would be advisable to reinvest those earnings back into your business.

Generating New Business Ideas

As a potential business owner, you need to ask yourself the following questions:

- Do I have the interest, expertise, and relevant skills to enable me to succeed in this emerging market?

- Can I identify a related business, service, or product need that no one else is providing or create a new need?

- Can I improve an existing product or service, as far as looking for ways to produce and sell it better and less expensively.

By taking a snapshot of current demographics, economic conditions, and technological information, you can generate some potential small business ideas. Of course, market research is needed to verify the viability of these ideas in your geographic area of interest. It all boils down to creating a specific idea, gathering evidence that it will succeed (based on market research), and knowing whether economic conditions favor your proposed idea.

Testing Out Your Business Idea

Once you have a business idea and have done some research, you're ready to test that idea out. Emily Koltnow and Lynne Dumas offer the following suggestions:

- Check out the competition: what they charge, what you might offer that they do not, and what will make your service or product better.

- If your business idea is a product, make a prototype and identify the cost of production. In the cost estimate include production costs, materials, labor, overhead, promotion, and profit.

- Talk with potential customers. Get their opinions: How do they feel about the price? Would they buy it? How many?

- If your business idea is a service, print a flyer or brochure as well as placing an ad in the local papers and see what reactions you get to your promotion.

- Identify a group of objective people and form an informal focus group to get feedback on your business idea. If you can afford it, there are professional market research companies that can do this for you.

••

Vincent exercised two interesting strategies for researching his target market and testing out his idea. He sent a 3,000-piece mailing to the community where he hoped to locate his bookstore. He included a quarter in each one (hoping to increase the response rate) and asked people to comment on how many paperbacks/hardbacks they bought recently and in which subject areas.

He got a 17 percent response rate (considered strong) and was surprised at how many people not only sent back the quarter (thinking he might need it), but also included personal suggestions to help him get started in his business venture.

Vincent also benefited from his MBA program, where he learned to use government census reports to determine who was buying what and when. He reviewed circulation records at the local library, which revealed that history and mystery (the focus of his intended specialty bookstore) together beat out all other categories. This certainly was encouraging to Vincent as he moved closer to making his business idea a reality.

•••

Should You Start a New Business, Buy an Existing Business, Invest in a Franchise, or Become a Consultant?

When considering any of these business options, be sure to get feedback from a team of advisors including an accountant, a lawyer, and a financial advisor. The pros and cons of starting a new business are listed here:

Pros: • For true entrepreneurs, the real goal and major appeal is in the creation of something new, not necessarily in the management aspect, so starting a new business is appealing.

Cons: • You need a good idea, potential customers, and knowledge of marketing, finance, and management to succeed.

• There is a high failure rate. (The Small Business Administration reports that 75 percent fail in a year, and 25 percent of survivors fail in the second year.)

• Most new businesses are privately financed with the owner's money and often are undercapitalized.

• It is not unusual for a new business owner to work at least 60, and possibly as many as 80, hours, 7 days a week, for the first year or so, which can create stress for yourself and your family.

• It is not as appealing if you are sales-oriented and are not as interested in creating as in selling.

Perhaps after reviewing the pros and cons of owning a business, you're thinking that you want to be self-employed but don't have an innovative idea or are not comfortable taking such a big risk. Then you could consider buying an already existing business or investing in a franchise. Both choices involve

To decide whether to open their own businesses, Mac, Patricia, and Allen all worked for related businesses for others.

Mac worked for a year and a half with a leader in the market research area of interest to him: the African-American consumer. It was his first exposure to the business world, and he was excited by it—enough so, that he went on to establish his own business.

Patricia, originally a music librarian, switched to being a law librarian and then went on to become a lawyer herself. She worked for five years in a law firm in her area of interest, the creative arts. She found the experience to be good training in preparing to move out on her own.

Allen, a dentist, worked for three years in someone else's practice and gained a good amount of knowledge about running a dental practice, which he was able to apply when he began his own practice.

In addition, Sandra spent her first year in her writing/publishing company on a part-time basis before leaving her job as a lawyer.

less risk, and there's less to learn the hard way, when compared to starting a new business. The pros and cons of buying an existing business follow:

Pros:
- There is reduced risk and a better chance of getting financial backing. Banks take a more favorable view because of the existing track record, i.e., the existence of customers, staff, supplies, facility, cash flow, etc.
- It is more attractive to a person with more interest in selling products than in setting up an operation or a marketing system or designing products.

Cons:
- The current owner might have liabilities he or she wishes to foist off on an unsuspecting buyer. Be sure to find out why the person is selling the business before making any commitment.
- It is not as appealing to an entrepreneur who likes to be original, creative, and innovative. This sort of business venture might not reflect enough personal vision.

The pros and cons of investing in a franchise follow:

Pros:
- The failure rate for a franchise business is less than 5 percent, according to the National Franchise Association.

- Operating costs are lower (franchisors buy in large quantities and can pass the savings on to individual franchises).

- Franchises receive plenty of business support, including advertising, accounting, hiring, and training. Franchisors with better quality franchises help with financing, legal assistance, site selection, and even management of construction.

- It is a relatively low-cost way to learn how to run a business and a good training ground for learning to operate your own business later.

Cons: - You're bound by the franchise agreement. Thus there is a loss of freedom and flexibility in operating the business.

- In exchange for the business support, the franchise must pay a fee, royalty, or a percentage of the gross.

- The success of each franchise is dependent, to a large extent, on the franchisor's business skills, determination, financial standing, and honesty.

For further information, consult the *Franchise Opportunities Handbook,* published by the U.S. Department of Commerce. The handbook lists most franchises registered in the United States and includes information such as number of franchises, product/service offered, costs, and what training is available.

You probably have heard the term *consultant* many times and might have wondered what exactly they do. Consultants are expert advisors who are contracted from outside an organization to help solve problems for a fee. Those who hire consultants include large, medium, and small companies; nonprofit organizations, such as associations; government agencies; elementary, junior, and senior high schools; colleges and universities; health care institutions; advertising agencies; public relations firms; and entertainment companies. The types of work consultants are hired to do include identifying and solving problems; providing expert knowledge; generating new ideas; convincing others to accept new ideas; helping identify growth areas; teaching new methods; and exploring ways and means of keeping up with the competition.

Consultants could be expert in a particular type of business or in a cluster of professional skills. For example, a consultant might be knowledgeable in accounting, human resource management, training and development, or data processing, or have particular talent in the area of communication and writing. Whatever your chosen area of expertise, in order to succeed you need to be a proven expert with at least five years of experience and a solid network of contacts who trust you and would contract for your services when they have a project to be completed.

As a consultant, you must be comfortable with yourself and able to continuously market or sell yourself and your skills. This requires good interpersonal, negotiating, presentational, and written communication skills, as well as sound technical knowledge in the field of interest.

••

Patricia combatted her fear of feeling alone (and cut expenses as well) in her legal practice by renting office space within an already existing, large law firm. Mac rented space in a friend's company and even got his phone line specially answered (sounding as if it was his company alone) by the secretary already in place.

••

Following are the pros and cons of working as a consultant:

Pros: • You can enhance the development of your network.

• Such work provides you with the opportunity to get familiar with companies and vice versa, which could lead to obtaining a full-time job.

Cons: • You really have to hustle. You are the salesperson as well as the product and service. If you stop hustling, you'll be out of business.

• You have to learn to cope with the rejection that can come from selling both yourself and your knowledge.

• You're only as good as your last job.

• You personally will have to get the work out on time, keep the books, pay the bills, bill customers, and hassle with delinquent accounts.

• Unless you have a clerical worker on hand, you will not enjoy the support that you once knew as a member of a larger organization. For example, if the fax breaks down, you have to get it fixed yourself.

• You might feel a sense of loss from no longer being part of a team effort.

• You might be less secure because you are no longer backed by the prestige and title of your former corporation.

- There is a lack of formalized structure, which is good for some and bad for others. You'll have to learn to adjust to a need for greater personal drive and motivation to get going and stay active in business.

- Because of the need to stay constantly active in order to generate business, your freedom is limited. Thus, you have to limit sick days and structure leisure time into your schedule after finishing an assignment and before prospecting for more work.

After reviewing the pros and cons of starting a new business, buying an existing business, investing in a franchise, and becoming a consultant, you are in a better position to judge which option better suits you. If you need more information to help you explore these options, you can contact the Small Business Administration, 1441 L Street N.W., Washington, DC 20416.

FIGURE 3.1

Work Values Satisfaction Self-Assessment

Directions: Rate each of the 80 work values as to their degree of importance, using the following choices:

> 5 High satisfaction
>
> 4 Above-average satisfaction
>
> 3 Average satisfaction
>
> 2 Below-average satisfaction
>
> 1 Low satisfaction

Follow these steps to complete the self-assessment. An example for category D, "The Job Itself," follows.

1. Focusing on one value at a time, rate your current level of satisfaction on the job by circling the appropriate number. Next, rate its importance to you. If you are currently unemployed, complete only the importance ratings.

2. When you have rated all 80 values, eliminate all work values that you rated as 1 or 2 (below-average to low) in **importance** by

"continued"

drawing a line through them. You will calculate your average level of satisfaction for each category, and including these would throw off the accuracy of your scores for values that aren't important to you in the first place.

3. For the remaining work values, multiply the satisfaction number by the importance number and write the result on the line in Column 1.

4. Within one category (A–G) at a time, total the work value **satisfaction** ratings only and divide by the number of work values being calculated (those rated 3 or above in importance). Write your average in the space provided after the category heading, in the parentheses and to the left of the /. In our example, the satisfaction scores for values rated 3 or above in importance totaled 53. We divided 53 by the number of values included (12), for an average satisfaction rating of 4.4.

5. Use the descriptors, low satisfaction through high satisfaction, to judge your average satisfaction level for each category (A–G).

   In our example, 4.4 is a rather high rating, halfway between 4 (above-average satisfaction) and 5 (high satisfaction). This would indicate that the person represented in our example has an above-average to high level of work value satisfaction in the category of the Job Itself, perhaps the most important category of the seven.

   Note in which categories you score the highest and the lowest. You might gain insight from the intensity of satisfaction for the seven categories of values. We'll return to discuss your results after completing the next steps in the scoring process.

6. For a more accurate category total score, compute the following:

   a. Add the scores listed in Column 1, for work values rated 3 or above in importance only. This becomes your Total Score (a). Each category (A–G) has its own separate Total Score (a).

      In our example, the Total Score (a) for the Job Itself equals 206.

   b. To calculate each category's Highest Possible Score (b), multiply your importance rating for each work value rated 3 or above in importance by 5 (the highest possible satisfaction score). Write the result on the line in Column 2. Add the scores in Column 2 and write the total at the bottom of Column 2.

   c. To complete the Satisfaction Percentage Score (a/b), divide each category's Total Score (a) by that category's Highest

"continued"

Possible Score (b). Write the percentage at the end of each category in the space provided, as well as to the right of the category heading, in the parentheses and to the right of the /.

In our example, 206 divided by 230 equals .895, which can be rounded up to 90 percent.

The Work Values Satisfaction Self-Assessment might appear a bit overwhelming at first. The best approach is to break it down into "bite-size" pieces. Consider doing one or two work value categories at a time. After just a few sittings, you'll have it completed. I think you'll be glad you did, for your values should play a key role in your career decision making.

Example

Level of Satisfaction	×	Level of Importance	=	Col-umn 1	Col-umn 2
Low Average High		Low Average High			

D. The Job Itself (4.4 / 90%)

1. The work is enjoyable and interesting.

1 2 3 4 (5) × 1 2 3 4 (5) = 25   25

2. I'm using my preferred skills and knowledge.

1 2 3 4 (5) × 1 2 3 4 (5) = 25   25

3. My job offers me appropriate growth in desired skills and knowledge.

1 2 3 (4) 5 × 1 2 (3) 4 5 = 12   15

4. I experience a sense of achievement on the job.

1 2 3 (4) 5 × 1 2 3 (4) 5 = 16   20

5. The work is intellectually challenging.

1 2 3 (4) 5 × 1 2 3 (4) 5 = 16   20

6. I have an opportunity to be creative in my work.

1 2 3 4 (5) × 1 2 3 4 (5) = 25   25

7. There is a variety of duties, a nice mix of responsibilities.

1 2 3 4 (5) × 1 2 3 (4) 5 = 20   20

8. The job entails a reasonable level of stress.

1 (2) 3 4 5 × 1 2 (3) 4 5 = 6   15

9. The work has an element of adventure; I perform

"continued"

	Level of Satisfaction ×	Level of Importance =	Column 1	Column 2
	Low Average High	Low Average High		
new, different, and exciting tasks.	1 2 3 ④ 5 × 1 ② 3 4 5 =			
10. The job provides the desired amount of social contact.	1 2 3 4 ⑤ × 1 2 ③ 4 5 =		15	15
11. I'm able to influence job duties to my liking.	1 2 3 4 ⑤ × 1 2 ③ 4 5 =		15	15
12. The job involves opportunities to travel.	1 ② 3 4 5 × ① 2 3 4 5 =			
13. The work is physically challenging.	1 ② 3 4 5 × ① 2 3 4 5 =			
14. I enjoy a familiar routine of daily tasks.	1 2 ③ 4 5 × 1 ② 3 4 5 =			
15. There's some action/ activity; I can move about on the job.	1 2 3 4 ⑤ × 1 2 ③ 4 5 =		15	15
16. The work allows me to be persuasive, convincing others to take certain actions.	1 2 3 ④ 5 × 1 ② 3 4 5 =			
17. Overall, the job is secure; there is little chance of becoming obsolete.	1 2 3 ④ 5 × 1 2 3 ④ 5 =		16	20

Satisfaction Total = 53 ÷ 12 = 4.4   Total Score (a) = 206

Highest Possible Score (b) = 230

The Job Itself Work Values Satisfaction Score (a/b) = 90%

	Level of Satisfaction ×	Level of Importance =	Column 1	Column 2
	Low Average High	Low Average High		
A. Company/Organization (/)				
1. The company is highly regarded in its field.	1 2 3 4 5 × 1 2 3 4 5 =			

"continued"

	Level of Satisfaction × Level of Importance = Col-umn 1	Col-umn 2
	Low Average High Low Average High	
2. The company is secure in its field; it belongs to a growth industry.	1 2 3 4 5 × 1 2 3 4 5 = ____	____
3. The company is experiencing growth.	1 2 3 4 5 × 1 2 3 4 5 = ____	____
4. The branch or division I work in is valued.	1 2 3 4 5 × 1 2 3 4 5 = ____	____
5. To a large extent, I agree with the setting and carrying out of company personnel policies.	1 2 3 4 5 × 1 2 3 4 5 = ____	____
6. The company does not discriminate based on gender, age, race, or sexual orientation.	1 2 3 4 5 × 1 2 3 4 5 = ____	____
7. Employees are able to observe important religious holidays and are allowed time off as appropriate.	1 2 3 4 5 × 1 2 3 4 5 = ____	____
8. The company adheres to a solid sense of ethics.	1 2 3 4 5 × 1 2 3 4 5 = ____	____
9. The geographic location of the company is desirable.	1 2 3 4 5 × 1 2 3 4 5 = ____	____
10. The company is loyal to long-term employees, whom they treat with respect and look to when promoting.	1 2 3 4 5 × 1 2 3 4 5 = ____	____

Satisfaction Total = ____ ÷ ____ = ____   Total Score (a) = ____

Highest Possible Score (b) =   ____

Company/Organization Work Values Satisfaction Score (a/b) = ____ %

"continued"

	Level of Satisfaction Low Average High	$\times$	Level of Importance Low Average High	$=$	Col- umn 1	Col- umn 2

B. Work Environment (/   )

1. The work setting is
   safe and healthy.   1 2 3 4 5 × 1 2 3 4 5 = ____ ____

2. The work setting is com-
   fortable and pleasant.   1 2 3 4 5 × 1 2 3 4 5 = ____ ____

3. Resources needed to
   get the job done are
   provided.   1 2 3 4 5 × 1 2 3 4 5 = ____ ____

4. The office space provided
   is suitable for meeting job
   requirements.   1 2 3 4 5 × 1 2 3 4 5 = ____ ____

5. The work hours are
   decent; they allow for
   some leisure time.   1 2 3 4 5 × 1 2 3 4 5 = ____ ____

6. The company dress code
   is comfortable for me.   1 2 3 4 5 × 1 2 3 4 5 = ____ ____

7. The distance to travel to
   work is reasonable.   1 2 3 4 5 × 1 2 3 4 5 = ____ ____

8. My co-workers are
   pleasant; there is a good
   work team feeling.   1 2 3 4 5 × 1 2 3 4 5 = ____ ____

9. Employee morale is
   upbeat.   1 2 3 4 5 × 1 2 3 4 5 = ____ ____

10. Back stabbing and other
    ruthless encounters are
    kept to a minimum.   1 2 3 4 5 × 1 2 3 4 5 = ____ ____

11. A healthy competitiveness
    exists among co-workers.   1 2 3 4 5 × 1 2 3 4 5 = ____ ____

12. There's a sense of belong-
    ing among employees; I
    can be recognized as a
    member of a group as

"continued"

	Level of Satisfaction Low Average High	×	Level of Importance Low Average High	=	Col- umn 1	Col- umn 2
a result of the work I perform.	1 2 3 4 5	×	1 2 3 4 5	=	____	____
13. In general, I am respected and looked up to on the job.	1 2 3 4 5	×	1 2 3 4 5	=	____	____

Satisfaction Total = ____ ÷ ____ = ____   Total Score (a) = ____

Highest Possible Score (b) =   ____

Work Environment Work Values Satisfaction Score (a/b) = ____ %

C. Supervisor Relations (/   )

1. My supervisor treats me with respect.	1 2 3 4 5	×	1 2 3 4 5	= ____	____
2. My supervisor thinks of me as a human being, not just someone to get the work done.	1 2 3 4 5	×	1 2 3 4 5	= ____	____
3. I am given appropriate recognition.	1 2 3 4 5	×	1 2 3 4 5	= ____	____
4. My supervisor is open to my suggestions.	1 2 3 4 5	×	1 2 3 4 5	= ____	____
5. My supervisor is accessible and approachable when needed.	1 2 3 4 5	×	1 2 3 4 5	= ____	____
6. I am dealt with honestly.	1 2 3 4 5	×	1 2 3 4 5	= ____	____
7. I am motivated with praise, not criticism.	1 2 3 4 5	×	1 2 3 4 5	= ____	____
8. I am allowed some degree of freedom in performing my work.	1 2 3 4 5	×	1 2 3 4 5	= ____	____
9. My supervisor is knowledgeable and skilled in my area of expertise.	1 2 3 4 5	×	1 2 3 4 5	= ____	____

"continued"

	Level of Satisfaction	×	Level of Importance	=	Col- umn 1	Col- umn 2
	Low Average High		Low Average High			

10. My supervisor is able to give me meaningful feed- back about my work.   1 2 3 4 5 × 1 2 3 4 5 = ____ ____

11. My supervisor possesses and upholds solid ethical practices.   1 2 3 4 5 × 1 2 3 4 5 = ____ ____

12. Overall, my supervisor is a competent manager.   1 2 3 4 5 × 1 2 3 4 5 = ____ ____

Satisfaction Total = ____ ÷ ____ = ____   Total Score (a) = ____

Highest Possible Score (b) = ____

Supervisor Relations Work Values Satisfaction Score (a/b) = ____ %

D. The Job Itself (/   )

1. The work is enjoyable and interesting.   1 2 3 4 5 × 1 2 3 4 5 = ____ ____

2. I'm using my preferred skills and knowledge.   1 2 3 4 5 × 1 2 3 4 5 = ____ ____

3. My job offers me appro- priate growth in desired skills and knowledge.   1 2 3 4 5 × 1 2 3 4 5 = ____ ____

4. I experience a sense of achievement on the job.   1 2 3 4 5 × 1 2 3 4 5 = ____ ____

5. The work is intellectually challenging.   1 2 3 4 5 × 1 2 3 4 5 = ____ ____

6. I have an opportunity to be creative in my work.   1 2 3 4 5 × 1 2 3 4 5 = ____ ____

7. There is a variety of duties, a nice mix of responsibilities.   1 2 3 4 5 × 1 2 3 4 5 = ____ ____

8. The job entails a rea- sonable level of stress.   1 2 3 4 5 × 1 2 3 4 5 = ____ ____

9. The work has an element of adventure; I perform

"continued"

	Level of Satisfaction	×	Level of Importance	=	Col-umn 1	Col-umn 2
	Low Average High		Low Average High			

new, different, and
exciting tasks.   1 2 3 4 5 × 1 2 3 4 5 = ____   ____

10. The job provides the
desired amount of
social contact.   1 2 3 4 5 × 1 2 3 4 5 = ____   ____

11. I'm able to influence job
duties to my liking.   1 2 3 4 5 × 1 2 3 4 5 = ____   ____

12. The job involves oppor-
tunities to travel.   1 2 3 4 5 × 1 2 3 4 5 = ____   ____

13. The work is physically
challenging.   1 2 3 4 5 × 1 2 3 4 5 = ____   ____

14. I enjoy a familiar
routine of daily tasks.   1 2 3 4 5 × 1 2 3 4 5 = ____   ____

15. There's some action/
activity; I can move
about on the job.   1 2 3 4 5 × 1 2 3 4 5 = ____   ____

16. The work allows me to
be persuasive, convinc-
ing others to take
certain actions.   1 2 3 4 5 × 1 2 3 4 5 = ____   ____

17. Overall, the job is secure;
there is little chance of
becoming obsolete.   1 2 3 4 5 × 1 2 3 4 5 = ____   ____

Satisfaction Total = ____ ÷ ____ = ____   Total Score (a) = ____

Highest Possible Score (b) =   ____

The Job Itself Work Values Satisfaction Score (a/b) = ____ %

E. Rewards/Benefits (/   )

1. My salary is fair and
competitive for the level
of responsibility.   1 2 3 4 5 × 1 2 3 4 5 = ____   ____

"continued"

	Level of Satisfaction	×	Level of Importance	=	Col-umn 1	Col-umn 2
	Low Average High		Low Average High			
2. Appropriate promotions have been awarded in a timely manner.	1 2 3 4 5	×	1 2 3 4 5	=	____	____
3. A decent medical insurance plan is provided.	1 2 3 4 5	×	1 2 3 4 5	=	____	____
4. A pension plan/retirement fund is provided.	1 2 3 4 5	×	1 2 3 4 5	=	____	____
5. Profit sharing is available.	1 2 3 4 5	×	1 2 3 4 5	=	____	____
6. An appropriate amount of vacation time is available.	1 2 3 4 5	×	1 2 3 4 5	=	____	____
7. An appropriate amount of sick leave is available.	1 2 3 4 5	×	1 2 3 4 5	=	____	____
8. Tuition reimbursement for continuing education or training is available.	1 2 3 4 5	×	1 2 3 4 5	=	____	____
9. The job includes the use of a company car.	1 2 3 4 5	×	1 2 3 4 5	=	____	____
10. An athletic club membership or discount is offered.	1 2 3 4 5	×	1 2 3 4 5	=	____	____
11. I am provided with a computer for home use.	1 2 3 4 5	×	1 2 3 4 5	=	____	____
12. There's good job security (considering the current status of the job market).	1 2 3 4 5	×	1 2 3 4 5	=	____	____

Satisfaction Total = ____ ÷ ____ = ____   Total Score (a) = ____

Highest Possible Score (b) = ____

Rewards/Benefits Work Values Satisfaction Score (a/b) = ____ %

F. **Professional Growth Opportunities (/   )**

1. There is potential for increasing autonomy and freedom in decision

"continued"

	Level of Satisfaction × Level of Importance	= Col-umn 1	Col-umn 2
	Low Average High Low Average High		
making (how to carry out job).	1 2 3 4 5 × 1 2 3 4 5 =	____	____
2. There is potential for increasing levels of respon-sibility (freedom to act and solve problems without close monitoring).	1 2 3 4 5 × 1 2 3 4 5 =	____	____
3. There is potential for an increasing leadership role (directing, managing, or supervising activities of others).	1 2 3 4 5 × 1 2 3 4 5 =	____	____
4. There is potential for promotion from within (job title or salary).	1 2 3 4 5 × 1 2 3 4 5 =	____	____
5. There is potential for increasing opportunities to have creative input in my work.	1 2 3 4 5 × 1 2 3 4 5 =	____	____
6. There is potential to achieve desired levels of status and prestige.	1 2 3 4 5 × 1 2 3 4 5 =	____	____
7. Continuing education is encouraged, and in-house people move laterally to enhance on-the-job growth.	1 2 3 4 5 × 1 2 3 4 5 =	____	____
8. Professional development, through participation in outside organizations/ activities, is encouraged.	1 2 3 4 5 × 1 2 3 4 5 =	____	____

Satisfaction Total = ____ ÷ ____ = ____   Total Score (a) = ____

Highest Possible Score (b) = ____

Professional Growth Opportunities Work Values Satisfaction Score (a/b) = ____ %

"continued"

	Level of Satisfaction	×	Level of Importance	=	Col-umn 1	Col-umn 2
	Low Average High		Low Average High			

G. Personal Development Goals (/   )

1. There's a sense of purpose in my work, helping me in fulfilling my life mission.   1 2 3 4 5 × 1 2 3 4 5 = ____ ____

2. I gain a sense of identity from my work.   1 2 3 4 5 × 1 2 3 4 5 = ____ ____

3. There's an opportunity for personal growth; I'm able to gain new knowledge.   1 2 3 4 5 × 1 2 3 4 5 = ____ ____

4. I'm able to help others in some way through my work.   1 2 3 4 5 × 1 2 3 4 5 = ____ ____

5. My work has a positive impact on my personal life. (It doesn't create excessive stress that carries over.)   1 2 3 4 5 × 1 2 3 4 5 = ____ ____

6. My work offers me a chance to influence others' opinions or decisions in positive ways.   1 2 3 4 5 × 1 2 3 4 5 = ____ ____

7. There's an opportunity to serve as a mentor to newer professionals in my field.   1 2 3 4 5 × 1 2 3 4 5 = ____ ____

8. My work helps me attain inner harmony and peace of mind.   1 2 3 4 5 × 1 2 3 4 5 = ____ ____

Satisfaction Total = ____ ÷ ____ = ____   Total Score (a) = ____

Highest Possible Score (b) = ____

Personal Development Work Values Satisfaction Score (a/b) = ____ %

"continued"

Category Scoring Results

Work Value Categories	Work Value Satisfaction Total Score
A. Company/Organization	_____ %
B. Work Environment	_____ %
C. Supervisor Relations	_____ %
D. The Job Itself	_____ %
E. Rewards/Benefits	_____ %
F. Professional Growth Opportunities	_____ %
G. Personal Development Goals	_____ %

Following are interpretations of the scores in each category:

90–100%   Congratulations! You are **highly satisfied** with this aspect of your job.

80–89%   You are experiencing **above average satisfaction** with this aspect of your job.

70–79%   You are feeling **average satisfaction** with this aspect of your job.

60–69%   You are experiencing **below average satisfaction** with this aspect of your job. This should serve as a warning signal for a problem area.

Below 60%   You have **low satisfaction** with this aspect of the job.

FIGURE 3.2

Entrepreneurial Personal Characteristics Self-Assessment

Directions: In this self-assessment you will rate the degree to which you believe you possess each of the 50 entrepreneurial personal characteristics. The response choices are as follows:

"continued"

5 High

4 Above-average

3 Average

2 Below-average

1 Low

1. Read through the entire list to get familiar with the characteristics.
   Try to be accurate in rating yourself. However, if you tend to be a perfectionist, pay close attention to how high (or low) you rate yourself. You don't have to be perfect to give yourself a 5, just a bit higher than "above average." On the other hand, if you tend to rate yourself too high, make an extra effort to be realistic in your self-ratings.

2. Circle the appropriate rating for each characteristic. Write the score in the space provided.

3. Within each category (A–H), add the ratings and write the total in Total Score (a).

4. Divide Total Score (a) by the number of characteristics in that category to calculate the Average Attainment Level. Write this number next to the category heading, in the parentheses and to the left of the /.
   In the example, the Average Attainment Level is 4.3, which falls between the above average (4) and high (5) rating levels.
   In addition to the Average Attainment Level, pay particular attention to any individual characteristics that you rated 3 or below. In the example, the person represented rated energy level with a degree attained of 3. This person would need to take a serious look at how an average attainment level for energy (mental, emotional, and physical), a major demand of having your own business, could impact on his or her possible success.

5. Compute your total score (a) as a percentage of the highest possible score (b). Multiply the number of characteristics in each category by the highest rating (5). Divide Total Score (a) by Highest Possible Score (b). Write the percentage next to the category heading, in the parentheses and to the right of the /.
   In our example, 30 divided by 35 equals .857, which can be rounded up to 86 percent.

"continued"

A word of caution. A high score in any one category is no guarantee of success at running your own business. You may have only one low score in a category, such as confidence, and still have a high overall category score. Yet unless you work on your confidence level, you could have a difficult time attempting to build a business of your own.

In the same vein, a low score is no guarantee of failure. You might grow and learn in weak areas or find a partner who is strong where you are weak.

Example

Degree Attained

Low   Average   High

E. Motivation/Attitude (4.3 /86%)

1. I am a self-starter. I take initiative in completing tasks.   1 2 3 4 ⑤ = 5

2. I have a high energy level to meet the tremendous mental, emotional, and physical demands of establishing and running a business.   1 2 ③ 4 5 = 3

3. I have a strong drive. I am compelled to move forward and accomplish goals.   1 2 3 4 ⑤ = 5

4. I am determined and inner-directed. I don't let setbacks or others' opinions (e.g., family) deter me from accomplishing goals.   1 2 3 ④ 5 = 4

5. I am enthusiastic by nature.   1 2 3 ④ 5 = 4

6. I am persistent at achieving goals.   1 2 3 4 ⑤ = 5

7. I am optimistic. I have a basic belief in myself.   1 2 3 ④ 5 = 4

Average Attainment Level = 30 ÷ 7 = 4.3 Total Score (a) = 30

Highest Possible Score (b) = 35

Motivation/Attitude Attainment Score (a/b) = 86%

"continued"

	Degree Attained		
	Low	Average	High

A. Idea Person (/   )

1. I am creative; I can generate   1 2 3 4 5   = ____
   ideas.

2. I always look for a better way to   1 2 3 4 5   = ____
   do things in an effort to improve.

3. I can develop an idea and make   1 2 3 4 5   = ____
   it work, based on market research,
   realistic goals, and constant feedback from the marketplace.

4. I am resourceful. When required   1 2 3 4 5   = ____
   information is not readily available,
   I am able to find out how and where
   to get it.

Average Attainment Level = ____ ÷ _4_ = ____ Total Score (a) = ____

Highest Possible Score (b) = _20_

Idea Person Attainment Score (a/b) = __%

B. Technical Knowledge (/   )

1. I have talent and expertise in an   1 2 3 4 5   = ____
   area of value to the marketplace.

2. I have solid business sense; I can   1 2 3 4 5   = ____
   spot opportunity readily and act
   on it appropriately.

3. I am always ready to learn more.   1 2 3 4 5   = ____

Average Attainment Level = ____ ÷ _3_ = ____ Total Score (a) = ____

Highest Possible Score (b) = _15_

Technical Knowledge Attainment Score (a/b) = __%

C. Management (/   )

1. I am excellent at organizing and   1 2 3 4 5   = ____
   planning, not only to get started,
   but to keep things going.

"continued"

	Degree Attained		
	Low Average High		
2. I can effectively manage time to meet the variety of demands of business, family, and social life.	1 2 3 4 5		= ___
3. I need to control and direct. I want freedom to initiate action and attain goals.	1 2 3 4 5		= ___
4. I can identify problems in the midst of confused and complex situations and work on solutions faster than most.	1 2 3 4 5		= ___
5. I am far-sighted as well as aware of important, immediate details. I can prioritize activities and tasks appropriately to achieve my overall goal.	1 2 3 4 5		= ___
6. I am able to weigh the pros and cons, make decisions, and live with the consequences.	1 2 3 4 5		= ___
7. I have enough financial and organizational ability to appropriately budget expenses and income.	1 2 3 4 5		= ___
8. I can delegate tasks effectively.	1 2 3 4 5		= ___
9. I am self-disciplined.	1 2 3 4 5		= ___

Average Attainment Level = ___ ÷ _9_ = ___ Total Score (a) = ___

Highest Possible Score (b) = _45_

Management Attainment Score (a/b) = ___%

D. Work Ethic (/)

1. I have a good reputation in community and business aspects of life.	1 2 3 4 5	= ___
2. I strive for a level of excellence in work, product, or services provided.	1 2 3 4 5	= ___

"continued"

	Degree Attained						
	Low		Average		High		

3. I am willing to take responsibility for all aspects of the business.   1 2 3 4 5   = ____

4. I can maintain my commitment to business success for countless hours with no guarantee of payoff, even if family and friends do not understand my slow progress.   1 2 3 4 5   = ____

5. I establish goals on a daily, weekly, monthly, and even yearly basis and pursue their accomplishment in a realistic manner.   1 2 3 4 5   = ____

6. I am attentive to detail.   1 2 3 4 5   = ____

7. I am honest in dealings with others: clients/customers, employees, and business associates.   1 2 3 4 5   = ____

8. I am able to make family and social life sacrifices in order to put in 60–80 hours per week for the first year or so.   1 2 3 4 5   = ____

Average Attainment Level = ____ ÷ __8__ = ____ Total Score (a) = ____

Highest Possible Score (b) = __40__

Work Ethic Attainment Score (a/b) = ___%

E. Motivation/Attitude (/   )

1. I am a self-starter. I take initiative in completing tasks.   1 2 3 4 5   = ____

2. I have a high energy level to meet the tremendous mental, emotional, and physical demands of establishing and running a business.   1 2 3 4 5   = ____

3. I have a strong drive. I am compelled to move forward and accomplish goals.   1 2 3 4 5   = ____

4. I am determined and inner-directed. I don't let setbacks or others' opinions   1 2 3 4 5   = ____

"continued"

	Degree Attained		
	Low	Average	High

(e.g., family) deter me from accomplishing goals.

5. I am enthusiastic by nature.   1 2 3 4 5   = ____

6. I am persistent at achieving goals.   1 2 3 4 5   = ____

7. I am optimistic. I have a basic belief   1 2 3 4 5   = ____
in myself.

Average Attainment Level = ____ ÷ _7_ = ____ Total Score (a) = ____

Highest Possible Score (b) = _35_

Motivation/Attitude Attainment Score (a/b) = __ %

F. **Personality (/   )**

1. I am independent and self-reliant.   1 2 3 4 5   = ____

2. I have faith in myself. I am willing   1 2 3 4 5   = ____
to take on challenges with no
guarantees.

3. I can exhibit considerable self-   1 2 3 4 5   = ____
control under difficult circumstances
and handle business anxieties and
pressures with relative ease.

4. I rarely lose objectivity. I can   1 2 3 4 5   = ____
accept things as they are and deal
with them.

5. I have a strong desire to excel,   1 2 3 4 5   = ____
accomplish goals, and be better
than others.

6. I am persuasive. I can communicate   1 2 3 4 5   = ____
to others the value of my product
or services in a convincing manner.

7. I can handle rejection and failure.   1 2 3 4 5   = ____
I am challenged rather than dis-
couraged by setbacks or failures.

8. I am not too proud to seek the   1 2 3 4 5   = ____
advice of others.

"continued"

	Degree Attained
	Low Average High

Average Attainment Level = ____ ÷ _8_ = ____ Total Score (a) = ____

Highest Possible Score (b) = _40_

Personality Attainment Score (a/b) = __%

G. Interpersonal Relations (/   )

1. I enjoy and pursue interactions and involvements with others, especially within the context of running a business. 1 2 3 4 5 = ____

2. I can work well with others in difficult situations. 1 2 3 4 5 = ____

3. I am more concerned with a person's accomplishments than his or her feelings. I choose experts rather than friends as business associates. 1 2 3 4 5 = ____

4. I am able to negotiate, whether with business associates, customers/clients, or even family members. I can compromise in working out arrangements in difficult situations. 1 2 3 4 5 = ____

Average Attainment Level = ____ ÷ _4_ = ____ Total Score (a) = ____

Highest Possible Score (b) = _20_

Interpersonal Relations Attainment Score (a/b) = __%

H. Life-Style (/   )

1. I enjoy challenges. I am attracted to situations that test my skills, knowledge and ability to solve problems. 1 2 3 4 5 = ____

2. I maintain a healthy life-style. 1 2 3 4 5 = ____

3. I am flexible enough to adapt to various demands. 1 2 3 4 5 = ____

"continued"

	Degree Attained		
	Low	Average	High

4. I am willing to take personal and financial risk.   1 2 3 4 5   = ____

5. I am flexible with life-style needs.   1 2 3 4 5   = ____

6. I can handle isolation.   1 2 3 4 5   = ____

7. I am comfortable without structure.   1 2 3 4 5   = ____

Average Attainment Level = ____ ÷ _7_ = ____ Total Score (a) = ____

Highest Possible Score (b) = _35_

Life-Style Attainment Score (a/b) = __ %

Category Scoring Results

Entrepreneurial Personal Characteristic Categories	Entrepreneurial Personal Characteristic Average Attainment and Percentage Scores
A. Idea Person	____ / ____ %
B. Technical Knowledge	____ / ____ %
C. Management	____ / ____ %
D. Work Ethic	____ / ____ %
E. Motivation/Attitude	____ / ____ %
F. Personality	____ / ____ %
G. Interpersonal Relations	____ / ____ %
H. Life-Style	____ / ____ %

Following are interpretations of the scores in each category:

90–100%   Congratulations! You've attained, to a high degree, the entrepreneurial characteristics in this category.

80–89%   You've attained, to an above-average degree, the entrepreneurial characteristics of this category.

70–79%   You've attained, to an average degree, the entrepreneurial characteristics of this category.

"continued"

60–69%   Your attainment of the entrepreneurial characteristics
                of this category is below average.

Below 60%   You indicate a low degree of attainment of the
                entrepreneurial characteristics of this category.

A Grand Total Percentage Attainment Score for the entire assessment
exercise can be computed by completing the following calculation:

Add the Total Scores (a) for Categories A–H: = _____

Divided by the sum of Highest Possible Scores (b): =   250

Grand Total Percentage Attainment Score = _____

CHAPTER *4*

UNDERSTANDING AND CONQUERING YOUR CAREER CHANGE FEARS

Procrastination

Procrastination is postponing, delaying, deferring action on, or putting off something. Not all procrastination is bad. It's only a problem when it becomes troublesome to you in some way.

Everybody procrastinates once in a while, but for some people, procrastination is a problem that can ruin relationships, cause emotional pain, and sabotage careers. You may have experienced this state of indecision yourself or with someone you are close to. Procrastination can be tremendously frustrating. Those close to the procrastinator cannot understand why it's taking so long for the person to decide and take some action. Those experiencing procrastination feel frozen in a state of indecision.

Procrastination and Career Decision Making

Listed below are a few of the general reasons why someone might procrastinate with respect to career decision making and some suggestions on how to deal with the difficulty.

Unclear Career Goal.   You may not be very clear about who you are and what you want for yourself. This could be an issue of identifying what is important to you—your interests, skills, values, and personality preferences—and combining them with related career information to generate some ideas for career goals. If that process doesn't work for you, then the issue could be a deeper one related to identify and self-esteem.

Variety of Interests and Abilities.

One might not think people with multiple interests and abilities would have difficulty in career decision making. However, their interests may be of equal importance, with no one option standing out as best. The person could decide on any number of directions and probably feels pulled in several. In this case, setting priorities could help you focus.

Or it could be a case of not wanting to let go of the other options that's keeping you from making a decision. If this applies to you, it's important to recognize that having it all is a much different issue than not knowing what career to go into. The challenge here would be to set priorities and to identify a career that includes a number of your top interests, if possible.

In addition, you could pursue other interests away from the job during leisure time as hobbies or avocational pursuits. If this approach does not work, counseling might be needed to deal with this "having it all" mentality. Try to "have as much as possible" instead.

Finding Fault with All Alternatives.

Perhaps, somehow, you find something wrong with each possible choice. No alternative looks appealing, so you decide not to act (or not to decide). We all know that every situation, every decision, has its pros and cons. Determine whether the aspects that you value the most regarding a potential career are more in the pros column or more in the cons column.

Once you are clear on your values and understand the various aspects of a particular job, you are in a position to assess whether most of your top values have the potential of being met. You can then proceed accordingly.

Possibilities for dealing with negative factors range from lessening their percentage to possibly removing them from the job description and replacing them with something else. Again, here's where research pays off. You need to be aware of your employer's needs, as well as your talents and skills, to be able to accomplish this challenging bit of negotiation.

Unsure of Self.

This whole career decision-making process can leave you in a nervous state, unsure of what to do. As mentioned previously, with change comes risk. It's natural to have some self-doubt. This is another reason to be certain that you have done your homework on yourself and have established a relevant, meaningful career goal. This will help remove some of the doubt.

In the process of establishing your career goal, which includes identifying your skills, you could seek out the opinion of experts in your field as to how they see your level of skill and potential success. This would also put you in a position of either knowing you had the skills necessary (relieving your doubt) or knowing you need further skill development.

Procrastinating in making a career decision could have its roots in fear: the fear of change, failing, or even success. Even perfectionism fits in here, because some of us won't do anything unless we can do it perfectly. Many of these fears are grounded in unrealistic thinking. Let's look at possible fears as well as perfectionism in order to better understand them.

Fear of Change

The average American will work for 10 different employers, keep each job 3.6 years, and change careers 3 times before retiring. With career-related and general forecasts of change, people who are flexible and adaptable will be better off. One might think that the only security is having the confidence to cope with the insecurity that accompanies change. In situations like these, real inner security means trusting yourself to be able to handle the unexpected.

Being afraid to change is natural. You're going from the familiar (even if dissatisfying) to the unfamiliar. Many people desire stability and dislike breaks in routine. Your identity and self-esteem might be tied to your surroundings, your security comes from predictable events, and you know what to expect. However, sometimes desire for routine can lead you to miss out on many of the possible satisfactions in life, including an enjoyable and rewarding career.

Even though change can often initially appear threatening, it can serve as a catalyst to go on to new and better possibilities. Although it is easier to just stay put, try to view change as an opportunity to allow new experiences into your life. If you hang in there, the new situation can also become comfortable, and you will have eliminated the dissatisfying aspect of your former position.

Whether you are forced to take action as a result of external factors or are internally motivated to do so, it is certain to involve some degree of change. Of course, if internally motivated you usually have the luxury of being able to plan for it, as opposed to externally motivated situations where you are taken by surprise.

Some other fears of potential career changers are listed here:

1. Disruption of a familiar and comfortable routine

2. Possible unanticipated events as a result of taking action

3. Risking job security in current position (when change is your choice)

4. Financial risks of being unemployed (when change is not your choice)

5. Self-doubt and the unknown

6. Validating whether you have the skills you thought you had by sticking your neck out in a new career

7. Losing status and sense of identity

8. Not getting along with new supervisor and co-workers

These concerns could lead career decision makers to make no decision at all or to choose inaction at a time when they are either losing their job or know it's best (or urgent, depending on their circumstances) to make a change.

To overcome your hesitation about career decision making, you need to face your fears. This implies taking risks. To take that step forward into the unknown, you need to be flexible enough, as well as courageous enough, to leave the familiar routine and try something new. You should improve your chances of success through sound planning, preparation, and research. As a result, you will help to make the unknown more known, which will lessen your fear.

However, if you are unsuccessful, it might mean getting hurt, experiencing rejection in not getting a job interview, feeling nervous while taking a test during the interview process and doing poorly, or finding out that your skills are judged to be not good enough.

As painful as these outcomes may be, try not to be afraid to fail. Failing is a learning experience. If you try your best and take a positive approach and still fail, at least you know you gave it your best shot. Recognize that you are only human, and forgive yourself for not being perfect. Then take the time to figure out what went wrong. Do everything within your power to remedy the situation, and then try again.

Change with regard to work involves important factors such as money, status, power, relationships, self-image, self-confidence, personal satisfaction, and other factors that shape our lives both directly and indirectly. This can result in a fair amount of worry, if not downright anxiety. However, worrying about change tends to cause more anxiety than the change itself.

Usually, change means giving something up, letting go in order to move forward. Letting go can be difficult. It could involve losing some sense of self. Often, letting go is the biggest block for some career changers who want it all.

Fear has a purpose. Once you accept and recognize it, it serves to alert you to take action to protect yourself from possible loss. One approach for coping with your fear of change is to imagine the worst possible result of your decision. What is so frightening about the change? If this happened, what would you do? Can you prevent this? How?

People who are most afraid of taking risks might experience high levels of anxiety that could interfere with their ability to realistically assess their interests and skills, see the various alternatives, and set and accomplish goals. If severe, there is probably a self-esteem and identity problem to be attended to first in order to benefit from career counseling.

On the other hand, if your fears are more within the norm, you need to recognize the phases involved in making a career change. By breaking down what seems to be an overwhelming problem into smaller, more manageable steps, you can help to eliminate much of the mystery and self-doubt involved in changing your career.

Making a meaningful career decision, one that fits well, takes a combination of understanding your interests, skills, values, personality preferences and career awareness (what's really involved in a particular job). When you accomplish a good match, you'll know it. It will feel right, and you'll be able to proceed with confidence. This will help to alleviate much of your fear about changing careers.

Fear of Failing

The fear of failing is probably the most common fear that keeps people from taking risks of all kinds. If you associate your self-worth with external success to an unrealistic degree, then you might be troubled by this fear. Many people who fear failing are concerned about being judged by others or by themselves. Perhaps they or others feel they're not living up to their own expectations, and their inner voice expresses disappointment. They often fear they'll be found to be deficient in some way and that their best attempts won't be satisfactory.

Often, those who fear failing at tasks view it as failing as a person. Society values success over failing and equates failure with inadequacy. Therefore, one might think, "If I perform well, that means I have a lot of ability, so I like myself and feel good about myself." This person considers his or her performance to be a direct measure of ability and worth. But if performance is the only measure of a person and nothing else is taken into account, self-esteem and confidence can be destroyed by failure. Self-worth cannot be measured by external success alone. You are no less a person if you don't succeed at what you try to do.

What is success anyway? Each of us would define it differently. Success is a subjective perception; it's what any one individual values. Often, those who fear failing measure themselves against an unrealistic standard of perfection of how successful, smart, or talented they think they should be and then fail to measure up. That's assuming they've tried in the first place. Such people often elect not to try. (If they can't attain these high expectations, why bother at all?)

The key to conquering the fear of failing is to ask yourself, "How do I define success?" Determine what measuring stick you're using to decide whether success has been achieved. Is your measuring stick realistic? Are you expecting perfection or close to it? If you can adjust how you judge yourself and attempt to be more realistic in both your expectations and measurement of success, you will be more inclined to take a chance in situations that you previously avoided. You will be on your way to overcoming your fear of failing.

With healthy self-esteem and confidence, you're not as vulnerable to others' opinion at times of failure. You'll be more inclined to pick yourself up, assess the situation, note what needs to be remedied, and try again. It's not to say that you won't feel bad; it's just that it won't feel like the end of the world.

••

Three of our career changers—Martha, Mac, and Victoria—reported fearing failing. Martha's biggest fear was going from dealing with children (in the classroom) to adults (employees, suppliers, and the customers). Not only did she succeed in her transition, but her teaching skills came in handy when instructing employees.

Mac wasn't sure how well he would relate with high school students as a counselor, after almost 30 years of being in business for himself and dealing only with adults. Mac was glad to find out that inner-city high school counselors are well respected by the students. They often have the last word about whether a student in trouble stays or goes. This, in combination with the type of person Mac is (easy to talk with, personable), helped Mac in making a successful transition.

Victoria feared making mistakes. Her career change created a risky situation. For 14 years she had a secure government position with seniority (even though it ended with a recent layoff). Now she was facing a corporate position with less security. Victoria helped to smooth her transition by doing well at free-lance work in technical writing for six months prior to making the complete move into a new position. In addition, she consulted with a friend who had recently made the same career change, and her positive experience also helped calm Victoria's fear.

••

Sidney Simon offers some possible consequences of fearing failing and how it affects us and our lives. The fear of failing:

• Reduces the number of available alternatives or keeps you from pursuing them.

- Persuades you to set easier goals and do less than your best.

- Leads you to create good reasons not to change (perhaps by painting a rosy picture of the here and now).

- Causes indecisiveness and confusion, which stop you from knowing what you really want.

- Keeps you from asking for help when you need it or accepting support from others when offered.

- Distorts your perception of your life and what you can do to make it better.

- Can keep you from asserting yourself, so you tend to settle for less.

- Can lead to the development of unhealthy habits and behavior patterns (e.g., substance abuse).

- Keeps you from taking risks and therefore experiencing possible growth.

Two Different Outlooks

Martin Seligman discusses how two different types of people, optimists and pessimists, respond to failure. Optimists see defeat as a temporary setback. They view it as a singular situation and do not generalize it to their whole being. They don't blame themselves. If things don't work out they realize that at least they've tried and make note of what needs further attention to help improve their chances of success when they try again. When optimists are confronted by a bad situation, they perceive it as a challenge and try even harder.

On the other hand, pessimists give up more easily and get depressed more often. Usually the problem lies in their habits of thinking—how they view events and their outlook. If you're more of a pessimist, then you need to develop strategies for correcting distorted thinking (the destructive things we say to ourselves when we experience a setback) and raising self-esteem and confidence. The goal is to go from helplessness to gaining personal control in your life, thereby allowing you a greater chance of experiencing success rather than failure.

Fear of Failing and the Career Change

Anyone would fear repeating past mistakes such as performing poorly on the job (more than we can handle, too much responsibility, etc.) or not getting along with co-workers or a supervisor. Past experiences like these can leave us feeling vulnerable if we have not worked on the aspect of ourselves needing attention: career goals, job or interpersonal skills, evaluation of job offers, or self-esteem and confidence leading to interviewing and presentation skills.

Fear of Success

As strange as "fear of success" might sound to some, to others it's a reality. For many of us, success represents the satisfaction of completing a goal with a sense of accomplishment. However, others give up just short of accomplishing their goal. Why? Some people are subconsciously worried that they might look too good and would therefore have to face some unpleasant consequences of recognition. That's being fearful of success.

Yes, even achieving success means facing change and the unknown. With fear of failing, we are afraid of losing our reputation, pride, sense of identity, job, or money, and so we might decide not to compete. With fear of success, one is actually afraid of winning. Central to this concern are the questions: "What will this level of achievement bring in the form of new responsibility, demands, or expectations (from family members, friends, colleagues, or employers)? Can I make it, if and when I get there?" "Will people treat me differently?" Thus, a fear of success can be part of a future fear of failing.

Jane Burka and Lenora Yuen present the following additional reasons for fearing success:

1. May have to work longer hours to live up to expectations, possibly becoming a workaholic. Need to gain better control of one's time.

2. May feel undeserving of success, not good enough to have what you want. This is usually grounded in low self-esteem, but your success might have actually caused problems for others. If so, try to remedy the situation and attempt to move one. If you're stuck in guilt, consider personal counseling.

3. Possible consequences of success include jealousy of others, loss of friends, and loneliness. People who fear success tend to assume responsibility for others' feelings. The most you can ask of yourself is to be conscious of how you're handling your success when around others.

4. Some fear being punished for their success (almost like a superstition). They might gain center stage and then be vulnerable to some form of challenge or criticism from others, revealing their imperfection.

5. Some can't even see success having a place in their lives. They see themselves as lacking the traits success requires. Again, this is a self-esteem issue.

Fear of Success and Gender

Simon discusses gender-related differences in the fear of success. For example, men might believe that as a result of being successful, they must live up to traditional expectations of working long hours to maintain success. This could make it difficult for some men to enjoy play and leisure, express tenderness, be open about doubts and insecurities, or ask for comfort. Women's experiences are even more complicated. As a result of success they fear social rejection, being seen as unfeminine (based on old cultural norms), and accusations of crossing the sex-role barrier.

Simon adds that it's common for an achieving woman whose power, status, and wealth might threaten the men (or significant others) in her life to be concerned that her success will cause the loss of a relationship. The fear of success can overwhelm her, and she might decide to stop achieving. She sabotages her own career goals or even leaves the work force ("rat race") to pursue less demanding and threatening interests.

A promotion or career change can complicate life with new responsibilities, the challenge of once again proving one's competency, and the need to gain the approval and acceptance of a new supervisor and co-workers. The key is to view changes as challenges and opportunities, rather than obstacles, so you can enjoy and build on your success.

Your success doesn't need to bring about the adverse consequences you fear. By developing your ability fully and achieving all you can, you're showing respect for your gifts as a human being and providing a healthy role model for others. It is true that some people in your life might have difficulty dealing with your success. However, others will take pride and share your joy in your success.

Perfectionism

Perfectionism is related more to unrealistic attitudes than to perfect behavior or performance. High achievers are usually not perfectionists. They realize that at times they will make mistakes or have a bad day. They usually set high goals for themselves, but they are able to tolerate disappointment. Rather than giving up in frustration, they know they can do better and work hard to do so.

Perfectionists usually expect more of themselves than is realistic. Everything must be perfect. Their impossibly high expectations cannot be met, but they refuse to accept anything less than exactly what they want. Therefore, they would rather not attempt to reach desired goals if perfection cannot be attained. It's not how high their standards are that make them perfectionists, but rather how unrealistic and inhibiting their standards are for them.

Just how does one become a perfectionist? One possibility is being taught early in life that self-worth is equal to success. If you grow up learning that nothing is good enough, eventually you see all efforts as inadequate.

Later on, the perfectionist becomes stuck when facing challenges that test skills or put work or ideas on the line. This, again, reflects low self-esteem and an overwhelming need for approval. The need for approval could result in inaction caused by fear of disapproval.

Are You a Perfectionist?

Two sets of characteristics are presented here to help you determine whether you are a perfectionist. The first is a list of general indicators of being a perfectionist and the second is a list of beliefs that perfectionists possess.

Ann Smith lists the following indicators of perfectionism:

1. Negative self-talk prevents enjoying still and quiet moments.

2. Feeling like you're never doing enough, having a long "To Do" list.

3. Obsessing about details of a task, anticipating problems beforehand, being unable to break tasks down into manageable pieces.

4. Being frustrated with and criticizing others' imperfection.

5. Practicing rigid, purposeless rituals in the name of organization, structure, cleanliness, or believing it is the right way (e.g., keeping the home in perfect order, ironing underwear, spending hours organizing activities and minutes doing them). Applied to job search activities, perfectionism might lead to constantly revising your resume but never sending it out because it isn't good enough.

6. Feeling the need to be the best when competing, yet never feeling satisfied with the outcome.

7. Having an all-or-nothing philosophy, believing in absolute terms that things are either right or wrong, always or never with no gray areas.

8. Struggling with spirituality, feeling unworthy and judged, needing or depending on God, but thinking you must be perfect to be accepted.

In addition, Burke and Yuen identify several beliefs of perfectionists:

1. Being ordinary is intolerable. Everything I do must be outstanding.

2. I must do everything myself. It's a sign of weakness to relieve myself of responsibility by getting assistance (e.g., career counseling).

3. There's only one correct solution to a problem, and it's my responsibility not to take action until I find it (resulting in doing nothing).

4. I must avoid any activity that would bring me into direct competition with others, because losing is intolerable.

5. As long as a project is incomplete, nothing has been accomplished.

6. Even small mistakes are catastrophic.

After reviewing the characteristics and beliefs of perfectionists, you probably have a better idea about your own degree of perfectionism (high, medium, low), and in what areas of your life it exhibits itself (work, family, love relationship, friends).

If you are a perfectionist to some degree, one suggestion is to imagine the worst case scenario for your career situation. Try to visualize it—what do you see? You might visualize a difficult interview, failing once on the job, not getting along with your new supervisor, or being shunned by fellow employees. It might help to remind yourself that although these fantasies are your fears, they're most likely exaggerated. However, let's assume they're not. Once your worst fears are visualized, what can you do to prepare to confront them?

Take, for example, changing careers and failing to perform adequately once on the job because of a lack of skills. If you're interested in a specific job, then your task is to identify exactly what skills are required and at what level of expertise. You need to measure the difference between that and your present skill level. Once you identify the skills you need to gain, and how and where you can gain them, you will be ready to seek employment in that career field once again.

Anxiety, Stress, or Depression

Fear and anxiety can cloud your thinking and produce a sense of dread and impending doom that reduces your ability to make decisions or take action. You may feel paralyzed and powerless because of your fears.

Many people react to fear and anxiety by avoiding anything that frightens them or makes them anxious. If a decision causes anxiety, one avoids making it. Fears are powerful. They can dictate how you live your life, limit your enjoyment or satisfaction, and cause you problems in trying to make changes in your career and life. Fears can obstruct the career change at any point of the process, from the initial setting of a career objective to the job search itself, including networking and job interviewing.

Work is an important part of our identity, so issues of low self-esteem, fears, anxiety, stress, and depression may result when adults are faced with the threat of change or loss of career. Let's take a closer look at anxiety and the stress it can cause.

Acceptance Anxiety

Changing careers entails a few types of anxiety. The first could be thought of as *acceptance anxiety*. To successfully make a career change, we need to gain the approval of those doing the hiring. For each of us, to different degrees, our sense of self-worth is bound up with the approval of others. The larger that degree, the more anxiety we will experience over being accepted for a particular job.

If we make the desired job or career change, we might continue to experience acceptance anxiety. We have some control over being accepted and liked by supervisors and co-workers, but it is far from complete. Beyond what we learn from the interview process, all we can do is to have a professional attitude, be committed to our work, and show respect for ourselves, our jobs, and others.

However, if poor interpersonal skills have hurt you in your efforts to get along with others in the past, then some corrective action on your part might be necessary. This could include personal counseling (individual or group), as well as communication courses or workshops.

Performance Anxiety

In addition to acceptance anxiety once on the job, there's also the possibility of performance anxiety. If you're unsure about how your skills match up to the requirements of the targeted job, you could seek feedback from experts in the field. They may be able to shed some light on the degree to which you have the required skills. Nevertheless, some people hesitate to put themselves to the test because of performance anxiety. Depending on the degree to which it exists, it could create a good deal of stress.

Frustration Anxiety

One other type of general anxiety comes into play when making a career change. Compromise is inevitable in any change; we gain something, yet we have to give up something else. The challenge is to make a change in which you value what you gain more than what you give up. Personal and financial sacrifices are often necessary to achieve your goals, dreams, and ambitions.

For example, a career changer has a job opportunity of greater interest that is more related to his or her long-range goal. However, there is an initial salary cut and less available leisure time. This person will have to weigh the pros (more interesting work leading toward overall career goal) against the cons (initial salary cut and loss of leisure time). Certainly, no one would be happy about the cons, but some people might become downright anxious over it. The thought of not getting all of one's needs met can cause frustration and anxiety.

If you currently suffer from anxiety, is it a normal amount or more severe? Try to recall a recent situation such as a job interview, in which you strongly desired particular results. Did you experience any of the following symptoms of severe anxiety?

- Dizziness

- Heavy perspiration

- Clammy hands

- Increased heart rate

- Rapid breathing

- Faintness

- Chest pain or pressure

Such severe anxiety does have its consequences. During a job interview it can certainly affect the content of your answers and the style in which you communicate your responses. Other consequences of severe anxiety include being less productive, inability to concentrate, overcompensating (which others can usually see through), and measuring yourself against an unrealistic standard.

Anxiety can bring on stress. Stress is what we experience when our body systems perceive and react to an event or situation as threatening or challenging. Therefore, the stress response is both psychological and physiological. The psychological stress may be experienced as anxiety, tension, depression, anger, fear, helplessness, hopelessness, or other emotions. Physiologically, stress is experienced as a variety of bodily responses: the heart beats a little too fast, blood pressure remains elevated, the stomach fails to digest properly, muscles stay tense, and breathing remains shallow. In time, a stress-related illness can develop. Among these familiar psychosomatic or psychogenic illnesses are headaches, ulcers, lower back pain, and hypertension.

Illnesses not caused by stress can be aggravated by it: asthma, arthritis, diabetes, epilepsy, and even the common cold. This is because stress depletes the body's resources and hinders its innate ability to restore and maintain healthy functioning. If excessive, stress can prevent you from attaining your career goal by lowering your energy, immune system, and confidence. Recognizing the signs of stress is the first step in reducing it.

Fortunately, we have the ability to trigger a mechanism that reverses the stress response: relaxation response. With relaxation of mind and body, physiological change automatically occurs: the heart rate slows down, blood pressure drops, breathing becomes calm, blood flow increases in hands and feet, muscles release tension, and there is also brain wave change. The processes involved in the stress response begin to return to normal functioning.

Body and mind respond equally to stress and relaxation, and with adequate amounts of each, a healthy balance will be maintained. The difficulty is that so often the balance is weighted heavily on the side of stress. We can counter this with techniques that promote deep relaxation.

Depression

At times, when unattended to, our worries and concerns can lead to being depressed. Depression is characterized by feelings of helplessness, hopelessness, inadequacy, and sadness. Some depression is to be expected in situations such as loss of one's job, a career setback, burnout with job or job search, adverse office politics, or inability to realize one's dream.

However, we must differentiate between mild depression, which is normal in certain circumstances and severe depression, which impedes one's ability to participate in career planning activities. There are certain "danger signs" used to distinguish between temporary, mild, and severe depression. If you have five of the following nine symptoms over a two-week period, then you are in a major depressive episode, according to the American Psychiatric Association:

- Depressed mood
- Loss of interest in usual activity
- Loss of appetite
- Insomnia
- Psychomotor retardation (slow thought or movement)
- Loss of energy
- Feelings of worthlessness and guilt
- Diminished ability to think and poor concentration
- Suicidal thought or attempt

If you are experiencing severe depression, obtain professional counseling without delay. Even if you are only moderately depressed, you need to know how to help yourself and when and where to seek help.

Your job success and an optimistic outlook go hand in hand. A confident, upbeat outlook increases your ability to make decisions, which can improve the quality of your life in general and your career specifically. You'll be better equipped to handle setbacks, because you'll view them as challenges and work hard to rise above them.

Relaxation and Stress Management

Relaxation is a skill. Like all skills, learning to relax involves instruction and practice. Let's review a few of the many approaches to managing stress through relaxation. To pursue any of these methods that sound interesting, get the books mentioned here, or one of many others on the topic. Courses and workshops on these methods are offered frequently in many areas.

A crucial first step before attempting any of these methods is to consult a physician about your physical preparedness to attempt these techniques. People with heart or respiratory conditions, back problems, or mental health issues, as well as pregnant women, should take special precautions.

We will briefly discuss progressive self-relaxation (PSR), sensory fantasy, Hatha yoga, concentrative meditation, hypnosis, biofeedback, systematic desensitization, and the threshold method.

Progressive self-relaxation (PSR) involves alternately tensing and relaxing different muscle groups until you've moved through your body and achieve a state of complete relaxation. Formal PSR requires that you listen to (or follow) a detailed set of instructions (scripts). There is usually a longer set for the first few weeks of training and then an abbreviated version. The instructions can be memorized or recorded on tape and played back during a relaxation session. Professionally recorded relaxation tapes can be found at bookstores, especially those specializing in East-West psychology, and related music outlets. A good source for PSR, including instructions and scripts, is *BT: Behavior Therapy: Strategies for Solving Problems in Living,* by Spencer Rathus and Jeffrey Nevid. After learning PSR and becoming familiar with the feeling of deep relaxation, you can learn other methods, such as sensory fantasy.

Sensory fantasy involves imagining a special place that was relaxing for you. For example, you might picture yourself at a favorite beach with no one else around. The more vividly you can imagine this scene, the more involved and relaxed the fantasy will be. It's suggested that you visit this special place for 15 minutes, then slowly return to the present. Allow a few minutes to adjust to your actual surroundings. This technique, if practiced regularly, can provide a reliable and effective way of achieving a relaxed state.

Hatha yoga means mastery of body and breath. *Pranayana,* the yogic science of breath control, is at the very heart of Hatha yoga practice. It's believed that stress leads to the contraction of respiratory muscles. Breathing becomes shallower and more restricted, resulting in the intake of less air and less oxygen. Through controlled yoga breathing, you may be able to raise your level of vitality, feel more conscious, tone your nervous system, and generally feel better. For a description of the physiological process of breathing, including basic facts related to the anatomy and physiology of respiration, consult *The Complete Yoga Book,* by James Hewitt.

Meditation is a general term applied to the methods of steadying, quieting, or opening the mind for the purpose of expanding states of consciousness, intuitive awareness, and deeper relaxation. Concentrative meditation is a yogic practice intended to calm and tone the nervous system and help you relax, thus protecting against stress. This is accomplished by focusing awareness on a fixed point and steadying your mind. Yoga and meditation instruction can be found in a variety of settings: East-West psychology centers, health clubs, adult education centers, and private instruction.

Hypnosis is a method of focusing your mind and then using your imagination and thoughts to stir feelings and to alter your behavior and attitude. In hypnosis, you are altering your internal world. When you change how you think and imagine things to be, your feelings and behavior can begin to change. Hypnosis is simply a focused state of attention and concentration that allows you to use more of the potential and power of your mind.

If you think you might benefit from hypnotherapy, you should discuss it with your psychologist, physician, or other health care professional. They should be informed enough to discuss with you the pros and cons of this approach in helping you better attain your goals. If your health care professional doesn't seem knowledgeable enough about hypnotherapy to give you a recommendation for or against it, then consult one of the professional associations listed here for referrals to trained hypnotherapy professionals:

American Society of Clinical Hypnosis
2250 E. Devon Avenue, Suite 331
Des Plaines, IL 60018

Society for Clinical and Experimental Hypnosis
129-A Kings Park Drive
Liverpool, New York 13088

Biofeedback is a treatment technique in which people are trained to improve their health by using signals from their own bodies. In the term *biofeedback,* the *bio* refers to the biological organs, the human being, and the *feedback* is provided by safe electronic instruments. These instruments are attached to various parts of the human body to measure the strength or intensity of a particular biological signal by a light, a meter, or a tone. For clients, the biofeedback machine acts as a kind of sixth sense that allows them to "see" or "hear" activity inside their bodies.

Many clients participating in biofeedback training who practice the skills of relaxation and stress management achieve significant symptom reduction and are able to reduce or eliminate related medication (biofeedback therapists work in conjunction with your personal physician). Clients often report a renewed sense of physical and mental well-being and improved self-image. If you think you might benefit from biofeedback training, you should discuss it with your physician or other health care professional. For further assistance, contact the Association for Applied Psychophysiology and Biofeedback, 10200 W. 44th Avenue, Suite 304, Wheat Ridge, CO 80033.

Systematic desensitization through visualization is an approach to help you clearly define the target situation that is causing anxiety, such as a job interview, and imagine yourself going through a series of steps of graduated difficulty, with each more closely approaching the situation you fear. At every step, relaxation techniques are used to help you cope with whatever is fearful for you at that stage. When you are able to imagine yourself in the frightening situation and remain completely relaxed for several minutes, you can then move on the next step. Eventually you will be able to remain completely relaxed as you picture yourself in the target situation. The desensitization process can rarely be accomplished in one sitting, or even in a few. A desensitization session should not last longer than an hour, and because several sessions may be required to overcome your fear, you may need a considerable length of time to complete a desensitization program. Figure 4.1 details an example of the desensitization process.

FIGURE 4.1

Overcoming Anxiety about the Job Interview through Desensitization

Approaching the Interview

1. Construct a hierarchy of fears by writing each incremental step in the job interview process on a 3 x 5 card. Each step should be only slightly more unsettling than the one before. Here is an example list of incremental steps:

   • Getting up, showering, dressing, and having breakfast

"continued"

- Leaving home, driving downtown (on the expressway, if applicable), or using public transportation

- Arriving at the office building where the interview will be conducted, parking in an indoor garage (if applicable)

- Entering the building, standing in the lobby, verifying the interview office location, taking the elevator to the appropriate floor

- Exiting the elevator, walking down the hallway, finding the office where the interview is to take place

- Entering the office, announcing yourself to the receptionist, having a seat

- Waiting to be called in for the interview

2. Number the cards 1 to 7, 1 for the least frightening step and 7 for the target situation. Begin each desensitization session by relaxing, using one of the methods previously discussed.

4. Once relaxed, read the first card in your numbered series. Try to accurately imagine the situation on the card. Develop a detailed scene using all your senses: see yourself in the situation, hear the sounds you might hear if actually there, feel the sensation, and smell the odors. Maintain this scene in your mind until you begin to feel frightened, then stop your imagining.

5. As you begin to feel fear, make your mind go blank or picture a peaceful, relaxing scene. Continue to practice your relaxation technique until your fear is replaced by a feeling of calm. This could take 2–10 minutes. If unable to achieve calm in 10 minutes, back up to the prior scene or create an incremental step between the prior step and the current step that you can handle.

6. Try to imagine the same feared situation again. Most likely you'll be able to keep it in mind longer now. When it does become uncomfortable, put the scene out of your mind and relax yourself again. Repeat this process until the situation no longer evokes fear.

7. When you are able to think about the situation for three consecutive times (for several minutes each time) without feeling any fear, then move on to the next card in the series and repeat the process. Continue through the cards using steps 1–6. As a result, you will be able to contemplate the target situation while remaining completely relaxed.

"continued"

Responding to Interview Questions

1. Write out every possible question you can anticipate that would make you uncomfortable.

2. Develop an answer for each, actually writing them out, then summarize your responses on index cards.

3. Study each question and related responses until you are comfortable in answering them.

4. Now you are ready to proceed in one of the two following ways:

   a. Order your cards from easiest to most difficult and use the desensitization approach just described. During your relaxed state, visualize yourself a success in all ways: appearance, speaking voice, and content of answers. You can even envision a positive response from your interviewer, using a tone that indicates you did well.

   b. Have someone role-play an interview with you, asking the questions in order of difficulty. This will make the desensitization more realistic for you.

The threshold method is useful when the target situation is one you can actually approach, in a gradual manner, without causing undue problems. This is not a mental exercise, but it is similar to desensitization in that it uses a series of graduated steps, each bringing you closer to the target situation. It's possible to use a job interview role-playing situation with the threshold method, if you can gradually approach the actual situation and control your fear and you are able to regain your composure by remaining in the situation for a reasonable length of time.

Overcoming Distorted Thinking

We've just taken a look at a variety of approaches to help you learn how to relax. Relaxation is a first step in dealing with anxiety, stress, and depressive moods caused by fears and related issues associated with changing careers. These methods, however, don't require paying attention to the thoughts that create your fears. We will now consider the principles of cognitive therapy, which helps to eliminate fear by challenging the irrational beliefs and illogical distortions that cause them.

Cognitive therapy argues that how you think largely determines how you feel and behave. Your emotional and behavioral responses to a situation are largely determined by how you perceive, interpret, and assign meaning to that event. Cognitive therapy attempts to change the way you think about events, in order to change the way you feel and behave. For example, someone who was laid off from a job after 10 years could feel overwhelmed with depression and a sense of unfairness. Or the person can decide that this is the "kick in the pants" he or she needed to start a new career.

People form concepts about themselves, others, and how the world operates. These concepts are reinforced by further learning experiences, and they, in turn, influence the formation of other beliefs, values, and attitudes. Cognitive therapists believe that it is these beliefs, values, and attitudes that are usually the driving force behind both emotions and behaviors.

When one suffers from distorted or faulty thinking, the results could be disturbed feelings (of discouragement, frustration, or depression) and undesirable behavior. Cognitive therapists believe that you can get better by learning a new set of cognitive skills.

This approach works well with the types of problems and issues that face those wanting to make a career change. Cognitive therapy can be of value in helping career changers to identify and overcome their roadblocks and to relieve inner conflicts that are impeding progress toward their career goal. For example, potential career changers might exaggerate current career problems, disqualify their positive attributes, or think in ways that increase their fears and limit their positive response to possible career transitions. Through cognitive therapy, you can learn to recognize distortions in your own thinking and then substitute a more natural, accurate perception as an alternative for these thoughts.

Three Common Forms of Career Change Negative Thinking

Most negative thinking that occurs in career planning falls into one of three categories.

1. Unrealistically high expectations for performance that can result in self-condemnation, anxiety, and guilt (should, ought to, and must statements):

   "I should not make mistakes."

   "Everyone must like and accept me."

2. Viewing oneself in a limiting way, in a self-deprecating manner:

"I can't change careers, I'm not smart enough to be successful in a job like that."

"If I change, I'll probably fail, because I'll be unable to achieve the support of my co-workers and my supervisor."

3.   Unrealistic expectations of other people or of life itself:

"I keep getting rejected in my job search. I'm not meant to be successful."

"Why continue with my job search—other employers will also reject me."

"Life shouldn't be this tough; getting a job should be easy."

As you become more aware of these areas of distorted thinking, try to be aware of how they apply to what you're thinking or feeling. In the area of career change, being held back by distorted thinking is a serious problem. Much of people's anxieties, fears, guilt, low self-esteem, and irrational behavior are generated from beliefs, attitudes, and expectations that are often unconscious and unexamined, yet play a large role in career changers' lives.

An important strategy that can be applied to a situation like this is reality testing. Most fears in the career change process originate from exaggerated views of what success really is, misconceptions about how many people do actually fail at a particular job, and not recognizing the extent to which your dedication, a solid work ethic, and good career planning can reduce the possibility of failing. Therefore, it makes sense to examine your thoughts in the light of reality and rationality.

Steps in Applying Cognitive Therapy

Five general steps can be taken in cognitive therapy, with a professional therapist, to challenge possible unrealistic and irrational thinking:

1.   Identify the feeling (e.g., fear of failing)

2.   Identify the thoughts, beliefs, and attitudes that are associated with the feeling

3.   Examine the thoughts in the light of reality and rationality

4.   Ask questions:

   a. Is there evidence of the truth of this belief?

   b. If there is no evidence, are there any other explanations?

    c. As bad as it seems, how is it in light of other terrible things that could happen?

    d. How likely is it that the dreadful consequences will occur?

    e. How reasonable are your expectations or standards for judging performance?

5.   Assign homework to test the validity of beliefs or ideas.

By following these steps, you might discover that you had an inaccurate view of your own ability, were using an unrealistic measuring stick to assess potential, or were overplaying the impact of changes in your life-style.

As effective as cognitive therapy can be, keep one thing in mind: When confronting long-held beliefs, ideas, values, or attitudes, you will often experience painful thought confusion. This confusion may give rise to anger, guilt, or helplessness and probably strong resistance to future introspection and exploration. Introspection and exploration can be thought of as a journey into unfamiliar territory. Whenever you travel into unfamiliar territory, it's not a bad idea to have a guide (professional personal counseling). The therapist is not someone who will do things for you, but rather someone who will help point things out, like road signs along the highway. You will still be the one to make the decisions and to take the necessary action.

Thus far we've looked at an overview of cognitive therapy and identified general steps in dealing with distorted thinking. Now let's examine two specific techniques that can be used within the context of cognitive therapy, constructive self-talk and the ABC method.

Constructive Self-Talk.
One thing you might do as you deal with the anxiety and stress of a career change, is make negative statements to yourself that promote a self-fulfilling prophecy. Here is an example of negative self-talk and a more constructive approach:

- **Old self-talk:** "I don't have enough patience to make it through the job search any longer. I can hardly take another rejection."

- **New self-talk:** "I *have just enough patience* to make it through the job search for tomorrow. I can handle one more possible rejection. If it occurs, I plan to . . . ."

Take the job search and break it down into more manageable pieces. Take one day at a time. This positive approach assesses what you have left to work with, not what you have lost. When the going gets tough, you will benefit most from actually saying to yourself, out loud, while you *visualize* it, "I have just enough __(of the resource I need)__ to __(reach my goal)__."

A worthwhile new habit is to learn how to encourage, not discourage yourself. Of course, you have to believe that you do have the inner resources you need. The word *believe* might trouble you if you find it difficult to truly believe in yourself. Recognize that self-esteem is the core of self-belief, and you can do something about raising your self-esteem.

The ABC Method.

ABC is a method developed by Albert Ellis, the founder of Rational Emotive Therapy (RET), which has much in common with cognitive therapy. When you encounter adversity, you react by thinking about it. Your thoughts then quickly form beliefs that have certain consequences. The beliefs are the direct cause of what you feel and what you do next. Your beliefs can be the difference between objecting and giving up, on the one hand, and positive thinking with constructive action, on the other.

The first step in applying the ABC method is to see the connection between adversity, belief, and consequence. Let's take, for example, a frustrated job searcher who has been experiencing a number of rejections following interviews.

A.   **Adversity:** The most recent rejection.

B.   **Beliefs:**

    I'm really not that good, everybody can see it, thus the rejection.

    I must come off terribly during the interview process.

    Most likely the type of job I'm pursuing is not a good match for me, so I'll never get hired.

    Why go on with this career change effort? Life just isn't fair.

C.   **Consequence:** This distorted thinking becomes a self-fulfilling prophecy, resulting in anxiety, stress, or depression.

By applying some cognitive therapy techniques, our job searcher can find the link between unfounded beliefs and the consequences. Distorted thinking leads to inaction and dejection, whereas more explanation can create energy and help bring about more positive results. Therefore, changing habitual beliefs becomes a priority. Two general ways to alter distorted thinking and beliefs, once you're aware of them, are to distract yourself when they occur and to dispute them, which is more effective in the long run, because you're less likely to experience a recurrence.

Disputation entails giving your distorted thoughts and beliefs an argument. By effectively disputing the beliefs that follow adversity, you can change your automatic (immediate) reaction from dejection and giving up to positive action.

Belief

I must come off terribly during the interview process.

Disputation

Not necessarily. The competition is also excellent, so of course I have some "no's" to go through before I reach that one, all important "yes".

For an excellent discussion of the disputation technique, see *Learned Optimism,* by Martin Seligman.

Increasing Your Self-Esteem

Self-esteem is a major factor in success or failure, in every aspect of your life, and especially in your career. Our self-concept influences all of our significant choices and decisions and therefore helps to shape the kind of life we create for ourselves. This includes how we view the world around us and what we consider to be potential career choices.

The development of your self-confidence and self-acceptance is related to how your parents, teachers, friends, and others around you reacted to you as you grew up. In addition, much of your own present sense of self-confidence comes from your career. A job well done can be self-satisfying and also generate positive feedback from those around you: supervisors, co-workers, family, and friends.

Low self-esteem leads to feelings of inadequacy, insecurity, self-doubt, lack of assertiveness, fear of failing, irrational beliefs, procrastination, and depression, all of which adversely affect one's efforts in changing careers.

The link between self-esteem and your career is so strong that any serious self-esteem issues should be the primary focus of counseling before any career planning work is done. Before undertaking career-related self-assessments (interests, values, skills, and related preferences), self-esteem issues must be addressed.

Adults with low self-esteem are likely to misjudge themselves. They are less likely to own their skills or feel entitled to their interests and dreams. Therefore, career planning efforts should be put on hold for a while, if possible, until a healthier frame of mind can be developed.

Living Consciously, Responsibly and Authentically

In *How to Raise Your Self-Esteem*, Nathaniel Brandon states that we can increase our self-esteem by living our lives consciously, responsibly, and authentically.

Living Consciously.   Living consciously is the basis of self-confidence and self-respect. To live consciously means to attempt to be aware of everything that leads to our actions, purpose, values, and goals and to act appropriately. Living consciously means taking responsibility for being aware of the decisions we need to make. In any given situation, living consciously means generating a state of mind that fits the task at hand.

In the situation of changing careers, living consciously could mean facing any current unhappiness and feelings of depression and the need to change, facing fears about changing careers, and then taking appropriate actions to help resolve these difficulties rather than denying and burying them. When you learn to accept fear, you cease to be a slave to it. You cannot overcome a fear whose reality you deny.

Living Responsibly.   Living responsibly means realizing that you are responsible for your choices and actions: how you spend your time, the level of consciousness you bring to your work, how you care for your body, the relationships you choose to enter or remain in, how you treat others, the meaning you give to your existence, your own happiness, and your life (materially, emotionally, intellectually, and spiritually).

Being responsible, in this context, means being the main causal agent in your life, not the recipient of blame or guilt. It's saying to yourself, for example, "Why do I make myself so lazy when it comes to my job search?" rather than, "Why am I so lazy?" This is not to say that one never suffers through the fault of others, or even accidents, or that you are responsible for everything that happens to you. You need to know what is within your control and what is not.

Where does your responsibility start and end in comparison to others you are dealing with? If you take responsibility for matters beyond your control, your self-esteem will be at risk. You'll fail to meet your own expectations. Likewise, if you fail to take responsibility for matters that are within your control, your self-esteem again will be at risk.

It is through actions that an attitude of self-responsibility is implemented and expressed. Ask yourself, "What actions will bring me closer to my goals?, advance my career?" By living consciously and taking responsibility you gain greater control over the direction of your life.

Living Authentically.   Good self-esteem also demands congruence, living authentically. To live authentically means being truthful to yourself and others. Honesty consists of respecting the difference between the real and the unreal. Yet many of us have shut down our inner self and have chosen to become unconscious. Thus, it takes courage and independence to attain authenticity, to face the good with the bad in our lives.

Living authentically incorporates the following traits and qualities:

- Usually honest with self and others

- Strive to be truthful when communicating with others

- Open about what it is that you love, admire, and enjoy

- If experiencing hurt or anger, you usually talk about it with honesty and dignity

- Honor your needs and interests by standing up for yourself

- Don't mind others' seeing your excitement

- Can acknowledge when you're wrong

- Present the self you feel on the inside the same as the self you present to the outside

To grow in self-esteem means leaving our comfort zone and entering the unknown. This entails risk, but all change involves some degree of risk.

The Reactions of Those Close to You

As you succeed in increasing your self-esteem by living more consciously, responsibly, and authentically, others around you will either adjust to your new self or attempt to maneuver you back into your old self-concept. This is because people are used to dealing with you in a certain way, and your change is making them readjust. Some relationships will remain intact, but others will not. Again, a part of change is letting go, and being realistic means accepting the fact that we can't have everything.

Healthy individuals with high self-esteem are not always liked, because they are usually more independent, outspoken, direct, and self-assertive. This can bring out envy and hostility in certain people, especially conventional types. Most people are somewhat insecure. If you're insecure and not very happy, it's hard to recognize and accept others who are secure and happy.

Don't confuse liking yourself and appreciating your own self-worth with being selfish and self-centered. It's the way you handle yourself with others that determines whether you are acting in a selfish or self-centered manner. Therefore, it is worthwhile to monitor yourself. The best guide for you to follow could be that if you live your life consciously, responsibly, and authentically (and treat others with respect), you must be on the right track.

Goal Setting

The Importance of Decision Making

Even though much that happens in our lives is by chance, it's important to recognize the power we do have to influence and control situations and events in meeting our goals. One way to illustrate this is to think back to some recent, positive development you experienced on the job. Was it the result of chance, or had you taken specific action that helped to bring about the positive result? Chances are that you made a decision along the way that influenced the positive outcome.

It might be helpful to take a look at your decision-making style at this point. Is the process you use satisfactory to you? When you review past major decisions, such as choice of education, spouse or significant other, job or a major purchase, what conclusion are you able to make about how you went about your decision making?

Effective decision making is influenced by information gathering, timing, and willingness to take a risk. Adequate information allows you not only to determine your alternatives, but also to access the pros and cons of each. If you did not have enough information in a particular decision, how did it affect the outcome? What might you do differently in the future? Your timing might have been just right, or perhaps it was off. You might have made a decision too quickly, only to regret it later, or too slowly, and missed out on valuable options. What might you do differently in the future to be better prepared and therefore respond in a more timely manner? In your past decisions, how much of a challenge were you willing to take? Perhaps too much, and you paid the price with negative results. Or maybe you accepted too little challenge, deciding to play it safe, and yet paying a price for that as well, in terms of less satisfaction.

You might also ask yourself, "Have my decisions been consistent with my values?" Your overall satisfaction and happiness will be enhanced when your decision making matches as closely as possible with the things, ideas, or beliefs that you value the most. Obviously, decisions most closely in line with your values have a greater chance of being carried through to completion.

Decision-Making Styles

Which style do you believe characterizes most of your important decisions? If after identifying your decision-making style you are not pleased with the way you have made decisions in the past, you now have an opportunity to change your style and apply some of what you learned here to present and future decisions. Following are some decision-making styles:

Planned: Gathering information and applying a methodical, deliberate, and judgmental approach that is balanced between cognitive and emotional factors in weighing the facts

Agonizing: Too involved with gathering information and analyzing the alternatives, getting lost in the data, so much so that it's difficult to make up your mind

Impulsive: Take action too quickly, usually the first alternative, based largely on emotion without gathering necessary information

Intuitive: Somewhat mystical, based on what "feels right," nonverbalized emotion

Avoidance:
- **No decision:** Fatalistic, leaving to fate, "It doesn't matter what I do."

- **Procrastinating:** Delaying, keep putting off, can't get started.

- **Accommodating:** Compliant, let someone else decide, "Whatever you say is fine with me."

Whichever decision-making style you normally use, try to adopt the planned style: gathering information and weighing the pros and cons of each alternative. This is important especially when it comes to your career, because the process requires time and thoughtful study. Following is a decision-making model that can help you carry through those changes and increase the possibility of becoming a more effective decision maker:

1. **Identify the decision that needs to be made precisely and completely.**
    What is the problem?
    How important is the decision?
    How soon must you decide?

2.   **Gather information and evaluate the quality of your data.**
     Is it complete?
     Is it unbiased?

3.   **List possible actions that you might take.**
     Brainstorm—identify every possible action.
     Discard those that are obviously unacceptable.

4.   **List the advantages and disadvantages of alternative choices.**
     What are the probable outcomes of each?
     What are other possible outcomes?

5.   **Weigh the pros and cons of the various actions carefully.**
     Which are consistent with your values?

6.   **Develop strategies to follow (similar to goal setting).**

The Role of Risk

All change involves some risk. The risk is the uncertainty of not knowing the outcome of the intended change in advance. This in turn could create anxiety that results from fearing the unknown.

Growth, simply cannot occur without taking chances. Growth takes you to uncharted territory, creating uncertainty and potential danger. This is part of the process of change. However, this doesn't mean you have to go out on a limb. Through examining your needs, recognizing your self-worth, accepting that you deserve the very best you can attain for yourself, applying a sound goal-setting strategy (see next section), and taking the responsibility for acting, you'll be able to approach taking risks in a sensible and viable manner, leading to the accomplishment of your goals.

The first step in deciding whether to attempt the risk of changing careers is to admit to yourself what degree of unhappiness your current position holds for you. Are you where you'd like to be? Do you think your career should be more than it is, that you should feel more satisfaction than you are? Think about times in the past that you have risked, whether at work, with family, or in a love relationship. Look to see what you feared and how you felt before taking the risk. What actions did you take that helped you push through your fears? Think about how these past experiences can help you with your current risk of changing careers.

Setting and Accomplishing Your Goals

Part of undertaking change is risking, and part of risking is dealing with the unfamiliar, thus creating fear and anxiety. This makes it important to understand what you can and can't control and to be realistic about what you can and can't achieve. You can get beyond fears and anxieties by exercising good, sound planning and taking smart, calculated risks.

Applying goal-setting criteria is a method you can use to accomplish more of what you want. Goal setting, if you take it seriously, is a process of taking greater control over your life. Three basic guidelines for goal setting are breaking a goal into smaller steps, staying flexible, and challenging yourself.

Breaking a Goal into Smaller Steps.

Over time, achieving a series of small successes can lead to feeling better about yourself as a result of accomplishing your goals. Therefore, start small. Break down larger goals into more manageable pieces.

Let's take the goal of revising your chronological resume into more of a functional/chronological combination. This is a good goal example because revising resumes often feels overwhelming at first. Because you're changing careers, this format (emphasizing your functional skills, with a chronological work history at the end) will serve your purposes more effectively than the chronological format, which emphasizes your past job titles and employers. Let's assume you have established an objective and have done some preliminary research into the skills required for the position you intend to apply for. In addition, you've assessed your skills from past positions.

First, we will break up this ambitious task into smaller, more manageable steps:

1. Purchase, or take out from a library, a resume guide that emphasizes functional resumes, such as Yana Parker's *Damn Good Resume Guide*. Spend a couple of days looking it over, noting resume examples that are for jobs similar to your objective. Specifically, note the major skill categories being emphasized and the action verb statements in each.

2. Identify the 3–5 major functional skill categories you wish to emphasize. This is where your skill assessment comes in handy, as you combine the skills you now have with the major transferable/functional skill categories that relate to your job objective.

3. Develop 2–4 skill statements, using action verbs, for each of your 3–5 major skill categories.

4. Develop a chronological section that includes past job titles, employers, and dates. No description is necessary here. This section shows

potential employers that you are not trying to hide gaps in your work history.

5.   Develop your education section with the usual information including special honors.

6.   Include other relevant information (professional association membership and activities, honors, related accomplishments).

7.   Have your resume professionally typed and printed.

Does changing the format of your resume seem less overwhelming to you now? Would you feel more inclined to give it a try with this approach? The idea here is to enhance the likelihood of your accomplishing your goals by taking each goal one manageable step at a time.

Even a long-range goal such as your job search can be broken down into month to month, week to week, and day to day manageable steps. The steps related to the job search, in addition to updating your resume, could include the following:

- Read up on interviewing skills and job search methods

- Attend networking-related meetings and seminars

- Contact employers

To break these goals into smaller steps, you need to sit down and figure out specifically what it is you want to do, how long it would take, and when you want to do it, and then put together your plan.

Staying Flexible.   As you go about accomplishing your goal, remember that sometimes circumstances and events alter your situation. You will need to readjust your goal, either the time you've allowed yourself, the method you intended to use, or other aspects. You must remain flexible so that when legitimate factors arise, you can alter the original goal to meet the new situation. In fact, if you're working on a long-range goal of a month or more, you can expect, at the very least, to make some weekly adjustments. These adjustments are usually minor and don't deviate from your original plan by a day or more, unless some major interruption occurs.

Challenging Yourself.   Try to include some challenge in your goals. When first starting out, it could be a small challenge. As you get more into it, gradually increase the challenge. In goal setting the possibility of failure actually has a positive side—it provides a challenge. There's a greater sense of accomplishment when risk is involved and failure is possible. Your level of satisfaction will usually be directly proportional to the amount of challenge you create. The accumulation of small successes can add up and help you feel better about yourself.

Criteria for Goal Setting

James McHolland presented the following criteria to assure that goals are achievable. As you set a goal, be sure it meets each criterion.

Desirable.   Do you really want to accomplish this goal? If you don't want to, the odds are pretty good that you won't. This shouldn't be a *should* or a *have to,* but rather a *want to.*

Believable.   Do you believe you can accomplish your goal? Is it realistic? Believing is a powerful aspect of goal setting. You want to set goals that are within your reach.

Achievable.   Do you see this goal as being possible to achieve? Do you have enough time to accomplish your goal. If you're not organized about your time, create a weekly schedule: block off all work hours, travel hours, family responsibilities, etc. Once a week, figure out what you need to accomplish during the following week. Estimate the time each goal will take, and plug them into the open slots of your schedule. Being organized with your time is a key ingredient in helping to ensure the accomplishment of your goals.

Measurable.   Is your goal stated in specific and concrete terms, so that it is clear when you have accomplished your goal? Stating that you will "work on your resume" is not specific and concrete. However, stating that "for the next three days, I will spend two hours per day developing skill statements of two major skill categories" is both specific and concrete. In this way, it will be clear when you've accomplished your goal.

Focus.   Is your goal presented without an alternative? Statements like, "I'll do some work on my resume or call for two information interviews," are not acceptable. Decide which you want to do more, set it as your goal, and then do it. Being clear and focused about your goal setting helps to ensure success.

Values.   Is the goal consistent with your value system? Maybe a high value of yours is family, and you have plans to be with them during the next day. Even though you hold changing careers high as a value, it might not rank as high as your family and your plans with them. However, you mistakenly planned to work on your resume on the same day, which might create a conflict with your family plans. It may be best to reschedule the resume writing goal to avoid a values conflict with your family plans.

Non-injurious.   Is the goal non-injurious to yourself and others? This criterion usually pertains to physical goals, such as exercise and diet plans. However, other goals could be injurious to self or others in physical or emotional ways. Perhaps your career goals are running you into the ground, causing undue additional stress. It would seem wise to reorganize the focus of your career planning efforts and establish a healthier pace.

Independent.   Are you depending on anyone else for the accomplishment of your goal? If so, you've just opened the door to not accomplishing your goal. State your goal in an independent manner, and rely on no one but yourself. Take full responsibility for accomplishing your goal.

If for some reason you don't accomplish your goal, try to figure out what happened. What kept you from accomplishing your goal? Review the criteria to see if the mishap can be explained by having not met certain criteria that you thought would be met. Make a note of the mishap, and as you set future goals, consider these experiences and pay particular attention to related criteria. Learn from your mistakes, use the criteria in a positive, not a punitive way, still helping to ensure future successes.

One suggestion is to keep a daily journal of what you accomplish. Evidence of small, steady actions recorded in your journal can help validate your progress. You'll be able to refer to it and see how your small, successful steps can add up. Keeping a daily journal is a method to help you see your real progress and increase your self-esteem. In the journal include the date, what was accomplished, and a few words about how you felt about it.

When you do accomplish your goals, it's a good idea to reward yourself in some manner. Perhaps you will allow yourself some small luxury that you seldom pursue. This could range from buying a new compact disc to dining at a French restaurant with someone special, and many things in between.

Developing Your Support System

A support system is a set of people who will listen, understand, and offer suggestions and feedback about your career changing and job search experience. Members of your support system should not make decisions or take actions for you. Rather, they serve as a sounding board for you to bounce ideas off of and receive additional points of view and insight.

Seeking support does not mean you're a failure, incompetent, or weak. It means that you've realized it's unrealistic to expect yourself to go through this experience alone. As long as you fulfill your responsibilities for your career change and don't expect others to do things for you that you should be doing for yourself, there's nothing wrong with seeking encouragement, feedback, and support from others along the way. In fact, at times you might get stuck in a step of the process, and members of your support system can help to get you back on track.

Choosing the Right People

Many different individuals can be part of your support system. However, not everyone has the right qualities to serve your best interests. Probably the most important quality to look for in potential support system members is being an objective listener. In addition to being a good listener, it is important to find someone who is mostly on your side and tries to see things from your point of view.

Of course, if you become unrealistic and irrational, a solid support system member will recognize this and point it out to you in a noncritical and nonjudgmental manner. Criticism and judgment are not supportive, as they tend to reinforce your critical view of yourself. In addition, unconditional praise is not really supportive either.

It's important for you to recognize the various strengths that your support system members have to offer. Examples follow of different strengths members could offer:

- Someone who is good to brainstorm business-related ideas with

- Someone who is adept at planning the job search strategy (from resume writing to networking to job interviewing)

- Someone who can listen when that's all you need and want

- Someone to schedule free time with to break up the stress a career change/job search can generate

People to exclude from your support system are those who have their own issues to deal with. This prevents them from being supportive in the way you might like. They could be competitive, jealous, threatened, or indifferent.

Gaining Family Support

Support of family members is most important for a career changer/job searcher, for you are never a career changer on your own. Those in your immediate family feel the impact as well, especially if you are married with children. Spouses, children, and significant others might be used to a certain life-style. It could be difficult for them to sacrifice in this area while you go about your career change. So this process is difficult for them as well as you. Career change can take time, especially if additional education or training is necessary. Family members' patience may waiver at times if they don't fully realize the ordeal this is for you.

The best way to gain family members' support is through communication. Keep them aware of your career change, every step of the way. Let them know the goals you plan to accomplish on a daily, weekly, even monthly basis. This shows some sense of direction and responsibility on your part, which can serve to help all of you. When your family members see you motivated and accomplishing your goals, it will be easier for them to make necessary sacrifices and be supportive toward you. Don't be afraid to let them know how they can help you and that you realize the impact this has on them as well.

The hardest time will come with you become stuck and are unsure of your next move. If family members are in the dark, it will be hard for them to remain patient and supportive. Be open about being stuck, but try to develop a plan to get unstuck and start taking steps in that direction. When family members see positive steps, even small ones, and are kept informed, they will usually hang in there with you. It's your responsibility not to be unreasonable, however, in your expectations of them. Be fair to yourself and them as well.

••

Being recently remarried helped Zephree, as it does most career changers, to be able to afford a large cut in salary in changing careers. Ed claims he would never have made it without his wife's income. Vincent credits his wife's emotional support as being most helpful. He adds, "If your spouse (or significant other) isn't behind you, you're not going to make it." Vincent's wife's encouragement along the way to the opening of his bookstore proved to be the caring and support he needed as he moved through his career transition.

Sandra got help from numerous family members with her publishing business. From her packaging needs to delivery and distribution services, family proved to be a key to Sandra's success.

••

Support Groups

There's something to be said about being part of a group that is going through the same life experience as you. Usually, career change support groups will consist of members at various stages of the process. Some will be just starting out on a job search, others will be well into the process, and still others will have completed the process and will soon be moving on. The members represent a wealth of experience that you as a member can tap into, as well as sharing what you know with them. Ten to twelve heads is surely better than one when it comes to problem solving.

Career change support groups can be found in a variety of settings:

- Adult continuing education centers

- Community colleges (most serve non-students)

- Universities (especially non-credit programs)

- Places of worship (churches and synagogues)

- HMO/hospital self-help/education programs

- Career counselors in private practice

- Social service agencies (e.g., Jewish Vocational Service)

- Community mental health centers

A few phone calls to career counselors in your area will help you identify related groups.

Group members can be sources of valuable information, insights into the process, and contacts for you to expand your network. It helps you avoid feeling alone as you go through the often difficult career change process. Of course, you must be brave enough to join one. Seeking out help can be hard for some. They don't like to admit they need it. It is not a weakness. The only related weakness here is being too stubborn to realize it's unrealistic to go through a career change on your own and therefore choosing not to seek help from others.

Getting Personal or Career Counseling Assistance

You may find that after reading all the suggestions in this chapter you're still somewhat stuck. Nothing seems to be helping you get back on track. You may be experiencing any of the following:

- Significant lack of confidence and self-esteem

- Continuing indecisiveness and procrastination

- An unwillingness to make a commitment toward one goal and having to then let go of other possibilities

- Your fears of change, failing, or success are controlling you, and you're stressed out

- You meet the clinical definition of depression provided earlier and see no change over a period of months

- Problems that are not directly career change related (substance abuse or spouse/significant other difficulties) that can negatively impact your career change process

In this case, you should consider pursuing either personal mental health assistance or professional career counseling, depending on your unique situation.

Personal Mental Health Assistance

One of the first issues you will want to know about a counselor or therapist is his or her approach to counseling. This can refer to either a formal counseling technique, following a certain theoretical approach, or simply to their own way of viewing problem solving.

Most effective counseling professionals combine features from different approaches to counseling, depending on the problem that the client may have at a given time. However, some counseling professionals do identify with a specific approach. Ask the counseling professional, "How do you see the problem I'm dealing with?" or "What form of counseling/therapy will you be using?"

Following are some suggested sources for information about and referrals to reputable counseling:

1. Check with family and friends with whom you're willing to be open.

2. Ask your personal physician.

3. Contact related professional associations.

4. Contact directors of counseling centers at local universities, colleges, and community colleges. (Often community college counselors will see non-students at a reduced rate as compared to those in private practice.)

5. Contact local universities that have a graduate level counseling psychology training program. Many of their faculty will have private practices, as well as being familiar with professional and community resources.

6. Contact the psychiatry department of local medical schools.

7. Contact faculty from undergraduate psychology departments at local universities, colleges, and community colleges.

8. If your city or state has community mental health centers, you could get help there. They might also be able to make a referral for you.

9. Your priest, pastor, or rabbi sometimes can provide services and make referrals as well.

10. The phone book has listings of counseling professionals in your area.

If you do pursue counseling, you should be able to decide after 6–8 visits whether it is "working." At this point, trust is important because you will be starting to reveal more and more about yourself. You might begin to feel a sense of relief and a sense of hope. Your problems might not feel "solved," but you should be starting to feel that they could be. You should feel in control of your counseling. "In control" means you're an active partner in this process. Self-disclosure needs to evolve at a pace that is comfortable for you. You may talk about whatever you wish; the subject is up to you. Your rapport with your counselor or therapist is crucial to your success in the counseling process. You should feel that you're being helped and that you are responsible for your progress.

Your sense of personal comfort with your counseling professional is most important. Ask yourself the following questions:

- Can I trust this person?

- Does he or she remember what I said?

- Does he or she have a sense of me as an individual?

- Am I being understood?

These questions will better enable you to assess the "fit." Don't feel compelled to stay in a situation that you feel isn't working. Seek out additional referrals and check them out. In addition to evaluating your professional counselor, be sure to do some self-evaluation as well. Are you being honest with yourself and the counselor? Do you sense that you're dealing with your important issues? Discomfort can be a healthy sign in this process, to a degree. It could indicate you're really facing your issues and being responsible about owning them and doing something about them.

NCDA Consumer Guidelines for Selecting a Career Counselor

The following was developed by the National Career Development Association to help career changers find an appropriate counselor.

Sometimes it seems that virtually everyone is a vocational coach, ready and anxious to give advice, suggestions, and directions. Unfortunately, all are not equally able to provide the kind of help people need in making decisions about what to do with their lives. Promises and luxurious trappings are poor substitutes for competency. Thus, the selection of a professional career counselor is a very important task. The following guidelines are offered to assist you in making this selection.

Credentials of the Professional Career Counselor. A

Nationally Certified Career Counselor (NCCC) signifies that the career counselor has achieved the highest certification in the profession. Further, it means that the career counselor has:

- Earned a graduate degree in counseling or in a related professional field from a regionally accredited higher education institution.

- Completed supervised counseling experience that included career counseling.

- Acquired a minimum of three years of full-time career development work experience.

- Obtained written endorsements of competence from a work supervisor and a professional colleague.

- Successfully completed a knowledge-based certification examination.

Other professional counselors may be trained in one- or two-year counselor preparation programs with specialties in career counseling and may be licensed or certified by national or state professional associations.

What Do Career Counselors Do?   The services of career counselors differ, depending on competence. A professional or Nationally Certified Career Counselor helps people make decisions and plans related to life/career directions. The strategies and techniques are tailored to the specific needs of the person seeking help. It is likely that the career counselor will do one or more of the following:

- Conduct individual and group personal counseling sessions to help clarify life/career goals.

- Administer and interpret tests and inventories to assess abilities and interests and to identify career options.

- Encourage exploratory activities through assignments and planning experiences.

- Utilize career planning systems and occupational information systems to help individuals better understand the world of work.

- Provide opportunities for improving decision-making skills.

- Assist in developing individualized career plans.

- Teach job-hunting strategies and skills and assist in the development of resumes.

- Help resolve potential personal conflicts on the job through practice in human relations skills.

- Assist in understanding the integration of work and other life roles.

- Provide support for persons experiencing job stress, job loss, and career transition.

Ask for a detailed explanation of services (career counseling, testing, employment search strategy planning, and resume writing). Make sure you understand the service, your degree of involvement, and any financial commitment.

Fees.   Select a counselor who is professionally trained and will let you choose the services you desire. Make certain you can terminate the services at any time, paying only for services rendered.

Promises.   Be skeptical of services that make promises of more money, better jobs, resumes that get speedy results, or an immediate solution to career problems.

Ethical Practices. A Professional or Nationally Certified Career Counselor is expected to follow ethical guidelines of such organizations as the National Career Development Association, the American Counseling Association, and the American Psychological Association. Professional codes of ethics advise against grandiose guarantees and promises, exorbitant fees, and breaches of confidentiality, among other things. You might wish to ask for a detailed explanation of services offered, your financial and time commitments, and a copy of the ethical guidelines used by the career counselor you are considering.

Package Deals and Contracts. The fact that an organization offers a package deal, in the form of a contract with a large up-front fee, in itself does not mean it is unethical. A recent survey of California career counselors revealed that the average number of appointments for career counseling clients was 4–5. Most likely this means two things are occurring.

First, career counseling clients are choosing, in many cases, not to complete the process with the counselor. They're either completing it on their own or decide to stay put in the current career situation. Career changers who are good at pencil-and-paper tasks might be less comfortable with face-to-face encounters with employers and tend to drop out of counseling. Second, career counselors may be having a difficult time maintaining a financially viable practice, continually having to market for new clients due to a quick turnover.

Therefore, a package deal with a competent and ethical career counselor locks the career changer into the process. They are less likely to drop out if it's already paid for. This is to their advantage, especially if they would have dropped out otherwise. A package deal also helps the career counselor to pay bills and maintain the practice. However, not everyone who offers a package deal is necessarily competent or ethical. That's why it's important to ask questions such as the following:

- What will be done, and by whom will it be done?
- Is there a cut-off point with regard to refunds? (If so, don't expect much after that date.)
- Is there an upper limit in the amount of time they will spend with you? Per week? For X number of months?

If there is a contract, don't sign it until you understand everything clearly and agree. (Have your lawyer take a look, as well.)

Obtaining a Career Counseling Referral. The following are sources that you could contact for a referral to a career counselor.

- **National Board of Certified Counselors:** Call or write for a list of National Certified Career Counselors (NCCC) in your area:

  National Board of Certified Counselors
  3-D Terrace Way
  Greensboro, NC 27403

- **Your Network of Contacts:** Ask around, to those you know, including family and friends, if anyone knows of a qualified career counselor.

- **Local College Career Counselor:** Contact career counselors at local community colleges or universities. They're likely to know of colleagues in the area who offer career counseling to the public. In fact, they themselves might also have a private practice, in addition to their college position.

- **Local College Placement Office:** Professional staff (Directors or Assistant Directors of Placement) will know of those in the community doing career counseling. Their offices can be known by a variety of names:

  - Placement Office

  - Career Placement Office

  - Career Planning and Placement Office

  - Career Planning and Development Office

  The university you graduated from might have services for its alumni. If you do not live in the area, you might still call the university for a referral to someone near you.

- **Social Service Organization Staff:** Contact places like the Jewish Vocational Service, Forty Plus, Operation Able, women's centers, etc. They might either provide the services you're looking for or provide a referral.

- **Other Options:** You can also try the following for a referral: your physician, your HMO staff, your employment assistance program staff, the *Yellow Pages,* or your business reference librarian.

Your First Contact with a Career Counselor.
Richard Bolles suggests making a visit to a potential counselor and leaving your wallet at home. When calling to make the appointment, Bolles recommends being upfront that this is an exploratory visit and you don't expect to be charged. If

you are able to arrange such a meeting, we support you in that effort. We definitely agree with Bolles's position here, especially for package deals. With a large fee, those offering package deals without a free initial appointment should be avoided.

However, for the individual counselor operating on an hourly appointment basis, offering free initial appointments might not be practical from a time perspective. Perhaps the counselor can give you 10–15 minutes on the phone to answer some questions and follow that up with service and fee information in writing. Moreover, Mary Burton and Richard Wedemeyer suggest that meeting the potential counselor for one session (and paying) is a worthwhile investment.

Regardless of how you make contact, you want answers to these basic questions:

- What are the specific services offered?

- Who is going to provide the services, and how long have they been doing it?

- What are the fees for these services?

- Can I pay as I go?

In addition, request the names of current or past clients that you may speak with. Counselors need the permission of the client before giving out their number, so a short amount of time is needed here.

Don't expect any guarantees. You can expect a lot of homework and a good coach who can guide you through the self-assessment phase and the job search as well (including resume writing, interviewing skills, and job search methods). He or she can lend objective insight and support, but cannot get you a job. You will have to go face to face with employers and convince them of your value. You might be capable of going through the career planning process on your own, but if you need help, then get it.

CHAPTER 5

STRATEGIES FOR IDENTIFYING CAREER OPTIONS

Perhaps the most difficult part of the career planning process for most career changers is identifying a target career. Often, adults feel ashamed to admit that they are confused about their career options. They wonder how someone at age 30, 40, or older could still be unsure about what to pursue in terms of a career. If you share this confusion, remember that as adults pass through different developmental stages, what once fit for them no longer does. Adults continue to change in terms of likes and dislikes, values, and even in approach to and philosophy of life.

You might realize that your former career no longer fits but still be confused as to what other occupation would be more appropriate. The first step, if you're confused, is to allow yourself to be confused! If you can allow yourself to be confused, you can then relax and get on with your career planning process more effectively.

This is where assessment and testing come into the process. One effective and successful approach for adult career changers, based on 20 years of experience in the career planning field, is a combination of an analysis of life experiences exercise and testing. This exercise incorporates identifying and prioritizing enjoyable experiences from all aspects of your life, including home and family, education, career, social, leisure, etc., and then taking a closer look at those you ranked the highest with regard to what interests were involved, skills used, values reflected, and personality preferences exercised. These become the nuts and bolts for generating career option ideas.

Two key tests, or inventories, are the Strong Interest Inventory (SII) and the Myers-Briggs Type Indicator (MBTI). These popular inventories show how similar your interests (SII) and your personality preferences (MBTI) are to people working happily, to some degree, in many different occupations (over 100 on the SII and over 200 on the MBTI).

The jobs scoring the highest for you on these inventories usually match up well with those generated from the analysis of life experience exercise. It is a powerfully confirming experience to see that your effort on the life experience exercise pays off with some viable possibilities. Often, testing alone leaves career changers wondering, "Well, what now?"

One potential problem with the SII and MBTI, however, is that they can be easily misinterpreted. Sometimes they are not interpreted at all; some counselors merely hand their clients the results. Not only is this a detriment to the client, but it is also unethical career counseling as well. The major area of concern is that a career changer will walk away thinking that these inventories are telling them they *should* go into one of their higher-scoring occupations. The inventories are not recommending a career direction. They simply indicate that your interests, or personality preferences, are similar to those of people happily employed in certain occupations and that perhaps you would enjoy the same occupations. The career changer must investigate these occupations further to verify whether or not they are viable career options.

No career decision should be made based on only one source of information, even if that source is as reputable as the SII or MBTI. However, after combining different, reliable sources that cover your interests, personality preferences, skills, and values, it's not unusual to begin to see certain patterns or themes in your results. Seeing these patterns can help to lessen your confusion and help you to focus on identifying meaningful career options.

In this chapter, we will focus on actual assessment results for a career changer whom we'll call Tony. This example will illustrate how to:

- Complete the analysis of life experience exercise, of which a major component is identifying your skills.

- Gain insights into your SII and MBTI results.

- Clarify your life and work values and understand their impact in your career decision making.

The goal is to identify career options in which most of your preferred criteria are somewhat in balance.

Analysis of Life Experience Exercise

The following exercise is similar to exercises found in *What Color Is Your Parachute?*, by Richard Bolles, (also published separately as *How to Create a Picture of Your Ideal Job or Next Career*); *Job and Career Building,* by Richard

Germann and Peter Arnold, and in *Career Satisfaction and Success,* by B. Haldane.

Identifying Your Significant Life Experiences

The key to success in this approach is being able to identify your most significant life experiences. The whole process depends on this first step. In this process, we will define *significant* to mean any experience in which you have accomplished something and enjoyed it (both aspects are required) from any area of your life: learning (formal education, formal training, or informal education), work, family, leisure, and social. Don't confuse *significant* with *grandiose* experiences, in which perhaps you were presented with an award or some type of honor. Your significant experience can be anything, as long as you enjoyed it, accomplished something, and were an active participant (rather than an observer). The average adult usually comes up with 35–40 significant life experiences.

The next step is to prioritize your experiences according to which ones you enjoyed the most. You will consider your top 10 or 12 experiences and ask yourself the following questions: Why are these my most significant experiences? What interests are involved? What skills am I using? What special knowledge am I applying? What preferences are indicated? What values are reflected? In addition, you will also look for patterns or themes among your top experiences. Examples of patterns could be helping others, being creative, managing or leading others, teaching/training others, problem solving, experiencing adventure, etc.

The best way to identify experiences is to refer to a list of skills. Bolles lists transferable skills, organized in the three categories of Things; People; and Information, Data, and Ideas. We've also provided the list below for you to refer to. Along with the list of skills you'll be using, you will need a sheet of paper listing the various areas of your life that the experiences can come from: learning/education, work, family, leisure, social, etc. Fill in pertinent information within each of these. For example, list formal (names of schools attended) and informal learning experiences, job titles (all the way back to high school, if you want), leisure activities, etc. You'll be referring to this list to help you focus during the experience brainstorming phase.

Now you're ready to identify experiences. Start with the major skill category you think you most enjoy. For example, let's look at management skills. Focus on one skill at a time. For example, in this category is the skill of being persuasive. Ask yourself, "When have I used persuasive skills and enjoyed using them, as well as experiencing a sense of accomplishment?"

Start with education. Can you recall any education experiences in which you used persuasive skills and enjoyed it? Perhaps you gave a persuasive

Sample List of Transferable/Functional Skills

Clerical Skills
bookkeeping
classifying
collecting
compiling
computing
examining
filing
organizing
recording
wordprocessing

Human Relation Skills
advising
assisting
counseling
empathizing
facilitating
guiding
listening
motivating
representing
serving

Research Skills
assessing
calculating
collecting
diagnosing
evaluating
examining
extrapolating
interviewing
investigating
synthesizing

Communication Skills
editing
explaining
influencing
interpreting
listening
mediating
promoting
speaking
translating
writing

Management Skills
communicating
consulting
coordinating
delegating
directing
evaluating
leading
negotiating
persuading
planning

Selling Skills
communicating
contacting
educating
informing
organizing
persuading
planning
presenting
promoting
scheduling

Creative Skills
designing
developing
establishing
illustrating
imagining
improvising
inventing
performing
revitalizing
visualizing

Public Relation Skills
conducting
consulting
informing
planning
presenting
promoting
representing
responding
researching
writing

Technical Skills
adjusting
aligning
assembling
drafting
engineering
installing
observing
operating
programming
repairing

Financial Skills
accounting
administering
allocating
auditing
balancing
budgeting
calculating
forecasting
investing
projecting

Problem Solving Skills
analyzing
appraising
diagnosing
examining
executing
planning
proving
reasoning
recognizing
validating

Training Skills
adapting
communicating
demonstrating
enabling
encouraging
evaluating
explaining
instructing
planning
stimulating

speech in your freshman Introduction to Speech course, on the importance of having the right to vote. You enjoyed giving the speech and felt you accomplished something, because in high school you were somewhat shy and would never have pictured yourself getting up in front of 20 people and giving a persuasive speech. Continue with the education category until you've identified all other significant experiences in which you used persuasive skills and enjoyed using them.

Activities from your education background that might be significant experiences include projects or presentations, a particular paper or assignment, your role in class discussion, or even persuading an instructor to change a grade. Don't forget to include extracurricular activities you participated in, ranging from athletics to arts to clubs and organizations.

The experiences you identify must be specific, rather than general. If you can describe *what* you did, *how* you did it, and what the *outcomes* or *results* were, you most likely have identified a specific experience. You'll see later that the description of how you did something leads into the identification of the skills you used. In our example, identifying the speech course is too general, but identifying the actual speech you gave is specific.

When you've completed the education category, continue brainstorming experiences in which you used persuasive skills from the remaining categories. For example, in a particular work experience you may have persuaded your supervisor or a group of co-workers to proceed on a certain project using your ideas. Perhaps you recall persuading your family to have a long overdue dinner together. Maybe you recall persuading a reluctant friend to join you in a game of tennis. Generate as many experiences as possible in which you used a certain skill and enjoyed using it from each major life category and then go on to the next major skill category and do the same.

You're probably thinking, "This is a lot of work." This is true; however, it's well worth it.

When you try this exercise, you'll quickly realize that it takes intense mental concentration. Don't be surprised if you're feeling wiped out in less than an hour. If that occurs, rather than sabotaging your career planning efforts by working at less than full capacity, put it down and come back to it when you can give it your full and fresh attention. How long can this take? Perhaps as many as 10–12 hours. People who work full time and are motivated about their career planning efforts seem to finish within two weeks. Many people take longer, depending on the time they have and their motivation level.

Keep a list of experiences as you brainstorm from the skill terminology and each your major life categories. It's difficult to remember everything from your past that might fit here. Looking at photo albums can sometimes help you to remember enjoyable experiences. Family members and friends might be able to help you recall experiences.

Upon completing the experience brainstorming exercise, you're ready for the next step. Take your list of experiences, however long, and attempt to identify the ten experiences in which you felt the most enjoyment and accomplishment.

Your Top 10 should represent some variety. If your Top 10 include more than two experiences that are somewhat the same, consider adding one or two more experiences. This might help to add some meaningful variety to your Top 10. However, you do want to note the intensity of the type of skills/experiences that had multiple Top 10 entries.

Let's turn now to our case study, beginning with a brief description of Tony. As we progress through the assessment process, much more information about Tony will be added. Tony is a 31-year-old Caucasian, with a bachelor's degree in finance and economics and an MBA with an emphasis in marketing. During the past five years, Tony has had five positions in the areas of media sales, account management, and finance (not a top interest). Generally speaking, all positions lacked creative input (which is a top interest). The two positions since finishing his MBA did not utilize the knowledge gained from it, which Tony values. Tony is a likable person with an outgoing and energized personality. Tony's primary goal when starting career counseling was to further validate his creative interest in advertising/marketing or identify any other possibilities. Tony's Top 10 life experiences follow:

1. **TV Game Show Contestant:** Tested knowledge, sense of showmanship

2. **Teaching Niece Multiplication Tables:** Helped her overcome anxiety

3. **Church Youth Group Advisor:** Related specifically to role of coordinating talent show

4. **Vitamin Product Class Presentation:** For undergraduate management class, researched product, wrote, acted, and videotaped

5. **Snack Product Commercial:** For business school (MBA) course, put together commercial targeted for a college population and was master of ceremonies

6. **Learned to Use Computer:** When working as a financial analyst

7. **Service Desk Manager:** In food store the day of the Super Bowl; able to handle crowd through speed and versatility

8. **Trip to Europe:** Specifically time spent backpacking; experienced different culture, language, and people

9. **Developed a Gourmet, All Natural Cat Food Business Plan:** Presentation for a business school (MBA) course

10. **Sky Diving:** Overcame fear

Because number 9 is similar to 4 and 5, we will include 11 to add variety.

11. **Creative Writing Class Paper:** Focused on relationship with brother

Writing Descriptive Stories on Your Top 10 Experiences

When you have identified your Top 10 experiences, write a couple of pages describing each one. For each experience, describe *what* you did (usually an introduction paragraph), *how* you did it (the main body of the story, giving a detailed, step-by-step description of what you did), and what the *outcomes* or *results* were (a concluding paragraph). If you haven't realized up to now why your experiences needed to be specific, you will at this point, as you try to describe step by step what you did. When an experience is too general it's impossible to generate a step-by-step description. Tony's description of experience number 4 is shown in Figure 5.1.

Identifying Your Transferable/Functional Skills

At this point, you are ready to identify your transferable/functional skills as they relate to your Top 10 experiences. You'll need a sheet of paper for each experience, with the title of the experience at the top of the page. Review carefully the skills you used in each experience. Read through your descriptive stories and as you identify skills used, write them in the margin, as shown in Figure 5.1. Use the skill listing from *What Color Is Your Parachute?* or the one provided on page 120 as a reference.

List as many skills as you can for each experience. Try for 10–15, but some experiences might have more or less. Don't shortchange yourself; after all, this is for you. Also list only the skills you enjoyed using. Prioritize the skills within each experience to identify those you enjoyed most and would like to use in your next career.

When completed, you should have ten lists of skills (or more, if you include more than ten experiences), prioritized in order of those you enjoy using the most. Now, look at the top of each list and ask yourself which of these skills are essential for you to use in your next career. Mark those you consider essential. However, in the interest of forcing you to make some differentiation among your top skills, try not to include more than 4–5 from each of your ten lists. If a skill is repeated in more than one experience, list it only once. Ultimately, these 30–40 top skills will be the ones we'll focus on in the next step of this process. Tony's prioritized list of the skills identified in the story follows, with essential skills marked with an asterisk:

FIGURE 5.1

Tony's Top 10 Experience Descriptive Story

As a student in my Executive Management (undergraduate) class, we were assigned to a group and were asked to come up with a presentation on a company. Myself and two others were assigned to work together. We brainstormed ideas and decided to put on an informational play about a particular vitamin company. We had to write our own parts and be prepared to answer questions.

Communicated with others generating ideas

One aspect of my responsibility was to give a financial report on the company for the last 4–5 years. I went to the business reference section of the university library and looked over annual reports and related information (product lines, etc.).

Researching, compiling, gathering information by studying resource

To get an idea of the company's financial status, I looked at information regarding net income over the past five years, in order to spot any trends, as well as gross profits and expense figures.

Computing, working with numbers, analyzing information, breaking it down

Once I completed taking notes from the resource materials, I sat down to prepare my 3-minute presentation. I wrote it out much like one would if preparing a speech. I also included five graphs, which the university service made into overheads to be used during my presentation.

Organizing thoughts, planning out a step-by-step process, business-related writing, visualization of information

I then memorized the presentation, word for word, paragraph by paragraph, and studied it for quite a while. The presentation was made to our class, and my 3-minute segment went well. It generated positive responses from the instructor and my fellow students.

Keeping track of details, good memory, communicating to a group, making a presentation

- Generating ideas*
- Making a visual presentation of information*
- Communicating with others, or group*
- Making presentations*
- Analyzing information, breaking it down*
- Business-related writing
- Keeping track of details, good memory
- Organizing thoughts, planning out a step-by-step process
- Researching, compiling, gather information by studying resources
- Computing, working with numbers

Formulating Your Personal Transferable/ Functional Skill Clusters

At this stage of the exercise, we will develop a way of organizing your top transferable/functional skills that will be more personally relevant using personal skill clusters. Personal skill clusters are natural groupings of your preferred skills. Clusters can be similar to the pattern or themes that your Top 10 experiences generated. The patterns or themes of Tony's experiences follows:

Teaching/Training/Advising	Business/Operations
2: Teaching Niece	6: Learned Computer
3: Youth Group Advisor	7: Service Manager
Business/Creative	**Adventuresome/Fun**
4: Vitamin Presentation	1: Game Show Contestant
5: Snack Product Commercial	8: Backpacking in Europe
9: Cat Food Business Plan	10: Sky Diving
Non-Business Creative	
11: Creative Writing Paper	

To create your personal skill clusters, make small strips of paper, just big enough to write a skill name on, and clear off a table for space to work. Write the name of each essential skill that you identified on a separate strip of paper.

Now try to form subgroups or clusters of similar skills. Think of the strips of paper as pieces of a puzzle. See if you can form 3–6 clusters of related skills. Check to see if any central theme might be related to your transferable skills. Arrange your clusters around each other by how they relate to one another.

Look at the example from Tony's skill clustering in Figure 5.2. He identified a major cluster of problem-solving skills that fed into two other

---

FIGURE 5.2

Tony's Personal Transferable Skill Clusters

Problem Solving

- Sizing up situations (10)
- Dealing with ideas, information, and concepts
- Able to handle a variety of tasks (3)
- Work self-directedly without supervision
- Think quickly (2)
- Improvising
- Analyzing/reasoning
- Using computers
- Taking risks

Creative

- Visualizing (4)
- Using imagination (3)
- Performing/entertaining (5)
- Making people laugh (2)
- Radio/TV presentations (2)

Instructing/Teaching/
Guiding and Training

Management/Supervision

- Leading others (2)
- Determining policy
- Control over project (3)
- Meeting goals/objectives
  and producing (4)
- Organizing time
- Addressing large/
  small groups

Human Relations

- Facilitating others' growth and development (2)
- Creating atmosphere of acceptance (2)
- Treating others as equals
- Listening
- Inspiring trust
- Sensitive and responsive to others' feelings (4)

clusters: creative and management/supervision. In addition, the cluster of human relations skills fed into all three of the previously mentioned clusters. Also, a central theme of instruction/teaching/guiding and training intersected all of the other four clusters. The numbers in parentheses indicate the intensity, or in how many of Tony's Top 10 experiences that skill was identified as essential.

Your Specific Content/Special Knowledge

We will call your favorite subjects, or fields of knowledge, your Specific Content/Special Knowledge skills. This represents a second type of skill to add to the transferable skills. Identify subjects you've learned about and liked best from your formal education (high school and college), on-the-job training, self-study, and continuing education activities. We've provided a list of Spe-cific Content/Special Knowledge skills below, or you can use the one in *What Color Is Your Parachute?* When you've identified those that apply to you, then prioritize the Specific Content/Special Knowledge you've identified

Sample List of
Specific Content/Special Knowledge Skills

advertising	history	public opinion
alcoholism	house building	quality control
bicycles	income taxes	real estate
biology	interior decorating	recreation
business management	Japan	religion
community organizing	journalism	retail
crime	kayaking	safety
customer service	linguistics	science
diets	labor relations	sociology
diseases	marketing	sports
employee relations	massage	teaching
environmental planning	meditation	technical writing
earthquakes	mathematics	theater
fiber optics	opera	toys
financial planning	outdoors	training
fund raising	photography	utilities
gardening	periodicals	video recorders
geography	philosophy	waste
government agencies	poverty	water resources
health care	psychology	wildlife

according to those you would most like to see involved in your next career. Tony's favorite Specific Content/Special Knowledge skills are as follows:

1. Broadcasting (talk show/news host)

2. Psychology (human behavior)

3. Positive mental attitude (how to achieve one)

4. Religion

5. Marketing (advertising/creative)

6. Acting

7. Management

8. Finance (planning corporate investments)

9. Marketing (research and development)

10. Marketing (packaging and distribution)

11. Account management (advertising field)

12. Philosophy (meaning of life)

13. Political science (politics)

14. Computers (word processing and Lotus)

15. Law (for the benefit of the public interest)

Additional Related Information

Personal Problems You Prefer to Deal With.   In this part of the exercise, you'll be considering which personal problems or services you may want to help others with. These can include areas such as personal growth, health, education, career, finances, relationships, or religion. You can refer to the list of personal problems in *What Color Is Your Parachute?* Identify those that you have knowledge of and prioritize according to which you would like to see involved in your next career. Tony's results are shown in Figure 5.3.

Products to Deal With or Help Produce.   Think about whether there are any particular products you might like to work with or help create. You can refer to the list provided in *What Color Is Your Parachute?*, or the one provided below. Check off those that apply to you and prioritize them in order

---

FIGURE 5.3

Tony's Preferences in Two Additional Areas

Personal Problems/Services to Help Others With

1. Worship

2. Acceptance (self and others)

3. Psychological healing (self and others)

4. Life/work planning

5. Broadcasting (news to public)

6. Personal insight (through therapy)

7. Hospital/health (administrator)

8. Nursing (animals)

9. Stewardship

10. Ethics

Products to Work With

1. Greeting cards (creative)

2. Books (production, contents, editing)

3. Magazines (same as above)

4. Newspapers (same as above)

5. Health Foods

6. Vitamins

7. Computers

8. Toiletries

9. Products (manufacture of)

10. Money

Sample List of Major Categories of Products

appliances	gardening
artistic	health
books	housewares
building materials	magazines
clothing	medical
computers	office equipment
cosmetics	sports/recreation
electronic equipment	stereos
food	television
furniture	toys
games	transportation

of their importance to you to be involved in your next career. Tony's preferred products are also shown in Figure 5.3.

We have now identified three additional areas—Specific Content/Special Knowledge, Personal Problems/Services, and Products—which we will combine with your top transferable/functional skills as well as recalling the patterns and themes related to your Top 10 experiences, in order to generate job/career ideas.

Generating Career Ideas

A crucial step in the career planning process is generating ideas and options based on one's self-assessment results. If you've actually made it to this point in the process alone, you're to be congratulated. Many career changers have difficulty completing this type of exercise on their own. Even if you have been able to generate the information up to this point on your own, it's not a bad idea to brainstorm specific career-related ideas and opinions with a career counselor.

Career options can be generated by combining your top ranked transferable skills with your top ranked specific content/special knowledge, personal problems/services, and products as well as the patterns and themes represented by your Top 10 experiences. For our example, we will concentrate on Tony's skills in problem solving through creative means, incorporating the management of others (including training activities) and projects. This captures most of Tony's preferred transferable skill areas.

One area that stood out in many of Tony's preferences was that of marketing/advertising. Tony's disappointment in previous marketing positions was that he hadn't had a change to utilize his MBA knowledge, especially in creative endeavors such as marketing plans for products (including production of commercials). The results here certainly confirmed Tony's interest in the marketing field. This career area involved his special knowledge areas 5, 9, and 10 (the advertising/creative, research and development, and packaging and distribution), and area 2, psychology (human behavior), would be involved as well. In addition, one of the four major themes from his Top 10 experiences was the creative side of the marketing business.

When he looked in the career resource books, possible career options include the following:

Advertising manager

Advertising agency manager

Creative director

Market research analyst

Brand/product management

Management positions are emphasized, because they incorporate many of Tony's preferred skills (leadership/supervision, human relations, and training). Tony believes that even though his life experience exercise information indicates interest in psychology/counseling, this interest could be satisfied through a management position. However, the position of industrial psychologist combines the interest in psychology and business. (At this point, we don't know whether Tony is currently qualified for any of these positions. That information will be developed in the research phase in Chapter 6.)

In addition to these marketing-related options, public relations and fund raising were also suggested to Tony because of the importance of dealing with people in promoting a product, service, or organization through presentations and writing. Even though writing did not appear as one of Tony's most preferred skills, it did have a heavy emphasis in his Top 10 experiences (4, 5, 9, and 11).

Tony also had an interest in communications, specifically as a newscaster or talk show host. This was evidenced by Tony's specific content/special knowledge areas 1 and 6 and area 5 in services. In fact, there were a number of performance/presentation-related Top 10 experiences (1, 4, 5, and 9). In addition, publication editor for greeting cards, books, magazines, or newspapers was suggested, based largely on their ranking 1–4 as products that Tony most preferred to work with. One additional position in this area that related to Tony's marketing background was that of circulation manager.

It was suggested to Tony that these various areas—marketing/advertising, brand/product management, public relations and fund raising, radio/TV talk show host, and publication editor—could be focused in any of the following areas of interest:

- Religion: #1 Service; #4 Special Knowledge

- Personal growth/motivation: #2, 3, 4, and 6 Services; #2, 3, and 12 Special Knowledges

- Health foods, diet, and exercise: #5, 6 Products; #7 Service

Therefore, any marketing of products or organizations (public relations and fund raising) could be related to these areas. Likewise, any publications or radio/TV talk shows could also be focused on these topics.

The list of options generated here is not meant to be exhaustive, but rather attempts to identify the major career paths that seem to stand out. Yet so many possibilities can still be overwhelming at first. The next phase of the assessment process, testing, will help Tony to focus in and narrow down options more effectively to those possibilities of greatest interest and preference. Try not to compare yourself to Tony's results. You might not have as many interests as he does (most of us don't), and thus you will have fewer options to consider.

Understanding Your Strong Interest Inventory Results

The Strong Interest Inventory (SII) based on the personality theory of John Holland, is targeted for teens and adults. The SII measures interests in a wide range of career areas, including professional, technical, non-profit, and vocational-technical. It's used to assist in making education and career decisions.

Subtests include sections on occupations, school subjects, activities, leisure activities, types of people, preference between two activities, and individual characteristics. Three major categories of scores are generated: 6 General Occupational Themes (GOT); 27 Basic Interest Scales (BIS); and 207 Occupational Scales (OS), made up of 105 female scales and 102 male scales.

Probably the most used interest inventory, the SII is perhaps also the most misinterpreted. If one's results are not interpreted appropriately, they can actually do more harm than good. In this section, we will discuss the SII to help you understand its three sets of scores and how to use the results for identifying related career options.

If you've taken the SII previously, then perhaps some insights gained here might shed some new light on your results. If you've never taken the inventory, you can use the guidelines provided here if you take it in the future. The SII is usually only available from career counseling professionals.

Holland's General Occupational Themes

Much of the SII is based on Holland's theory of vocational type. Part of Holland's theory suggests that work environments attract people with similar interests and, in a sense, become people environments. Holland's research showed that vocational-related interests could be grouped into six broad categories and that each category can be described by a General Occupational Theme:

1. Realistic: Physical performing, outdoors, things and objects, mechanical activities

2. Investigative: Science and math related, analytic and abstract reasoning activities

3. Artistic: Any aspect of the arts (painting, drawing, sculpting, etc., theater, dance, singing, writing, playing a musical instrument) as well as just being creative in the sense of using your own ideas to do things

4. Social: Working primarily with people in a helping and guiding (social service) context such as teacher, counselor, or clergy

5.   Enterprising: Working primarily with people but in a leadership context, using persuasive skills, often with a business/sales emphasis

6.   Conventional: Highly ordered and organized, interested in structured activities, like to know what's expected of them, often related to jobs involving office/clerical activities in business-related fields and usually not in a leadership role

Figure 5.4 illustrates the relationship between the six GOTs. Those most similar to each other can be found next to each other. For example, both Social and Enterprising occupations are primarily working with people, but in different contexts. Social is more helping/social service related, and Enterprising is more leadership/business related. Therefore, they are closely related and next to each other on the hexagon.

Also, the GOTs most dissimilar to each other are found directly across from each other on the hexagon. For example, Realistic (working primarily with things and objects) is across from Social (primarily working with people). In

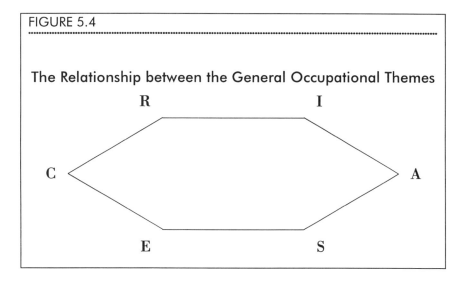

FIGURE 5.4

The Relationship between the General Occupational Themes

R   I

C   A

E   S

addition, Artistic types, who are creative and tend to be loose about structure, are across from Conventional types, who like to know what's expected of them and prefer structure.

Holland's theory suggests that people can be described in terms of the Holland GOTs, as can work environments and the people within them. Therefore, if you can identify which of the GOTs you relate to the strongest, then you could match your results to those of satisfied workers in different occupations for possible career options to consider. Holland's theory states that if a work environment suits your personality, you're likely to experience greater success, stability, and satisfaction.

Major work activities that jobs consist of can be described by the Holland GOTs. One-, two-, or three-letter codes (from RIASEC) can be used to describe related activities. The first letter would be the area of heaviest emphasis in that job, the second letter the second strongest area, etc. Usually the most important areas of a job can be described by the first two letters of its GOT code, and the third letter describes an area of lesser importance.

Let's look at the example of landscape architect. Its three-letter GOT code is AIR: Artistic, Investigative, and Realistic. Artistic, being the strongest theme, involves the design/creative aspect of being a landscape architect. Investigative is related to the scientific aspect, that of plants, soil, degree of sunlight, and weather conditions. The Realistic aspect relates to the instruments and tools used by a landscape architect.

Therefore, in addition to matching GOTs with persons happily employed in different occupations, you could also match up to the major activities involved in occupations as well.

Much of the information about interpreting your SII results can be found in the *User's Guide for the SII* by Jo-Ida Hansen. Most career counselors will have this book. Your six GOT scores are based on a small percentage of the 325 SII items you responded to; therefore, they might not be reliable. If you sense that they are inaccurate, don't be surprised. There is an alternative way to calculate these scores, which we'll discuss later in the chapter.

Your numerical score for each GOT indicates how much interest you have in each, as compared to the same and opposite sex in the general population. Because men and women score somewhat differently on some of these themes, a descriptive statement is added to your score, which is based on a comparison with your same sex in the general population. Research has shown same-sex comparisons to be somewhat more accurate. Therefore, for a combined comparison (to your same and opposite sex in the general population), you have the numerical score. For comparison to your same sex only, you have the descriptive statement.

The range for GOT scores is roughly from 30 to 70, with the average person scoring 50. However, the percentage of your Like responses (on the SII one chooses from Like, Indifferent, and Dislike response possibilities) can influence your GOT scores. The greater number of Like responses increased the chance of your having higher GOT scores, and vice versa. Check your percentage of Like, Indifferent, and Dislike responses on page 1, bottom right of the Profile Report. The same information can be found on other report formats for the SII.

A high percentage of Like responses (60 percent or above) can elevate your GOT scores (many high scores), and a low percentage (25 percent or below) can deflate your GOT scores (many low scores). Scores primarily in the average range can generate what is called a flat profile. We'll talk later in this section about elevated, deflated, and flat profiles. For now, pay attention to whatever is scoring the highest, regardless of the numerical scores. Even though this suggestion rubs against some of our societal norms (we're very score conscious), it's an appropriate approach for now. Tony's GOT scores are reported here, in order of the highest scoring. This reporting format, three sets of scores separated and reported from highest to lowest, will help you to see patterns or related themes among the scores. This is especially true for the next two sets we'll be looking at, the Basic Interest Scales (BIS) and the Occupational Scales (OS).

Social:	(55) Moderately high
Investigative:	(55) Average
Conventional:	(47) Average
Artistic:	(41) Moderately low
Realistic:	(36) Very low
Enterprising:	(33) Very low

We will wait to interpret Tony's GOT scores until we get to the OS scores. However, if you reflect on Tony's previous assessment results, the analysis of life experiences, you will notice how low his Artistic score is.

Basic Interest Scales

The 27 Basic Interest Scales (BIS) are organized by the GOT they relate to the strongest, as shown:

Realistic	Social
Agriculture	Teaching
Nature	Social service
Adventure	Athletics
Military activities	Domestic arts
Mechanical activities	Religious activities
Investigative	**Enterprising**
Science	Public speaking
Mathematics	Law/politics
Medical science	Merchandising
Medical service	Sales
	Business]management
Artistic	**Conventional**
Music/drama	Office practices
Art	Data management
Writing	Computer activities
Applied arts	
Culinary arts	

Similar to the GOT scores, the average adult scores about 50 on the BISs, with most people scoring between 30 and 70. If you score higher than 50 on a BIS, then you have responded with more consistent preference for activities related to that BIS. As a result, that would be an area to look upon as a focus of your interest and to perhaps incorporate as information in your career decision making.

The opposite is true for low BIS scores. Low numerical scores mean that when compared to same- and opposite-sex members' average scores, you show a low amount of interest in that BIS's activities. You can compare yourself to the average score of your same sex alone by the interpretive statement provided (Average, Moderately High, etc.).

Your results on the BISs might not be a big surprise to you. If the inventory is valid (if it measures what it claims to), it's really feeding back to you how you responded (Like, Indifferent, or Dislike) to various job titles, school subjects, activities, etc. It's somewhat like looking in a mirror, if you answered truthfully to the inventory items after some careful thinking. You probably already realized that you had interest in your higher-scoring BISs, but you might not have realized how strong that interest was when compared with same- and opposite-sex members in the general population.

You might discover that your scores on some of the BISs appear to be inconsistent with scores on related Occupational Scales (OS), to be discussed next. Perhaps you scored high on the Medical Science BIS and low on the OS of Physician. (For your information, the BIS of Science is more research-oriented and Medical Service is more social-oriented.) What this usually means is that although you have an interest in the subject matter of an occupation, you share very few other likes and dislikes with people in that occupation and you might not enjoy the daily routine of that occupation.

Generating Career Ideas

BIS information is useful for brainstorming career (and avocational) possibilities. In fact, you might be so used to looking at an avocational interest as only a hobby that you have never tried to fit it in as a career possibility. Many adults overlook their hobbies, the things they enjoy most during their leisure time, when planning careers. Yet many adults who do change careers bring the new career much closer to the hobby-related areas of their lives than the previous career. It's not surprising to find them much more satisfied in their work.

The BIS results do not decipher for you vocational from avocational interests. That is left up to you to determine. In other words, which do you want to try to involve in a career, which are just related to leisure, and which might be both career and leisure-related interests? Following are Tony's BIS results. The top 11 of 27 scales capture all of Tony's average and above scoring BISs.

	Score	Rating	Interest Scale	Theme Code
1.	(64)	High	Religious activities	S
2.	(62)	High	Public speaking	E
3.	(58)	Mod. High	Social services	S
4.	(54)	Average	Law/politics	E
5.	(54)	Average	Teaching	S
6.	(52)	Average	Writing	A
7.	(51)	Average	Music/drama	A
8.	(48)	Average	Science	I
9.	(48)	Average	Medical science	I
10.	(47)	Average	Nature	R
11.	(47)	Average	Adventure	R

Even though Tony had significant evidence of a social service interest from his life experience exercise, he believed at first that it would be satisfied by a management position. The interaction with staff (instructing, training, and the human relations component) he thought would satisfy his social service interest. Yet the social service BIS was third highest of 27 scales, and religious activities was the highest BIS (and #1 Service from the life experience exercise).

These two BISs can certainly be combined, as Tony did in his church youth group advising. It could also potentially be brought together by becoming a member of the clergy. Tony needs to explore the areas of social service and possibly teaching (#5 BIS and major skill cluster from life experience exercise). When considering teaching, Tony could look at other higher-scoring BISs for ideas of what subject matter to teach: Religion (#1), Political Science (#4), Writing (#6), Music/Drama (#7), Science (#8 and #9), and Outdoor Education (#10 and #11).

Tony's interest in writing is verified by its being #6 of 27 BISs. You'll recall that three of his Top 10 (and #11) life experiences involved writing. Of the four experiences, three were in the marketing field (product business plans and commercials), and the other was more of a generally creative, human relations focus, about his relationship with his brother.

The field of law (#4 BIS) incorporates much writing, and Tony's interest from the life experience exercise (Political Science #13 and Law #15 Specific Content/Special Knowledge) was verified. He could even specialize in environmental law (Nature #10 BIS). Writing can also be linked with Theater/Drama (#7 BIS), a strong interest of Tony's. Tony pursued acting right after completing his career counseling/testing and assessment. In addition, Tony could combine his interest in writing with Science (#8 BIS), which relates to an earlier career choice Tony once had, that of a veterinarian.

Earlier, in the life experience exercise, we suggested public relations and fund raising for Tony to consider. Two related Enterprising BIS scores were high for Tony, Public Speaking (#2) and Law/Politics (#4). Because both positions are highly persuasive (an E trait), there seems to be some support here from the two Enterprising BISs.

Public speaking can also be combined with Drama (#7 BIS) to support Tony's interest in Broadcasting (#1 Special Knowledge and #5 Service), specifically talk show host or news broadcaster, which includes secondary areas of writing (also involved heavily in public relations and fund raising) and politics (news). In fact, as we're getting more familiar with Tony and his wide range of interests, you could almost picture him as a talk show host where he could pursue many topics of interest.

Science (#8) and Medical Science (#9) showed up in Tony's top BIS scores. The only prior evidence of this area from the life experience exercise was #5 and #6 Products (Health Foods and Vitamins), #7 Service (Hospital/Health Administrator) and #8 Service (Nursing Animals). It seems from Tony's results that this could be a secondary area of interest, following others that ranked higher in the life experience exercise, such as advertising/creative, public relations, fund raising, and publication editor. Tony could focus work in these four areas in science-related products, services, or organizations.

Remember that three of Tony's Top 10 life experiences were adverturesome in nature: sky diving, back-packing in Europe, and game show contestant. Adventure ranked as #11 of the BISs. This would indicate that Tony enjoys a challenge, taking risks, and being spontaneous. This interest can be pursued in a career or avocationally (as the three experiences were). It's an "Average" rating as a BIS. Tony should consider whether an underlying sense of adventure is desired on the job, as it has already been evidenced off the job.

Occupational Scales

The third set of scores reported on the SII are the Occupational Scales (OS), perhaps the scores that those taking the SII are most interested in (and perhaps the aspect that is most often misinterpreted or not interpreted at all). The OS compare your interests to those of the same and opposite sex, happily employed in just over 100 occupations. These 200–300 members of an occupational group are usually members of a professional association related to their occupation. They meet the following criteria:

- Between 25 and 60 years old

- In the occupation for at least 3 years

- Have reported that they enjoy their jobs

- Meet some form of minimal standard of occupation performance, such as certification, licensure, or advanced degree

- Pursue their occupation with typical tasks and duties and not in some unusual way

On the SII Profile Report, both your same- and opposite-sex OS comparison scores are reported. However, as with the GOTs and BISs, your same-sex comparison scores are more likely to be good predictors for you than are scales for the other sex.

On the SII Profile Report, your score for each scale is printed in numerals for those scales normed for your sex and is also plotted graphically with an asterisk. The opposite-sex numerical score is also reported, but not graphically. The graphic display can be confusing, therefore, pull the scores out of the GOT structure and simply list them from highest to lowest as we did with the two previous sets of scores.

Someone who scores 50 on a given scale has responded to the SII items in the same way the average member of that occupation does and falls under the interpretive comment of "Similar." Following is a list of score ranges and related interpretive comments:

Score	Interpretive Comment
14 or below	Very dissimilar
15-24	Dissimilar
25-29	Moderately dissimilar
30-39	Mid-range
40-44	Moderately similar
45-54	Similar
55 or higher	Very similar

Scores in the moderately similar or higher range (40 or above) on same-sex normed scales are the most useful. Usually, your Top 20 OSs will capture all your moderately similar scores and above; if they do not, lengthen your list to include those as well.

One set of new information reported with OS scores is the one-, two-, or three-letter GOT code designation for members of that occupation. These are listed to the right of the OS name with Tony's OS scores. When a one-letter code is listed, it can at times be confusing. For example, male and female florists are described with a one-code letter: Enterprising. This is mainly because, in this case, they are business owners. Chances are that most florists have a strong **Artistic** side as well, but the statistical analysis done by Consulting Psychologist Press doesn't show it as high enough to include here. Similarly, male and female lawyers are classified as **Artistic**. Writing is a major part of being a lawyer (as is being creative in case preparation and presentation), so you could understand the OS code of A. However, there is probably also an Enterprising (persuasive) side to them as well.

Therefore, only one GOT is sometimes presented to describe an occupation even though there is usually another that plays a big part. If any of your higher-scoring OSs are coded with just one GOT, you can ask yourself, "What might that next letter be?" This approach might help your OS results make greater sense to you.

Listing the scores in order of highest to lowest helps us to see possible patterns among your higher OS scores, both by occupational title and by GOT code designation. For example, Tony's Top 20 OS scores follow:

	Score	Rating	Occupational Scale	Theme Code
1.	(55)	Very similar	Guidance counselor	S
2.	(53)	Similar	Broadcaster	A
3.	(50)	Similar	Social worker	SA
4.	(49)	Similar	Social science teacher	S
5.	(48)	Similar	Minister	SA
6.	(48)	Similar	College professor	I
7.	(48)	Similar	Advertising executive	A
8.	(48)	Similar	Public relations director	A
9.	(47)	Similar	Speech pathologist	SAI
10.	(46)	Similar	Psychologist	IA
11.	(46)	Similar	Marketing executive	EI
12.	(45)	Similar	Recreation leader	SE
13.	(44)	Moderately similar	Investment manager	ECI
14.	(43)	Moderately similar	YMCA director	SE
15.	(43)	Moderately similar	Dietitian	CSE
16.	(43)	Moderately similar	Chiropractor	I
17.	(43)	Moderately similar	Physician	IA
18.	(42)	Moderately similar	Lawyer	A
19.	(42)	Moderately similar	Public administrator	AS
20.	(41)	Moderately similar	Elected public official	E

Of the Top 10 OS GOT code designations, 3 include SA together, 2 with S alone, 4 with A, and 3 with I. In fact, 9 of the Top 10 include S or A. here we see a common situation in which one's GOT scores do not seem accurate, largely due to the fact that only a small number of the 325 best items (less than 10 percent) are used to compute these scores.

If you think your GOT scores are not accurate, you might want to try the alternative method in Figure 5.5 for calculating your GOT scores to see whether

---

FIGURE 5.5

··

Verifying Tony's General Occupational Theme (GOT) Score Results Based on His Top 20 SII Occupational Scale GOT Designations

	R	I	A	S	E	C
Number of times it appears as first letter × 3	—	4 × 3 = 12	6 × 3 = 18	7 × 3 = 21	3 × 3 = 9	1 × 3 = 3
Number of times it appears as second letter × 2	—	1 × 2 = 2	5 × 2 = 10	2 × 2 = 4	2 × 2 = 4	1 × 2 = 2
Number of times it appears as third letter × 1	—	2 × 1 = 2	—	—	—	—
Total Points	0	16	28	25	13	5

---

it yields scores you agree with more. We'll use the OS GOT code designation to calculate these alternative GOT scores. Let's look at Tony's results as an example. Basically, we will tally the number of times each letter (RIASEC) appears as a first, second, or third letter in the GOT code designations for each of your Top 20 OSs, In Tony's case, the new results are quite different (and fit better) than the original scores, as shown:

SII GOT Scores			Alternative GOT Scores	
55	MH	Social	28	Artistic
55	AVG	Investigative	25	Social
47	AVG	Conventional	16	Investigative
41	ML	Artistic	13	Enterprising
36	ML	Realistic	5	Conventional
33	ML	Enterprising	0	Realistic

Here Artistic jumps from fourth-highest to the highest scoring GOT. Social drops to second, yet it is still high, being only three points below Artistic. Investigative still places third. Enterprising is now just three points behind I, which is a jump from previously coming in last. Conventional drops, and Realistic is somewhat out of the picture. Up to this point, ASI (with E rising) seems to be a more accurate description for Tony's interests than the previous SIC (with E last). Let's move on now and take a closer look at Tony's higher OS scores and see what they might mean.

Most of the specific occupations and patterns we suggested to Tony after the analysis of life experience exercise are confirmed by his Top 20 OS scores. The advertising creative or marketing area is supported by:

- Advertising executive   (#7)   Similar

- Marketing executive   (#11)   Similar

- Investment manager   (#13)   Moderately similar

The public relations/fund raising area is supported by:

- Public relations director   (#8)   Similar

- (There is no fund raiser OS on the SII.)

Tony's interest in Broadcasting is supported by:

- Broadcaster   (#2)   Similar

The Helping Others/Social Service area is supported by:

- Guidance counselor   (#1)   Very similar

- Social worker   (#3)   Similar
- Minister   (#5)   Similar
- Psychologist   (#10)   Similar

There are underlying relationships to:

- Social science teacher   (#4)   Similar
- College professor   (#6)   Similar
- Recreation leader   (#12)   Similar
- YMCA director   (#14)   Moderately similar

Tony's interest in Law/Politics is supported by:

- Lawyer   (#18)   Moderately similar
- Public administrator   (#19)   Moderately similar
- Elected public official   (#20)   Moderately similar

In addition, the Medical/Science area was still appearing as represented by:

- Dietitian   (#15)   Moderately similar
- Chiropractor   (#16)   Moderately similar
- Physician   (#17)   Moderately similar

Therefore, the major areas of advertising/marketing/creative, public relations/ fund raising, broadcasting, teaching/training, and social service suggested as a result of the analysis of life experience exercise are all supported by the fact that their related SII OS scored in the Top 20 (with most in the similar range).

It might be beneficial to describe how we're using the term support. Tony's interest in these four areas are all similar (from moderate to very, though mostly in-between) to the interests of happily employed, same-sex members of those occupations. Does that mean that Tony should go into one of these occupations? Not exactly; the key word is *should*. For example, when Tony's interests are compared to males in more than 100 different occupations on the SII, they're similar to the interests of advertising executives, and because they like their job, maybe Tony would also like that job. The key word here is *maybe*, not *should*.

Tony, or anybody else, including yourself, would have to check it out, first by reading up on that particular job in a career resource book. In addition, if you are still interested in a certain occupation, you need to begin talking to persons employed in that occupation to gather more information and to begin to build your network of contacts.

Tony did some investigating of this nature for the occupation of industrial psychologist. Through reading and talking with people, Tony verified that indeed, this occupation did incorporate many of his numerous interests. However, he also verified that he would need a second master's degree in order to qualify. Tony decided that at this point in his life he was not willing to study for a second master's degree.

So what do you do when something you think you're interested in has a low-scoring (mid-range or below) OS score? First of all, you should never make a career decision based on only one information source, including the SII. However, a low-scoring OS score in an occupation of interest to you should be considered a signal warning you to investigate further before making a decision. Your job becomes one of trying to find out why your interests are being reported as somewhat dissimilar to same-sex members of that occupation.

In Tony's case, the only major area of interest not showing up in the Top 20 OS scores was that of publication editor. The closest related OS is reporter, which was in the mid-range of similarity, with a score of 37. Remember that Tony's BIS score for writing was sixth highest of 23, yet still only an average amount of interest when compared to the same sex in the general population.

In discussing this with Tony, he confirmed an interest in writing but mainly in the creative aspect involved with advertising/marketing campaigns. Tony expressed a lack of desire to use writing skills as a major occupational skill. He is not confident about his ability to write, which explains why it did not show up in the skill assessment portion of the analysis of life experiences exercise. Tony once considered law school, but he changed his mind when he learned of the prominent role of writing in that occupation.

Recall that Tony ranked books, magazines, and newspapers highly (2-4) as products he would like to work with. Where was he coming from? Tony would like to be in a position to determine the contents of the publication but not necessarily be the one to edit (perhaps owner/publisher). With that information, we can eliminate publication editor from Tony's list of options, unless he owns the publication and works with a staff of editors to plan and organize its contents. With respect to this one general-interest area whose related OS score was lower, Tony made sense out of it and now can move on with his career decision making. When you eliminate something as a choice, be sure you know why and what you're basing that decision on.

Tony had also determined that he didn't want to pursue a social services career. As mentioned earlier, his interests in human relations, mentoring, teaching, and training could be satisfied to a large degree through a management position. He has successfully combined two major interest areas, religion and social service, through his church youth group advising. He planned to continue doing that as an avocational pursuit.

Tony was beginning to focus back on the area of advertising/marketing/ creative as a primary career goal. His OS scores support this area of interest. In fact, it's not unusual to find that the SII strongly supports career options generated by the analysis of life experience exercise.

In summary, there are two ways to view the OS results. You can look at the higher-scoring, specific OSs and consider those as options. Or, as we've suggested all along, identify the patterns of your higher-scoring OSs. In Tony's case, it's an artistic/social pattern, so it would make sense for Tony to attempt to include these types of activities in his career choice and avocational interests as well.

Understanding Your Myers-Briggs Type Indicator Results

Although not specifically designed as a career assessment instrument, the Myers-Briggs Type Indicator (MBTI) has been widely applied in the career development field, helping college students and adults toward more informed career decisions. The MBTI is adapted from Carl Jung's theory of psychological type. The MBTI attempts to measure Jung's ideas about perception, judgment, and attitude in human personality, referred to as *personality type*.

The assumption behind the MBTI with regard to its use in career planning is that individuals are motivated to select careers by:

- Opportunities to express their preferences

- The promise of greater job satisfaction

- Rewards for using preference strengths

- A perception that they will find the tasks and problems of the occupation challenging and interesting

Personality typing, as defied by Myers and Briggs, assumes that much of our personality can be defined by dividing it into four independent preference areas or scales: energizing, attending, deciding, and living. Within each scale we have a preference for one of two opposites that define the scale. This makes for a total of 16 different combinations, each of which defines one particular and unique personality type.

Description of the Four Preference Scales

Extroversion/Introversion (E/I).

This scale measures how you are energized, where you prefer to focus your attention. People who prefer extroversion direct their energy to the outside world of people, activities, or things. They prefer to communicate more by talking than by writing and need to experience the world in order to understand it—thus a preference for action. People who prefer introversion focus more on their inner world of ideas, emotions, or impressions, like to understand the world before experiencing it. They think about what to do before acting.

Sensing/Intuition (S/N).

This scale measures what you pay attention to and how you acquire information. Sensing indicates a preference for using your five senses to notice what is real. Two key words that describe sensing types are *realistic* and *practical*. Intuition indicates a preference for using your imagination, looking beyond your five senses to see new possibilities and ways of doing things. Thus this type values imagination and inspiration.

Thinking/Feeling (T/F).

This scale measures how you make decisions. Thinking types make decisions objectively, in a logical manner, by analyzing and weighing the evidence. The term *Feeling* does not refer to feelings/emotions. Feeling types, when making decisions, consider what is important to them based on their personal value system.

Judgment/Perception (J/P).

This scale measures how you act in and relate to the outer world, your attitude, and the life-style you prefer. The term *Judgment* does not refer to being judgmental. Those who take a judging attitude have a preference for living in a planned and organized way. They like things settled, making decisions, coming to closure, and then carrying on. Those who prefer a perceptive attitude have a preference for living in a more spontaneous and flexible manner, staying open to experience. They are confident in their ability to adapt.

Interpreting Individual Scale Scores

The MBTI generates two scores for each of the four bipolar scales. One score, the raw score, indicates the direction of your preference (which of the bipolar measures you prefer on each of the four scales) and is indicated by that scale's one-letter symbol.

The second score, which is numerical, shows how strong or intense your preference is. This score can be misinterpreted. Some assume that strength of preference (higher numerical score) implies excellence. This is not the case. A larger score simply means that the person, if forced to choose, is more clear about what he or she prefers. The four levels of preference strength and intensity, corresponding numerical scores, and descriptions of MBTI examinees' reaction to each follow.

Very Clear Preference (41 or higher, or 31 for Feeling). These examinees usually agree that they hold the preferences as reported by the MBTI, as well as related attitudes and skills.

Clear Preference (21-39, or 29 for Feeling). This indicates, with reasonable probability, that the examinee holds and acts on the reported preference.

Moderate Preference (11-19). The examinee scoring at this level may still most often agree with the description of the reported preference but should be asked if he or she agrees with the interpretation.

Slight Preference (1-9). This could indicate a split within the examinee. Low scores are often a reflection of tension between the two opposite poles of the preference. It does not indicate equal excellence in, or a command of, both poles of the preference, as is the reaction of some examinees. Tony's scores on the four individual scales follow:

- Extroversion/Introversion (E/I): **E**–19, moderate to clear preference

- Sensing/Intuition (S/N): **N**–31, clear preference

- Thinking/Feeling (T/F): **F**–37, very clear preference

- Judgment/Perception (J/P): **J**–23, clear preference

Tony's scores reflect rather clear preferences. It's not unusual for most who take the MBTI to have at least one scale of the four in which the direction and strength of preference is close or almost equal. However, in Tony's case the direction of his preferences are quite clear.

Thus, how you respond on the MBTI determines your preferences, and the preferred bipolar dimensions (E or I, S or N, T or F, and J or P) form your four-letter type. There are 16 possible four-letter types, for which detailed personality profiles have been assembled. There seems to be widespread agreement by those who study personality typing, as well as those who take the inventory, that these profiles closely describe the real personality of most people once the four-letter type is determined.

Understanding Your Four-Letter Type

In order to better understand your four-letter type, let's take a look at Tony's as an example. Tony's four-letter type is **ENFJ**—extroverted, intuitive, feeling, and judging—with all four being clear preferences most of the time. We could describe Tony's type as an extrovert (E), someone who is energized by what goes on around him, who prefers intuition (N), imagination, and inspiration for perceiving and acquiring information. He decides with feeling (F), based on his personal value system, and takes a judging (J), planned, and organized attitude toward the outer world.

The opposite of Tony's four-letter type is **ISTP.** ISTP's are introverts (I), energized by their inner world of ideas and concepts, who prefer to process information through their senses (S). They choose to use thinking (T), logical reasoning, to make decisions. They use a perceptive (P), spontaneous, and flexible, attitude toward the outer world.

For an expanded description of your four-letter type, consult *Manual: A Guide to the Development and Use of the MBTI,* by Isabel Briggs Myers and Mary McCauley, or *Introduction to Type,* by Isabel Briggs Myers. In addition, the *MBTI Type Booklets* are individual booklets, one for each of the 16 four-letter types.

MBTI and Career Decision Making

The Perception and Judgment Functions.   People are usually attracted to, and more satisfied in, jobs or careers that provide opportunities to express and use their preferences. The combination of your perception (SN) and judgment (TF) functions, the second and third letters of your four-letter type code, are considered to be the most important with regard to career decision making. The types of preferences these two functions assess make a difference in the kind of work you will do best and enjoy the most. If your daily work has the most need for the kind of perception and deciding that you prefer, the greater the chance that you will experience job satisfaction.

Four combinations can be generated from these two functions:

- **ST, Sensing plus Thinking:** This person is interested in the realities of a given situation and makes decisions by logical analysis. The most satisfaction may be found in occupations where there's an analysis of facts on an impersonal level, such as applied science, business administration, banking, law enforcement, production, and construction.

- **SF, Sensing plus Feeling:** This type is interested in reality that can be observed, makes decisions with personal warmth, and is sensitive to others. Satisfaction may be found in occupations such as health care, community service, teaching, supervision, religious service, office work, and sales.

- **NF, Intuition plus Feeling:** These types also make decisions with personal warmth, but they are more interested in possibilities for projects and people than in facts. Occupations recommended for this group include behavioral science, research, literature, art and music, religious service, health care, and teaching.

- **NT, Intuition plus Thinking:** Persons of this type are also interested in possibilities but handle them by applying objective analysis and problem solving. Occupations usually satisfying to this type include physical science, research, management, computers, law, engineering, and technical work.

••

We've already pointed out that Tony was beginning to focus on the creative side of the advertising/marketing field, which his clear preference for Intuitive supports. The creative, imaginative process in advertising matches well with Intuitive types like Tony.

Just ahead you'll see that we also recommend that Tony channel his management interest into a smaller organization (enhancing the possibility of being able to act on his values) working toward some humanitarian cause. This environment relates to Tony's very clear preference for Feeling.

••

Even though your major career field of interest is bound to be directly related to the kind of perception and judgment you prefer, your other preferences also play an important role.

Extroversion/Introversion.
This scale pertains to where you would most like to focus and use your preferred perception and judgment functions. It could help you to decide on a specific work environment or particular organization within a given field. What would your preference be? In

the outer world of people and things (E) or inwardly, within your own private inner world of impressions or ideas (I)?

● ●

Tony is energized by his interactions with people, evidenced by his moderate to clear preference for Extroversion. This seems a good match for the usual lively work atmosphere in advertising. This is perhaps a clue to Tony that the "smaller" organization not be too small.

● ●

Judgment/Perception.　This scale helps you to determine how you would like to go about your job. Would you prefer to be planning operations, organizing activities, and possibly shut off as soon as you observed enough to make a decision (J)? Or would you prefer to be allowed to be more flexible, spontaneous, able to be open to new possibilities, allowed to suspend judgment in order to take another look and perhaps gain additional information prior to making a decision (P)?

● ●

Tony's clear preference for Judging indicates he likes to plan, be structured in his approach and make decisions—which will help in managing himself and others. However, the creative process like that in advertising may need a more flexible and spontaneous approach at times. This issue was brought up with Tony and he noted the potential conflict. Tony made it a goal to be more balanced in his approach to work and to be alert for situations that were better dealt with in a more "open to possibilities" manner.

● ●

The Career Report

One of the newer score reporting formats for the MBTI is the Career Report, which identifies occupations most often selected by people who are the same MBTI type as you. The database used for comparing your preferences is drawn from over 60,000 MBTI users in 208 different occupations. If you took a form of the MBTI other than the Career Report, you can ask your career counselor to order it for you from Consulting Psychologists Press

(1-800-624-1765). You could also get similar information from the *MBTI Manual,* Appendix D. There you will find 16 lists, representing all MBTI types, with the same 185 occupational groups listed on each, from highest to lowest, by the percentage of workers in that occupation with that type.

Probably the highlight of the Career Report, as far as examinees are concerned, is that it presents two lists of occupations:

1. The 50 most popular occupations (rank ordered beginning with the most attractive) for your MBTI type

2. The 25 least popular occupations (with the lowest percentage) for your type

It's suggested that you look over the top 25 percent of all occupational groups (of the 208) for a possible career focus, thus the reason for a list of the top 50.

This is similar to the Strong Interest Inventory Occupational Scales discussed earlier. It gives you a chance to compare how you responded on the MBTI (your preferences) to those of workers in a wide variety of occupations. However, workers participating in the SII were asked whether they liked their jobs, and only those who answered positively were included. This makes the Occupational Scales somewhat more powerful, because you know you are comparing your interests to happily employed workers. Therefore, there is a greater chance that you might also enjoy that work as well.

Only a subset of 33,000 members of the comparison groups (out of 60,000) reported on the MBTI Career Report were asked to what degree they were satisfied with their work:

- 36 percent responded they had a lot of satisfaction

- 26 percent responded that their level of satisfaction was okay

- 4 percent responded that there was not much satisfaction

- 35 percent chose not to respond

The *MBTI Manual* suggests that the impact of individuals who were not satisfied with their jobs on the rankings of the occupational samples is probably minimal.

Let's see what kind of support Tony can get from these results for the career areas he's still considering. Following are career areas that came through strongly on the analysis of life experiences exercise and the SII and are still of some interest to Tony, with related occupations from the Career Report Top 50 and its related position (highest percentage of ENFJs) on that list.

Social Service Related.

Religious:
1. Director of religious education
2. Specialized Protestant minister
3. Clergy, all denominations
4. Protestant minister
6. Rabbi
7. Priest or monk
20. Roman Catholic priest
25. Religious workers (all denominations)

Counseling:
9. Certified psychodramatist
12. Counselor: suicide or crisis
14. Counselor: runaway youth
15. Counselor: school
23. Counselor
40. Psychologist

Teaching/
Training:
8. Teacher: health
11. Teacher: art, drama, or music
39. Health education practitioner

Advertising/Marketing/Creative.

36. Marketing professional (only related comparison group)

Public Relations/Fund Raising.

48. Public relations worker or publicity writer (only related comparison group)

Broadcasting/Acting.

9. Certified psychodramatist (acting combined with counseling)
10. Actor
24. Artist or entertainer (only related comparison groups)

You'll notice a great deal of similarity between the MBTI's listing of related occupations and the SII's higher-scoring Occupational Scales for Tony.

The MBTI Career Report results strongly support Tony's main career interests. His preferences show a strong similarity to those of workers in the career areas of interest to him. The career area of interest to Tony that did not appear in the Top 50 list was that of managers and administrators. You might recall that Tony believed many of his social service, human relations, and teaching/training interests could be satisfied through a management position.

Interpreting Lower-Scoring Occupations of Choice.

What if an occupation of interest to you places lower down on your list (not in the Top 50)? For example, looking at the ENFJ list, we find clergy (all denominations) at the top with 17.79 percent of 534 workers scoring ENFJ. Now, you may think, "What's so high about 17-18 percent?" Remember that there are 16 possible subgroups making up each occupation's group of workers. If the workers were equally distributed among the 16 types, there would be only 6.25 percent of each type in each occupation. Therefore, you can see that 17-18% is a very high percentage representation under these circumstances.

The *MBTI Manual* states that a client should never be discouraged from entering an occupation on the basis that he or she is not the right type. No career decision should be based on any one source of information, even if it's an excellent source like the SII or the MBTI. However, it would be prudent for someone whose desired occupational choice is showing up lower on the SII OSs list or the MBTI occupational listings to investigate why this is occurring

A first step in this investigative effort of researching a possible discrepancy between your MBTI type and a preferred occupation is to check the *Atlas of Type Tables,* by Gerald Macdaid et al. Here you'll find one page for each occupation that the MBTI reports on. On this page is a breakdown of all 16 MBTI types and their percentages of workers in that occupation. Therefore, you can immediately see how your type compares to the other 15, as far as percentage of workers in that particular occupation.

The benefit of this visual presentation is that what you thought was a lower representation of your type might have still been the fifth or sixth highest type of the 16 possible for a particular occupation. In addition, when you note which types are the highest, there might be only a one-letter (or scale) difference to your type, and it just happens to be on a scale that you scored only a slight preference on. If you changed that one letter, your new type is among the highest represented for that occupation. However, if you have all clear preferences, as does Tony, switching letters would not be appropriate. What would be appropriate is to discuss with your career counselor just how that one scale might impact that particular job and its suitability for you. Three of four top scoring scales can be a close match depending on the emphasis of that scale in the particular occupation you're considering.

Let's look at the one area that scored lower for Tony, that of managers and administrators, a broad sampling of 7,463. Looking at the appropriate page in the *Atlas of Types,* we find that Tony's type, ENFJ, ranks eighth highest among the 16 types for the group of managers and administrators, with a representation of 4.92 percent. Initially, that doesn't sound like much, yet a closer look produces some interesting information.

The three highest scoring types for this occupational group, with 17.04 percent, 14.94 percent, and 10.06 percent, respectively, were ESTJ, ISTJ, and ENTJ. What do these three have in common? Yes, you get it, "T." When you think about it, a decision-making approach based more on one's personal values (F) could create some management difficulties when the bottom line often takes priority. This was Tony's most clear preference of the four scales, so let's keep looking.

The fourth and fifth highest scoring types, with 7.32 percent and 6.93 percent, respectively, were ESFJ and ENFP. What do you notice here? The first time "F" appears, first with S and then with N, as in Tony's type, ENFJ. So now we have reached the point where three of Tony's four scale preferences are appearing. It certainly seems worth the time to speak to Tony about his reaction to all this. How does he see his F decision-making style impeding or not impeding potential management positions? Are there any management positions that might have a better chance of fitting Tony's particular type?

Recall that some of Tony's highest values were of a religious, helping others, and ethical nature. Perhaps he could find a job in a smaller firm (less of the cold, impersonal, larger corporate atmosphere) involved directly with a cause or purpose related somehow to his highest values (such as public relations/fund raising for a non-profit). An additional possibility for Tony to consider would be a small business of his own related to one of the areas he's interested in, such as an advertising/marketing consultant specializing in non-profits and related causes.

Consulting the *Atlas of Types* is a good first step. If the answer is found here, so much the better. If not, then try researching the careers in published sources and by talking to people. There might be some reason, perhaps not clear up to this point, why a particular occupation scored lower for you. Therefore, careful review of career resource materials and talking with people already employed in that occupation could help identify where the discrepancy might be. If you're still interested in that occupation after careful and knowledgeable consideration, at least you've chosen it aware that the fit might not be right, rather than having unrealistic expectations.

What If You Don't Like Your MBTI Type?   It is possible that after identifying your MBTI type, some aspect might not be pleasing to you. Perhaps you saw yourself in a different light and, after discussing your MBTI results with your career counselor, decided that the MBTI might be accurate. Well, you'll be glad to know that your type is not written in stone. You can develop aspects of yourself that scored lower than what you would have liked. You should discuss with your career counselor aspects of yourself you would like to improve. Between the two of you, you should be able to come up with strategies for accomplishing that.

Other personality inventories I recommend include Sixteen Personality Factor (16PF) Questionnaire, the Personal Career Development Profile (PCDP), and the California Psychological Inventory (CPI).

Assessing Your Work and Life Values

Work Values

Work values are directly related to your level of satisfaction on the job, depending on the degree to which they are being fulfilled. If you haven't yet completed the Work Values Satisfaction Self-Assessment in Chapter 3, whether currently employed or not, this would be a good time to do so. The following list of work values is somewhat condensed from the 80 involved in the self-assessment in Chapter 3:

Achievement	Personal growth
Co-workers	Physical activity
Creativity	Prestige
Location/distance	Recognition
Formal/informal dress code	Respect
Fringe benefits	Responsibility
Helping others/altruism	Routine activity
Hours	Salary
Independence	Supervisor relations
Intellectual reasoning	Surroundings/physical environment
Job security	Travel
Leadership	Upward mobility
	Variety of duties
_____	_____
_____	_____
_____	_____

Add any other work-related values you can think of, and then prioritize them according to those values that are most important to you. If you've completed the self-assessment in Chapter 3, then your results here should be consistent with those.

Life Values

Following are 34 life values:

Autonomy/Freedom of life-style	Leisure time
Aesthetics	Morality
Helping others/altruism	Nature
Career	Personal growth
Creativity	Physical appearance
Education	Pleasure
Emotional growth/well-being	Popularity
Family	Power
Financial security	Prestige
Friends	Recognition
Health/physical fitness	Religion/spirituality
Honesty	Respect
Intellectual growth	Self-awareness
Justice/fairness	Self-confidence
Knowledge	Skill
Love relationship	Travel
_____	Wisdom
_____	_____
_____	_____
_____	_____

Look the list over. Are there any life values not on the list? If so, add these values to the list. Now identify, in order of priority, your Top 10 life values. You'll soon realize that this is a difficult task, because they're all important values to most of us. It's hard to let go of any of these values, which the prioritizing forces you to do.

To help you zero in on your top life values, we have provided the Values in Life Questionnaire in Figure 5.6. It is adapted from John McHolland's work with the Human Potential Seminar, a structured, small-group approach designed to help participants gain greater control in their lives, as well as to increase their self-esteem. Complete the Values in Life Questionnaire by answering the questions (give them careful thought) and then noting what life values are represented by your responses. In other words, what do your responses indicate about what's important to you?

By completing the Values in Life Questionnaire, you will become more focused about your most important life values and better prepared to prioritize them. However, before you start prioritizing, be sure to add any values to the list that you are interested in. Following are Tony's Top 10 life and work values and some thoughts on how they might impact his career decision making:

Life Values	Work Values
1. Religion/spirituality	1. Personal growth
2. Emotional growth/well-being	2. Achievement
3. Health/physical fitness	3. Intellectual reasoning
4. Self-awareness/confidence	4. Upward mobility
5. Morality	5. Salary
6. Family	6. Supervisor relations
7. Honesty	7. Creativity
8. Career	8. Co-workers
9. Love relationship	9. Helping others/altruism
10. Financial security	10. Leadership

FIGURE 5.6
....

Values in Life Questionnaire

1. Write down 2–3 decisions or choices (small or big) that you've made recently.

2. List 2–3 activities or experiences (ordinary ones are fine) that you've participated in over the past few weeks.

3. Identify 2–3 experiences or times in your life when you felt the most "alive" as a person.

4. Cite 2–3 satisfactions, achievements, or successes you've had in the last couple of weeks.

5. What 2–3 experiences or situations usually make you feel angry? (The opposite of this is your value.)

6. If you could be granted three wishes (none of which can be for additional wishes), what would yours be?

7. Happiness is: _____ .

8. If you had one week left to live, how would you spend it? Where? With whom? Doing what?

9. If you were to die in 10 years, what three things would you want people to remember you for? (or) What would you like to accomplish with your life in the next 10 years?

When in the process of career decision making and trying to identify a field of interest, it's a good idea to take a look at your life values and as, "Will this field impede in any way (directly or indirectly) the attainment of my life values?"

With respect to Tony's values in life, there's a strong ethical component (religion/spirituality, morality, and honesty). Tony needs to find an organization whose corporate mission or culture is somewhat consistent with these values in order for Tony to feel a greater possibility of his attaining these life values. Of course, activities outside of work can lead to the attainment of these values also (e.g., church youth group advising). However, if there's a strong values clash on the job, it could take a heavy toll on Tony's health and happiness.

If Tony is going to search for a creative job in advertising/marketing (the direction in which he is leaning), then he would fit best in an organization that operates along ethical principles. Tony also emphasizes emotional growth, self-awareness, and health/fitness as top life values. Will a potential employer place unreasonably high demands on Tony as far as hours to be worked or job-related stress, thus impacting attainment of these values? That would also be important for him to check out, because these stresses can affect two other highly ranked life values, family and love relationship.

In reviewing Tony's top tanked work values, it seems that, ideally, he would like a job in which he could achieve through creative activities, resulting in personal and intellectual growth, as well as helping others (supervisor, co-workers, and clients); and eventually attain a leadership role (involving upward mobility and related salary increases).

Therefore, as Tony looks into different organizations for possible employment, this becomes more or less his checklist of the ten most important values to look for. Some are not easy to assess (e.g., supervisor/co-worker relations and attaining a leadership role). However, he can make every effort during the interviewing process to check out these types of concerns. This research can uncover such things as corporate philosophy and mission, hiring, compensation and promotion trends, and related facts.

Tony can now add this value information to the other criteria he has already identified: interests, transferable/functional and specific content/special knowledge skills, and personality preferences. All of these become important areas of consideration when assessing future career possibilities.

Assessing Your Transferable/Functional, Specific Content/Special Knowledge and Adaptive/Self-Management Skills

As part of the analysis of life experience exercise, we showed you how we helped Tony to assess his transferable/functional skills, as well as to identify his preferred specific content/special knowledge skills. With regard to Tony's transferable/functional skills, he identified these from his Top 10 life experiences as the skills he thought would be essential for him to use in his next job/career.

If you did the analysis of life experience exercise for yourself, then you know how involved it was. If not, you can attempt it now. Regardless of when you completed it, now or earlier, here are a few more steps to add.

Review the skills in your Top 10 life experiences that you classified as essential and used to form your personal skill clusters. Ask yourself which of these you possess to a strong degree (not necessarily perfect), and which you would like to improve in. In addition, review the skills list in *What Color Is Your Parachute?* to identify any skills that were not represented in your Top 10 life experiences that you would like to identify now as skills you want to consider using in your next job/career. Make a note of them with your other skills assessment results. Decide which of these skills you have to a strong degree and which you'd like to improve in. Review the skills list for those you do not feel you possess but would like to learn. Some can be job/career related and others can be avocationally related.

Now you're ready to classify your transferable/functional skills into three categories:

1.   Skills you have to a strong degree (not necessarily perfect)

2.   Skills you have and would like to improve in

3.   Skills you do not possess but would like to learn

If you're having a difficult time judging the level of skill you possess, consider talking with experts in the field that you're hoping to apply those skills in to get a better handle on your level of expertise. In addition, look for the *Career Ability Placement Survey* (CAPS), by Lila Knapp and Robert Knapp. It's designed to compare your abilities to entry requirements in most occupations. Also, both the *Dictionary of Occupational Titles* and the *Enhanced Guide for Occupational Exploration,* by Marilyn Maze and Donald Mayall, have skill level codes for each job description, which can aid you in judging how close your skills are to the recommended levels.

If you possess enough skill to gain an entry-level position, then you can claim to have that skill, even though you know in the future you'll probably want to learn more and improve in that skill. If you haven't yet acquired the level of skill necessary for an entry-level position in the career field of interest to you, then you can classify that as a skill you have but want to improve in.

This helps to round out the assessment of your transferable/functional skills. It would be wise to do the same for your specific content/special knowledge skills. Determine what subject or content areas you possess to a strong degree, which you would like to learn more about, and whether there are any areas in which your knowledge is minimal and you would like to learn about.

What If I Didn't Complete the Analysis of Life Experience Exercise?

If you know, for whatever reason, that you're not going to complete the analysis of life experience exercise, then at least take this following minimal step. Review the skills list in *What Color Is Your Parachute?*, or another suitable resource, and list those skills you think you possess to a high degree, those you would like to improve in, and those you currently do not have but would like to learn. When you've completed this step, identify those you want to have involved in your next career and those that are more avocationally or leisure related.

For those skills you now have, which you desire to involve in your next career, prioritize them according to the ones you want to use the most. You should also identify specific content/special knowledge skills. It's quick to do, and when added to your most preferred transferable/functional skills will help add some focus to your career decision making. Of course, you can't decide on a career on skills alone, so you should add the other important elements we've discussed up to now: interests, personality preferences, and life and work values.

There is a third type of skill in addition to your transferable/functional and specific content/special knowledge skills, which are referred to as *adaptive/self-management* skills. These skills, also thought of as personal traits and qualities, describe how you adapt to and survive in your environment (home, job, etc.), as well as the style in which you use your other skills to accomplish what you set out to do.

Following is a list of **34** adaptive/self-management skills:

Accurate	Logical
Adaptable	Orderly
Adventurous	Patient
Analytical	Persuasive
Businesslike	Practical
Cheerful	Productive
Confident	Professional
Considerate	Realistic
Decisive	Responsible
Dependable	Self-starting
Ethical	Sensitive
Fair-minded	Spontaneous
Friendly	Tactful
Helpful	Thorough
Imaginative	Tolerant
Independent	Trustworthy
Intelligent	Truthful

Note the ones you believe characterize how you go about doing what you need to do, on and off the job. Add to the list any additional descriptive terms that describe your style of doing things.

Bringing Together Your Transferable/Functional, Specific Content/Special Knowledge, and Adaptive/Self-Management Skills

In the analysis of life experiences exercise, we brainstormed career ideas for Tony, our case study, by combining his transferrable/functional and specific content/special knowledge skills. Now we can add some of his adaptive/self-management skills to that.

Here's an example focused on the career area that Tony seems to be most interested in at the present time, as his assessment and testing phase of the process is about to be completed.

> . . . . to be imaginatively (adapt./slf.mang.) creative (tran./func.) in a cheerful and friendly (adapt./slf.mang.) manner, in the writing, producing, and directing (tran./func.) of adventurous and ethical (adapt./slf.mang.) commercials and advertising campaigns (spec.cont./sp.know.) in the advertising/marketing field.

As you identify your three sets of skills, this would be a good exercise to do, especially if you're having difficulty coming up with career ideas. Try different combinations of your transferable/functional and specific content/special knowledge skills.

In Tony's situation, perhaps he could target environment-related or small to mid-sized import/export corporations for pursuing his advertising/marketing interest, or an advertising firm that works with these types of businesses. After all, these are considered two of the "hot" areas for the 1990s. If the job market is so tight that Tony can't find his ideal type of work, he might have to adjust to consider what were secondary areas of choice. In the teaching/training area, Tony could consider the field of employee training, another growing area.

This step, brainstorming options based on current trends, is most important, especially in times of change, corporate downsizing, and related ramifications. Flexibility is the key. If you lose your job, similar ones might not be available. You might have to realign your goals and figure out new ways and directions in which to apply your skills and knowledge.

If Tony wanted to target a particular demographic trend, it could be the growing singles population. Currently, 70 million adults (40 percent) are unmarried, divorced, or widowed. Travel in particular is expected to grow with respect to the single population. This becomes another possible outlet for Tony's interests in advertising/marketing, employee training, non-profits, public relations, and fund raising.

Be creative in how you look at yourself, your skills, and your options. Those who will succeed in this belt-tightening, changing job market are the ones who are able to adapt, adjust, and change in order to stay employable. Other skill assessment instruments I recommend include the EUREKA Skills Inventory, the Career Ability Placement Survey (CAPS), and the Personal Skills Map (PSM).

Part *II*

The Job Search: Strategies for Dealing with Challenges

CHAPTER *6*

GETTING ADDITIONAL EDUCATION, TRAINING, OR EXPERIENCE

Research Your Career Goal

The only way for you to know whether you are lacking in education, training, or experience is by first having a clear career goal, beginning with an assessment like that in Chapter 5.

Once you have completed the assessment process, you still might not be clear about your objective. Some people are more confused than before they began because they are aware of many more possibilities than they had been considering. This is healthy confusion.

As a result, you might be considering a few different career goals. To help narrow down the possibilities, you need to do your research. The following detailed descriptions of career resources will help you identify valuable sources of information.

The Guide for Occupational Exploration (GOE). The GOE classifies jobs into 12 Interest Areas, 66 Work Groups, and 348 Subgroups, with reference to over 12,000 specific job titles. The main idea is to identify which Work Groups you have the most interest in. You can then find specific, related job titles with DOT numbers. In the front of the GOE it shows you how to translate your preferred interests, values, activities, school subjects, work experience, and military occupational specialties into related Work Groups.

Figure 6.1 provides the GOE table of contents. Beside each Interest Area title, we've provided the related Holland RIASEC theme(s) to help you identify interest areas.

For example, if your strongest Holland theme is Artistic, you could look at Interest Area 01: Artistic. When you look up a Work Group in the GOE, you'll

FIGURE 6.1

Interest Areas and Work Groups from the Guide for Occupational Exploration (GOE)

01:	**Artistic (A)**	06:04	Elemental Work: Industrial
01:01	Literary Arts	07:	**Business Detail (C)**
01:02	Visual Arts	07:01	Administrative Detail
01:03	Performing Arts: Drama	07:02	Mathematical Detail
01:04	Performing Arts: Music	07:03	Financial Detail
01:05	Performing Arts: Dance	07:04	Oral Communications
01:06	Craft Arts	07:05	Records Processing
01:07	Elemental Arts	07:06	Clerical Machine Operation
01:08	Modeling	07:07	Clerical Handling
02:	**Scientific (I)**	08:	**Selling (E)**
02:01	Physical Sciences	08:01	Sales Technology
02:02	Life Sciences	08:02	General Sales
02:03	Medical Sciences	08:03	Vending
02:04	Laboratory Technology	09:	**Accommodating (S)**
03:	**Plants and Animals (R/S)**	09:01	Hospitality Services
03:01	Managerial Work: Plants & Animals	09:02	Barbering and Beauty Services
03:02	General Supervision: Plants & Animals	09:03	Passenger Services
		09:04	Customer Services
03:03	Animal Training and Service	09:05	Attendant Services
03:04	Elemental Work: Plants/Animals	10:	**Humanitarian (S)**
04:	**Protective (R/S)**	10:01	Social Services
04:01	Safety and Law Enforcement	10:02	Nursing, Therapy, & Special Teaching
04:02	Security Services		
05:	**Mechanical (R)**	10:03	Child and Adult Care
05:01	Engineering	11:	**Leading-Influencing (E/I or E)**
05:02	Managerial Work: Mechanical	11:01	Mathematics & Statistics (E/I)
05:03	Engineering Technology	11:02	Educational & Library Services (E/I)
05:04	Air & Water Vehicle Operation	11:03	Social Research (E/I)
05:05	Craft Technology	11:04	Law (E)
05:06	Systems Operation	11:05	Business Administration
05:07	Quality Control	11:06	Finance (E)
05:08	Land and Water Vehicle	11:07	Service Administration (E)
05:09	Materials Control	11:08	Communication (E)
05:10	Crafts	11:09	Promotion (E)
05:11	Equipment Operation	11:10	Regulations Enforcement (E)
05:12	Elemental Work: Mechanical	11:11	Business Management (E)
06:	**Mechanical (R)**	11:12	Contracts and Claims (E)
06:01	Production Technology	12:	**Physical Performing (R)**
06:02	Production Work	12:01	Sports
06:03	Quality Control	12:02	Physical Feats

find a general overview of jobs classified in that Work Group, some hints that can help you tell how interested you might be in those jobs, and requirements for related skills, education, or training. Other sources of RIASEC scores include the Harrington O'Shea CDM System, the Career Assessment Inventory, and the Self-Directed Search.

Next, you'll find a list of specific job titles with a nine-digit DOT number. The first three and last three digits are for classification purposes and are explained in the introduction of the DOT. The middle three digits describe the level of skill required (the lower the number, the higher the skill required) for working with data (fourth digit), people (fifth digit), and things (sixth) on that job. The skill levels (0–9) for each area are also described in the introduction to the DOT.

The Dictionary of Occupational Titles (DOT). The DOT is organized numerically, not alphabetically. It provides (in two volumes) detailed job descriptions for over 12,000 jobs and references to over 20,000 job titles. It would be worth your time to look up related Work Groups in the GOE, scan the list of specific job titles, and look up in the DOT any jobs that sound interesting. When you look up a job in the DOT, scan the other jobs listed on the prior, same, or following pages. They are often closely related, and you might be interested in those as well. In addition, the latest edition of the DOT (1991) provides the following information with each job description: specific vocational preparation requirements, general education development (consisting of reasoning, mathematical, and language development requirements), and the physical demands involved.

If you're not clear about what's entailed, don't eliminate any possible job until you check the DOT description. This step does take time, but it means that you will know, with confidence, that you covered all the bases, leaving no stone unturned. That's a good feeling to have.

As you review the DOT job descriptions, it's a good idea to keep some notes on the pros and cons of each job you're looking up. This will come in handy later as you proceed to narrow down your list of options.

Of course, you can look up any Work Group whose title alone strikes you as interesting. In addition, in the back of the GOE is an index that will identify Work Group number and DOT number for any job title you might already have in mind. The DOT also has an index where job titles can be looked up to find DOT numbers.

The Enhanced Guide for Occupational Exploration (EGOE). The EGOE has fewer jobs listed for each Work Group, compared to the GOE, but it also includes the DOT job description for those jobs. Where the GOE refers to the 12,000 jobs described in the DOT, the EGOE lists 2,500 jobs (representing 95 percent of employed workers) with their DOT job description, all in one volume. Jobs can be identified by the process

just described (preferred Holland themes and related Interest Areas), as well as by alphabetical order by using the index.

Once you look up a specific job with its DOT description, a wealth of additional information is available in the form of codes (all of which are described in the front of the EGOE). The information covers general education development (in reasoning, mathematics, and language), specific vocational preparation, educational degree requirements, aptitudes (general learning, verbal ability, numerical, form perception, clerical perception, motor coordination, finger dexterity, manual dexterity, eye-hand-foot coordination, and color discrimination), temperaments (personality characteristics), stress demands, physical requirements, type of work environment, salary, and job outlook.

If you're interested in identifying all related job titles within a particular Work Group, you'll want to consult the GOE. If you think the most common job titles in that Work Group would be sufficient, then the EGOE (with the DOT descriptions included) will serve your purposes.

The Occupational Outlook Handbook (OOH).

Once you've looked up related jobs in the GOE/DOT or EGOE and can identify those you're most interested in, then you're ready to use the *Occupational Outlook Handbook* (OOH) to gather information that goes beyond the DOT job description.

In the OOH you'll find 250 jobs (representing 80 percent of the work force) described in greater detail. Categories of information include the following:

- Nature of the work (This is similar to the DOT description, but usually a bit longer.)

- Places of employment (The more work settings of interest, the greater the chance of finding employment.)

- Training, other qualifications, and advancement (It is important to understand how one can qualify.)

- Employment outlook (The OOH is updated every two years, but the employment outlook information is general, for the whole country, and thus not localized for your specific area. Therefore, take note of national trends but check out the facts where you live or might want to live.)

- Earnings and related benefits (Always note what year's edition of the OOH you're looking at and calculate the effect of inflation on salaries listed in older editions.)

- Work conditions (It describes what you can expect with this type of job, but conditions vary from setting to setting.)

- Related occupations (This is another way of expanding your options and increasing your awareness of the world of work.)
- Sources of additional information (Usually these are the related professional associations to which one can send for information.)

•••

After being laid off from a social work related, nonprofit position, Victoria took her writing/editing interest to technical editing in a corporate setting. The transition was facilitated with additional coursework.

•••

Specific Career-Focused Books

If, after reading the OOH information on a particular job, you're still interested in finding out more, you can check the library (or bookstore) for books focused on that particular career. Look for titles like *Careers in . . .* or *Opportunities in . . . .* The publisher of this book, VGM Career Horizons, has 150 titles in its *Opportunities in . . .* series.

Books of this nature can help you get even more familiar with the career area you're interested in by identifying various positions (public and private), locations (urban, suburban, and rural), and work settings (small, medium, and large firms) and how they differ from one another with regard to the work performed, type of clientele served, salary and benefits, and more.

Informational Interviewing

When you've completed these steps and are still interested in increasing your knowledge about a certain career, then it's time to talk with as many people as you can who are working in that career field, in as many different work settings as you can find them in. Informational interviewing is a way of getting your more in-depth questions answered and to build your network of professional contacts as well.

A key part of your research is to find out what skills are required in the type of work you're considering. In addition, what requirements are there related to education, training, or experience that one must have to be able to pursue employment in that career area? Once you have that information, you're in a better position to judge where you stand in relation to those requirements.

Even if you have determined that certain education, training, or experience is necessary, be sure to find out whether there are any exceptions to that rule. If you can identify exceptions, try to contact someone in that situation to find out everything you can about possible exceptions. Returning to school is a big time and money commitment, so you want to be absolutely sure that it's necessary in order for you to gain employment in the career area you desire.

It's not unusual for career changers, after identifying what they most want to do, to realize the need to gain additional education or training. (We'll deal with the possibility of needing additional experience later.)

••

Six of our ten career changers pursued further education to upgrade their skills in order to qualify to make their desired career changes:

- Ed and Patricia: law school

- Allen: dental school

- Victoria: technical writing certificate program

- Larry: degree in training

- Zephree: currently completing degree in criminal justice, toward her goal of becoming a juvenile probation officer

••

Here are some possible reasons for returning for additional education or training:

- To gain additional knowledge in a particular subject area related to your new career goal

- To complete a degree required for entry into a new career

- To prepare for a licensing or certification examination in your new career area

- To meet requirements for entrance into a graduate program necessary for your new career goal

- To stay competitive

Dealing with Your Fears Related to Further Education or Training

For adults who have not been in school for 15 or more years, the thought of returning to school can be anxiety producing. Some common fears of returning adult students with regard to returning to college are discussed here.

Will I Survive Academically?

Perhaps the greatest fear of returning adult students is, "Do I have the ability necessary to survive college (or other educational/training experience)?" Usually, some reality testing has to occur to help calm this fear. Just how hard or difficult will this be? We will assume that you haven't gotten to this point without doing your homework. In other words, you've made a decision to pursue a new career goal based on the identification of attributes that you possess and enjoy.

If so, then the choice you've made should be somewhere in the ball park of your abilities and skills. If not, you are at least clear on what skills you need to develop. Either way, let's identify some strategies that might help to lessen your fears of returning to college. (Most would apply to other related training as well.)

Speak with Instructors.   Visit a local college and seek out instructors in the departments that you would be pursuing coursework in. Ask them about the courses you're interested in taking, what's involved (assignments, papers, exams, etc.), what books you will be reading, and anything they can offer to help you better understand the expectations regarding student performance. You'll be able to judge your potential better based on information, rather than speculation.

Sit in on Some Classes.   If you happen to make a good contact with an instructor, maybe he or she will let you sit in on a class or two. Finding out how an actual class proceeds should be interesting for someone who either never has been to college or is returning after many years' absence. Visiting beginning courses in a program would be the wisest approach. This would help you avoid feeling overwhelmed by the advanced knowledge in a field you're just beginning to learn about. Taking a beginning-level course could also be a way of testing out your interest and academic ability. However, we would suggest checking out the strategies listed here first, before making that decision.

Ask a Friend Who Has Been in School Recently. Check with your network of contacts for those who have been in, or returned to, college recently. Ask them about their experiences. Could they share with you any assignments, papers, or exams they've completed? (Again, for beginning-level courses, if possible.) Chances are that your anxieties will be lessened. You'll realize that time and effort are required for assignments and exams, but it is definitely within reach of your talents and abilities.

However, you might still feel inadequate about certain abilities. Therefore, these assignments or exams still have you worried. If so, most colleges have developmental courses in writing, reading, and mathematics. If you need help in any of these areas, you could initially avoid coursework related to it while you enroll in related developmental courses to build up your skill levels to those needed.

Study skills is another area that returning adult college students are concerned about. There are specific workshops, tutoring, and courses offered to help college students develop appropriate study skills and thus ease the transition back to college. This could be an excellent choice for a first-time college course, especially if you have been out of school for a long period.

Visit the Returning Adult Student Office. Many college campuses have an office whose staff assists returning adult students with their transition back to college. Services come in the form of individual counseling, group counseling, support groups, workshops, etc. Their assistance can help you to become more informed about resources available to you and how to take advantage of them. If an office like this is not available to you on the campus you're attending, seek out the assistance of a counselor in a counseling center or office. He or she can usually provide much of the same information for you. If someone else is designated on your campus to do so, the counselor can usually point the way.

In the end, you'll probably realize that your motivation and drive can be more important than your intelligence level when it comes to earning a college degree. Therefore, if you've done solid research on yourself and the career area you're pursuing, there should be no problem for you in feeling motivated. Chances are that you are downright excited about the possibility of learning and growing in an area of interest and value to you.

Feeling Out of Place with Younger Students

Statistics reveal that over 50 percent of college students today are over 25. About one-third are over 30, and the level increases for graduate-level programs. Adults returning to college is a more common phenomenon than ever before. There is the opportunity to connect with all types of new people, of a variety of age groups and ethnic backgrounds.

Most college instructors will tell you how happy they are to have returning adult students in their classes. The maturity level and experience they bring is refreshing and invigorating and definitely adds to the classroom experience for everyone. Often, some of the traditional-age college students lack maturity and commitment to the educational process. They are only concerned with getting through the program, grabbing their degree, and trying to gain employment. Therefore, where returning adults wonder whether they can keep up with younger students, it's quite the opposite of reality. It's the younger students who are challenged to keep up with the commitment to excellence that most returning adults value.

•••

Both Patricia (law) and Allen (dental) returned to a professional school at an age that most would think not likely, 36 and 30, respectively. In addition, with respect to the role of family support, Sandra's family tried to talk her into staying with the field of law rather than changing to become a book publisher, because they saw it as a significant position of status for a female. Patricia's family tried to talk her out of going into law school because of her age.

•••

Getting College Credit for What You Already Know

As you prepare to enter or return to college, you'll be glad to know that there are alternative methods for gaining college credit besides the traditional classroom approach, including portfolio assessment, life experience for credit, and credit by examination.

Portfolio assessment involves documenting your experiences through performance, recommendation, or both to show that you've mastered certain abilities and skills. Experiences can be drawn from employment; community service or volunteer work; independent study and reading; non-college training, courses, or workshops; and other related accomplishments. Many traditional colleges have special life experience for credit programs designed for returning adult students. A good reference to check is *Bear's Guide to Earning Non-Traditional College Degrees,* by John Bear. It includes programs in both traditional and alternative col-leges. You could also contact the Association for Experiential Education, C.U. Box 249, Boulder, CO 80309 for information on alternative education.

●●●

Zephree is currently finishing her undergraduate degree, at the age of 42, in criminal justice. She works full time and is enrolled in a special program for adults that grants credit for life experience via a portfolio assessment. It's programs like these that help many students accomplish their desired career changes in a more timely manner.

●●●

Programs of this nature can possibly save a year, or two, of college that you would have spent in a traditional program. It also allows you to take the courses that are most important to you, because there are fewer general educational course requirements to fulfill. However, it is not an easy task. Developing a portfolio takes time and dedication. Some schools offer workshops and courses to assist in this process. If you want to get a better idea of what's involved, read *Earning College Credit for What You Know,* by Susan Simosko. For information on the process approved by the American Council of Education for gaining credit for learning outside the classroom, write or call the American Council on Education, Program on Non-Collegiate Sponsored Instruction, One Dupont Circle, Washington, DC 20036.

Ask the college admissions counselor for schools where you intend to apply about earning credit through examination. Following are a few of the prominent programs in this category.

- College Level Examination Program (CLEP)
- ACT–Proficiency Examination Program (ACT–PEP)
- DANTES (Defense Activity for Non-Traditional Educational Support)
- Advanced Placement Program (APP)
- PONSI (Program on Non-Sponsored Instruction)

If More Experience Is Necessary

Perhaps, as a result of your research into the career you're most interested in, you discovered it wasn't a matter of college coursework or a degree where you fell short. Rather, you were able to identify the need for experience, using certain skills, maybe in a particular work environment. In this situation, there are a few possibilities to check out for gaining necessary experience.

Internship

Both profit and nonprofit organizations offer the opportunity for you to gain work experience in exchange for your services at a lower rate of pay, usually for a year or two. If this type of opportunity fits for you, then it could be most worthwhile for both parties—if you can afford to do it. Perhaps a current job could be worked on a more flexible schedule, or reduced hours, thus making an internship opportunity more of a possibility. Consult the *National Directory of Internships,* published annually by the National Society for Internships and Experiential Education, or *Internships,* published by Peterson's Guides.

Volunteering

Don't think you have to work a lot of hours to be welcomed as a volunteer. Volunteering is experiencing a new wave of popularity. Volunteers are often welcomed even if only available for a few hours a week. It is definitely worth checking out to see if it could meet your needs for gaining additional experience in a career area of interest. This could be an excellent way to check out your career area of interest while polishing skills and gaining meaningful experience (as well as increasing your network of contacts). There's usually an office on college campuses that serves as a resource center for volunteer activities, both on campus and in the surrounding area.

Part-Time Work

Another avenue to consider for gaining needed additional experience is part-time work, which would probably pay more than an internship. What it really depends on is the type of experience you're looking for and how that's possibly attained. The appealing aspect of part-time work is that you can continue with your full-time job or college coursework, depending on which you are involved in.

All three of the approaches presented here (internships, volunteering, and part-time work) might offer a chance for you to gain the experience you need for the career area you're interested in. They can help you in further checking out the career field and work environment, develop some meaningful professional contacts, as well as guiding your decision making and leading to the attainment of your career goals.

CHAPTER 7

TIME AND MONEY

In this chapter, we will focus on the challenge of finding the time and money you will need for your career change. Being organized about your time can be the difference between success and failure. You can enhance the accomplishment of your goals when you are organized about your time and can plan, more effectively, to complete the goals you set out to accomplish.

Taking Control of Your Time

Each of us has our own way of dealing with the subject of time management. For some, our current time management techniques are sufficient—we're on top of the tasks we need to complete. However, others need tips on spending time effectively.

How Do You Spend It?

Before you can exercise effective time management techniques, you need to recognize how you currently spend your time. This can be easily done by simply sitting down and thinking about what and when you do what you do, as well as by keeping a log of the activities you take part in, including those related to work, family, social, and leisure aspects of your life. You might be surprised to find you have more free time than you thought (or time you can make available by sacrificing less important activities, like watching television).

●●●

Both Ed and Patricia attended law school part-time, at night, for four years while working full time in jobs related to the law to some degree (criminal law clerk and law librarian, respectively).

●●●

Develop a Weekly Schedule

The next step is to develop a schedule for each day of the week, indicating time that is already committed. This could include your work schedule or course schedule. Be sure to add in the time for commuting back and forth.

Next, block off those days and times when something regular occurs: family dinners on weekends, bowling night, exercise time, time alone for yourself, or organization meetings. Keep in mind that none of this is written in stone. You'll need to remain flexible about scheduling activities. You might decide as your goals become clearer that cutbacks are needed in some areas, as far as time demands. However, it's wise to always have some time scheduled (even if less than usual) with those people of greatest importance to you, as well as some time alone for yourself.

Once you have figured out how you spend your time in a typical week, you're more clear about what time is available for the new tasks you are encountering: college (or other related training) or job searching while still employed. If you are unemployed, you could be spending 40–80 hours a week on your search, whereas if employed full time, you could be spending 15–25 hours per week. Here's what we suggest you do next.

Set Your Goals

Every Sunday, sit down with your weekly schedule and figure out what you want to get done that following week. If you're back in school, what work needs to be accomplished in terms of readings, papers, etc.? If you're job searching, what contacts need to be initiated, which need to be followed up on, what readings might you complete, and other related tasks?

Then take the goals you want to accomplish and estimate the time needed for each. Next, plug these goals into the time slots available on your schedule. This is where your juggling skills might come into play. In addition, if time is tight, you'll need to set priorities and let go of some activities in favor of your educational/training or job search goals.

As you develop your plans on Sunday for the upcoming week, write out each day's goals and times to work on them. Carry these daily schedules or To Do lists with you every day for easy reference. This will prevent the feeling of all your intended goals spinning around in your head. Write it all down, carry it with you for easy reference, and save yourself one big headache.

Stay Flexible

You'll need to remain flexible with regard to your weekly schedule. It's not unusual for circumstances to change, thereby creating the need to revise your schedule. In fact, it's not unusual to make small revisions each day on your goals if they took shorter or longer to accomplish than anticipated or if other legitimate priorities came up.

So don't consider your goals as being written in stone. However, you'll know better than anyone else how you are really doing with respect to your goals. Are you making excuses or procrastinating? Or are you doing every-thing within your power to accomplish your goals and reach for the success that you have decided you want for yourself?

Finding the Time for Education, Training, or Experience

With work and family responsibilities, it's no surprise that finding time to return to college is a concern. This issue can be approached from a couple of different directions.

First of all, delivery methods for offering college credits have changed over the years. Classes no longer take place only in the traditional classroom. Options exist for workplace, self-instruction, home study, television, and related approaches, which are referred to as *distance education* options. This implies that living and learning take place away from the central campus. Some traditional colleges have one or more of these types of programs (though most are found at alternative schools), as well as evening, weekend, and summer intensive programs. Contact the following organizations for further distance education information.

National Distance Learning Center (NDLC)
Owensboro, KY 42301

United States Distance Learning Association (USDLA)
Box 5106
San Ramon, CA 94583

Second, planning is important. Once your career goal is clearly established and related education/training requirements are identified, it's important to plan out your college program in a manner that is sensible for you, pertaining to your current ability and skill levels and what you can handle with regard to your other responsibilities. Figure two hours of study time for every hour of class time, for starters. This will probably lessen as you go. Counselors and faculty can assist you with this step. If you have never applied solid time management techniques to accomplish your goals, this would be a good time to start.

The demands on your time when returning to school are very similar to time demands for carrying on a job search or starting your own business. It's important to communicate with your significant others what your plans are and what the related demands on your time will be. Being organized about your time will also help ensure that your studies don't interfere with your current work situation. In fact, it's probably a good idea, if feasible, to inform your supervisor about your educational plans and what you hope to accomplish. Your employer may even be willing to help pay for it, though it usually has to relate to your current job.

Job Searching While Employed

When you first read the words, "Job Searching While Employed," your initial reaction might have been, "Impossible!" You might think that if you're working full time, 9 a.m. to 5 p.m., those are the only times one can job search. Therefore, since you're working, it can't be done.

Stay Employed

Don't quit your job, if at all possible. Unfortunately, there is still a negative stereotype attached to the unemployed by many employers, as unfair as it might seem. Employers tend to mistrust the unemployed. ("If you're so talented, why aren't you working?")

It's similar to when you first applied for credit. No one would give you credit unless you already had it, which makes it difficult getting your first credit card. In this scenario, employers are unwilling at times to hire the unemployed, so you cannot get a job unless you already have one. However, if you have some type of special training employers are looking for, they may weigh that as more important than your unemployment status.

If all that sounds a bit insane, we agree, But if it's the reality out there, then it's important to be aware of it and to hang on to your current job. If your current job becomes unbearable and it would be a serious mistake to stay on for reasons related to stress, for example, then try to find temporary or interim work.

Making Contacts

As you identify people you want to talk with, either those you already know or people whom others in your network refer you to, you'll want to write them a letter stating your interest in the career area. The letter adds that as a potential career changer, you would appreciate talking with them about their experiences. The letter is followed up with a call within a week or ten days.

The call should happen during the day. If you have some privacy in your current position and can manage to complete some calls during the day, fine. However, you might be in a position in which that's just not possible. In that case, you might be able to get some calling done on a coffee or lunch break, from a phone booth if necessary. If you want to contact someone in a management position, chances are that they get in before 9 a.m., and you might catch them then. The purpose of the call is to set up a mutually convenient meeting time.

These informational meetings will also need to be strategically planned around work. We suggest early breakfast or lunch meetings (or early weekday evenings and even possibly Saturdays, if they prefer). You could offer to treat as a way of thanking your contact for taking the time to meet with you. The cost can be kept manageable by selecting appropriate types of eating establishments.

Interviewing for Hire

When it comes to job interviews, the situation changes a bit. These are a priority, and you could consider using personal or vacation days for them. Some delicate timing issues arise at this point. The potential new employer wants to see you for a first or follow-up interview. How do you handle it? Well, if it's a first interview, try to do it at their convenience. If it's a follow-up interview, it's fine for you to try to schedule at a convenient time for you. You might be hesitant to ask for a day and time most convenient for you and may be different from what was offered. However, keep in mind that if a prospective employer is interested in you, he or she will understand your situation and try to be flexible in scheduling a mutually convenient time for your follow-up interview. Let the potential hiring employer know that your first responsibility is with your current employer. We believe any employer worth working for will respect and even be encouraged by your sense of professionalism and responsibility.

Finding Money for Education or Training

A number of variables determine how much money you'll need to finance your education. These factors include whether the school you're considering is public or private, offers two-year or four-year programs, or is in your state or out of state. You should know that there's no age restriction on financial aid from the federal government. Also, the less money you have the more loans and grants are possible. Finally, community colleges or less expensive state universities can be good options for you.

Some alternative colleges can be expensive, but due to their accelerated pace are twice as fast to complete as traditional private colleges. Therefore, the cost at alternative colleges could actually be less. In addition, when compared to the cost of traditional state colleges, after adding travel, parking, and fees such as athletic and recreation fees not usually part of alternative programs, they might not be that much more.

Sources of funding your return to college include the following:

- State/federal financial aid

- Loans (from banks, friends, or relatives)

- Employer reimbursement

- Scholarships

- Fellowships

It's a good idea, as soon as you know what schools you'll be choosing from, to read the financial aid section of their catalogs and then to contact the financial aid offices and follow through on applying for financial aid. We suggest to apply to more than one school, because each school will have its own restrictions or policies on awarding student aid.

Processing of financial aid applications usually takes 4–6 weeks, so you can see the importance of being organized. Often, applicants receive money from a combination of aid programs of which most are determined on need and must be maintained with certain grade point averages and credit hour completion rates. Check with the schools you're interested in for possible differences.

If you're currently working full time, chances are that you won't qualify on a need basis (even though you might really need it). However, there are still federal and state sponsored loan programs that do not depend on need and usually do not have to be paid back till you stop attending college. These programs have relatively low interest rates. They are offered in conjunction with banks, so check around.

Be sure to check with your employer to find out whether a program exists to help reimburse you for your college expenses. Usually, if a program exists, your employer will expect that your coursework relates to your job (some firms might apply this more liberally that others) and that certain grades be achieved. If your employer does offer this benefit, find out whether you can attend private or public colleges, or whether there's a certain dollar amount you have to spend per year.

In addition, check with the financial aid office to see if any in-house scholarships are available that might relate to you (e.g., returning adult students, women, minorities, etc.). These can be highly competitive but are worth checking into. Also, if you belong to any professional organizations, there might be scholarships available for members.

Other sources for possible financing of college costs include the following:

- Religious, civic, fraternal, or service organizations (Chamber of Commerce, Rotary, Elks, Kiwanis, American Legion, B'nai B'rith)
- Special-interest groups related to women, religion, or ethnic background
- Personal loans from family or friends, with interest included but less than a personal bank loan

If all else fails, a home equity loan is a possibility to consider, as well as a loan from an insurance policy. Both usually have interest rates lower than personal bank loans.

••

The career changers who funded their return for education through the GI Bill were former servicemen:

- Allen for dental school
- Larry for a degree in training
- Mac for his master's in counseling

••

If it's possible for you to start your coursework at a community college before moving on to a four-year college, you might consider doing so. This alternative will be less expensive and allows you to get started with your studies as well. You might also check into the feasibility of on-the-job training for accomplishing the goals you have in mind.

Financing Your Job Search

Obviously, your employment status will determine a great deal about how you will finance your career change. If you're employed, you have a paycheck coming in, but it will make your job search longer, perhaps an average of 6–8 months (if you devote 15–25 hours a week to your search). This can vary depending on the field you're pursuing employment in and your level of motivation, as well as the job search techniques used. If you are unemployed and devote 40–60 hours a week to your job search, you can probably cut the length of time in half, to about 3–4 months, on average. Of course, the downside is no income.

Back to the Budget

Therefore, if you are unemployed, the issue becomes much larger than financing just your job search—it becomes one of survival as well. Probably the best first step to take is to get a handle on whatever sources of money you have and then take a look at your living expenses as well as job search costs.

Start the budget process by identifying your sources of cash. Possible sources include the following:

- Savings
- Securities, stock
- Loans (home equity and insurance policies)
- Unemployment compensation
- Severance
- Loans from friends and relatives
- Sale of personal items (camera, stereo, second TV, second car, etc.)

Once you've calculated your available cash, you need to do the same for your living expenses. (We'll worry about job search costs a bit later.) As you begin to review your expenses, ask yourself where you can cut back. Areas for possible cutbacks could include new clothes (unless you need some for your job search), food (eating in and out), utilities, entertainment, and possibly housing, if it becomes necessary. A few suggestions follow:

- Don't sell your house unless absolutely necessary. With rising costs, you might never be able to afford one again.

- Don't let go of any insurance on your home, car, or health.

- Payment of larger debts might be negotiable. Talk with your creditors and perhaps make arrangements to pay at least the interest owed for a short time.

- It might be tempting to run up credit card bills. Resist this, unless absolutely necessary, perhaps using it for job search expenses rather than actual life expenses (food, shelter, transportation).

Need Additional Cash?

Even with tightening up, your expenses might still be more than you have available to you. If you tapped out all your sources, you might be able to find an interim, temporary, or part-time job. If you can afford it, we suggest part-time (up to 30 hours per week) in order to give you daytime hours for your job search. If you are squeezed for dollars, this might be the best alternative. It will take a load off your mind, and you'll be able to more fully concentrate on your job search. You'll feel more confident and increase your chances of accepting the best possible offer rather than jumping at the first decent offer. Let's look at the possibilities related to interim or part-time work.

Temporary Work.   The temporary work market has experienced huge growth. With downsizing, many companies still experience the same amount, or more, of work to get done. Rather than hiring new employees, they've turned to either calling back those they cut (if still available) or, more likely, making use of temporary services. In this way, the employer saves on the costs of benefits (usually not provided for temporary help), especially health insurance. Yet it still helps employees who otherwise could be out of a job. However, it's not unusual, these days, for temporary agencies to offer group insurance for their workers.

Having spread across most job fields, temporary work is likely to be available in an area related to your career interests. This can provide you with the opportunity to increase your skills, develop your network of contacts, and perhaps even attain a full-time position at the location where you're working.

Part-Time Work.   You might be able to find part-time work in your career field, but probably at a lower level. Part-time work in an unrelated field often requires little skill or experience and is easier to find. Part-time work in your field has its advantages, the same as listed for temporary work. In addition, if your last full-time job doesn't generate a good reference for you, then the temporary or part-time job might.

Even if your part-time of temporary job is unrelated to your career goals, it can still serve a purpose by stopping the gap between jobs or ending the loss of income. Perhaps it's not something you're crazy about doing, but if the situation warrants it, you should be ready to face reality.

Whatever interim job you take, temporary or part-time (related or unrelated to your career goals), try your best to have some flexibility in daytime hours for your job search. Certain jobs fall more naturally into this category: bar and restaurant work, cab driving, and retail sales. So you're asking, "How does it look to potential employers that you're working at a lower-level position with reduced responsibility and wages?" Let's rephrase the question to, "How does it look to a potential employer that under an extremely tight job market, in order to meet your expenses, you were responsible enough to find work, be employed, and continue your job search, even if that work is at a lower level?"

I believe most employers would be understanding and respectful, as long as what you describe as a tight job market is true for your career field. Try to market yourself so that they can see that you have the knowledge and skills they're looking for in the first place.

If all else fails, there's always the alternative of public aid to help you get through this temporary period of unemployment. If you have misgivings or consider this a handout, be sure to do all you can in your job search efforts to shorten your unemployment period, and accept what your government is offering to you to help you get back on your feet. If you've worked hard in your prior jobs, you deserve some help.

Your Job Search Expenses

We urge you in your carer change to get out there, talk to as many people as you can in the job you're targeting for yourself, in as many different work settings as you can find them, in order to build your network of contacts and gain desired employment. However, this approach does not come without its expenses. Here are some of the more common expenses that you can expect to encounter, using primarily the networking approach to job searching:

- Appropriate clothing
- Professional organization memberships
- Professional meetings, seminars, workshops
- Professional and trade publications
- Information interview meals

- Office equipment or access to it

- Transportation

These costs can add up, so you'll want to budget them with your other expenses. Only you are in a position to judge how that might be done. However, if you're having a hard time on your own, even with these suggestions, you might want to consult with a financial advisor to come up with a sound financial plan. Inquire at your bank; perhaps they can provide this assistance.

When Changing Careers Means a Cut in Salary

We've been talking about figuring out your budget, and now it comes in handy once again. It's time to take an even closer look and calculate the lowest possible amount of money you're willing to work for. This becomes evident after doing the most belt-tightening that is possible. Of course, this figure needs to be combined with the reality of salaries that you can expect to be offered for your levels of skill and experience in the particular career field you're looking in.

••

In making his career change, Larry knew he'd be taking an initial salary cut, he just didn't know exactly how much. So he sat down with his wife, and they figured out what a bare-bones budget would look like. In other words, just how low could they go, knowing that there was the potential of future salary growth in such a position. This way he would know how to respond, as far as how acceptable forthcoming salary offers might be.

The salary he was offered was a few thousand short of Larry's bottom line (remember, he was responsible for a wife and three children). The change was important to Larry, but he accepted the position and made up the difference with a loan from his insurance policy that carried a low rate of interest.

As a result of good financial planning, Larry could proceed confidently, even though the new salary was a tough cut. He knew his family's bills would be paid, even if things would be tight for a while. His research on salaries for the position he accepted with this particular firm indicated that he could expect significant raises in a reasonable amount of time. They would be able to regain their standard of living and possibly surpass it in the not-too-distant future.

••

Know Your Bottom Line

As you proceed in pursuing your career change, you might experience a reduction in pay. With this possibility in mind, you need to know just how low you're willing (and able) to go, so that you are in a position to respond appropriately. If not, the danger exists that you will mistakenly accept a salary offer that makes your minimally acceptable life-style difficult to attain, resulting in dissatisfaction with your new position.

Be Clear on Your Objective

The other important factor in dealing with the possibility of a cut in salary as a result of changing careers is to make sure that this career objective is the one you want. Because if a salary cut is necessary to get started in that field, you'll be much more willing to face that reality if you know in your heart that the increased satisfaction (and perhaps family time as well), compared to your former position will make it worthwhile.

Once you've identified your career goal, learn as much as you can about the salary range that you can expect from a position of that nature. You will also want to research potential employers. The objective here would be to learn as much as possible about their financial status, track record, and prospects for the future. This will help you to know what kind of salary offer you might expect from an organization if the opportunity arises. Could it be the average for this type of position or below or above average?

If you discover that your desired career change would leave you below your minimally acceptable income level, then some additional thinking on your part is necessary. First, ask yourself, "As a result of my research on myself and careers, is this career goal still my first choice?" If you answer yes, then the next step is to figure out how to raise your income level to what you identified as minimally acceptable. Consider the following questions:

1. How big is the gap between your minimally acceptable salary level and the salary of the new position?

2. How long can you expect that gap to exist? Based on your research, if all goes well in the new position, when might you expect a raise and about how much of one?

3. What can you negotiate with new employers as far as the following:

    Use of a company car

    Six-month salary review

    Opportunities for advancement

4. Will your new job help you to develop the skills needed, or do you already have enough to possibly have your own part-time consulting practice on the side? This can be done in a large variety of fields: accounting, public relations, training, marketing, graphic arts, personnel, etc. This will make it a bit easier to accept the lower than desired full-time job salary.

By taking into account the variety of factors mentioned here, you can better judge the feasibility of accepting this offer, which is to some degree below your lowest acceptable salary level.

Look for the Brighter Side

A lower salary is tough to accept, both psychologically and monetarily. However, consider that you've done your homework and you're sure this is the career goal you want to attain. We operate from the philosophical point of view that if we're doing what we like the most, it's usually what we're best at. This leads to success, which in turn leads, in most cases, to some form of financial prosperity as well.

Your research on your career goal, as well as conversations with your new potential employer, might indicate that this financial crisis will not last long. You're confident that over time, within reason, your salary will become more acceptable and perhaps, sooner than you realized, even surpass your former salary. Keep this in mind as well. Many adult career changers who change to more satisfying careers claim they never regretted making the change, despite lower salaries.

Also, a most important factor is that you need to have a respect for this new position, that is you feel it is in itself a respectable job. By respect, we mean there's a good match with your higher ranked life and work values. Therefore, what you consider to be most important is involved either directly or indirectly with this new position, thus making it respectable to you and for you. This, too, will help in accepting a lower than desired starting salary. Finally, assuming you do find greater satisfaction in your new position, you'll probably also experience greater physical and mental health, which perhaps is more valuable than anything.

CHAPTER 8

STRATEGIES FOR DEALING WITH A TIGHT JOB MARKET

Staying Abreast of the Trends

In this chapter, we will first discuss how economic, societal, demographic, and technological trends affect the job market and highlight some general and specific occupational forecasts for the 1990s and beyond. Then we'll suggest strategies for how you can best prepare yourself to deal effectively with these trends and forecasts, thereby increasing your chances for success. We'll also discuss strategies for changing your career within your present place of employment, developing your networking skills, researching employers in the library, and job searching long distance.

Economic Trends

High Unemployment. Recession and corporate restructuring (downsizing, mergers, acquisitions, etc.) have led to relocation of industries, downturns in specific industries, and even industry and plant shutdowns. This, in combination with political decisions on tax laws, national health insurance, welfare reform, defense cutbacks, foreign trade, and domestic budget deficits, has led to layoffs, firings, voluntary separations, and forced retirements.

High unemployment is a result, because most new jobs require high levels of education and skill. Many unemployed people lack the necessary skills to function in an emerging post-industrial high-tech society. In fact, up to 75 percent of the unemployed lack basic skills and thus need remedial training prior to job skills training.

Therefore, high unemployment exists simultaneously with a labor short-age. There are two extremes: high-level, skilled jobs and unemployed workers with low-level skills. Those with lower skills do not like taking lower-paying service jobs or don't know how to find a job that matches their level of skill and experience.

Small Business Growth.   Another result of the vast restructuring of corporate America is the growth of small businesses. Many displaced mid-level managers (and even those who survived downsizings but feel insecure about their future) have opted to start their own businesses. The leaner cor-porations now outsource much of their work, formerly completed in-house, which helps lead the way for successful small businesses.

Since 1970, an estimated 66 percent of new jobs have been with compa-nies of 100 or fewer employees. In the future, up to 75 percent of new jobs will be with companies of 20 or fewer employees. It is estimated that 11.5 million people will be self-employed by the year 2005, a 15 percent increase from 1992 and twice what it was in 1970.

A Global Economy.   As most of us realize, the economy of the present and the future is global. Foreign trade is increasing, especially with compa-nies doing business in Asia and Europe, yet the United States is experiencing a huge trade deficit. Our imports are ahead of our exports, which means more money is going out than is coming in. This leads to a decrease in jobs as a result of buying the goods of others, not our own.

If less money is coming in (both from sales inside and outside the United States), it will keep businesses from expanding, thus hurting job growth here. Also hurting job growth is unprecedented debt, on three levels: national, cor-porate, and personal. The global economy has also eliminated geographic boundaries of business activities, resulting in some jobs being transported overseas.

Decline of Major Cities in Northeast and North Central United States.   A result of current economic trends finds old urban cen-ters of the Northeast and North Central regions, mainly manufacturing and related service industries, experiencing decline and high levels of unemploy-ment. Growth is currently found in suburban and semi-rural areas of cities located in the Southwest, West, Southeast, and Northwest (and a few cities in the East). Population as well as wealth and economic activity will continue to shift into these areas, based on high-tech communication and service indus-tries that require an educated labor force.

Societal Trends

These trends include those that reflect current interests, values, and habits of society at large.

The Environment.   More and more Americans are becoming environmentally aware and concerned. This strong emphasis on environmental issues impacts many sectors of our economy, including government agencies, manufacturing, engineering consulting firms, and waste handling and recycling businesses. This, in turn, affects environmental conservation–related careers in such areas as chemistry, biology, geology, engineering, computer science, finance, law, and even fund raising.

Health and Fitness.   In addition to increased environmental awareness, Americans are more health and fitness conscious in the 1990s. This push to be slim, trim, and healthy is creating jobs in areas such as health clubs; fitness equipment; clothing; exercise physiology and athletic training; physical therapy; recreation-related activities and equipment; food content, packaging, and design; restaurant and fast-foot menus; dietary supplements; and more.

Aging of the Population.   The aging population means that there are more retirees with more leisure time and other needs related to housing, health care, shopping, senior care, travel, and entertainment.

More Singles.   More people are electing to delay or forego marriage, and more divorced individuals are joining their ranks. This results in more discretionary income to spend on themselves.

Double Incomes, No Children.   Also added to groups with increased spending options are those who do marry but wait longer to have children or choose not to have children. We see much of this discretionary spending taking place in leisure and entertainment areas such as health clubs, travel, movies, cultural events and activities, TVs, VCRs, stereos, fast food, packaging and marketing of food products, and more.

Baby Boomers and Their Children.   By the year 2005, 76 million plus baby boomers (born between 1946 and 1964) will be between 41 and 59 years of age, and their children will be growing up. This development has already had and will continue to have ramifications for child care, education, clothes, toys/games, and furniture, among other things.

Schools in Crisis.   Another societal trend is the crisis of our public school systems. For a variety of reasons—poor management, lack of funding, high dropout rates, lack of solid family structure and parental guidance—students are coming out of the elementary and secondary public school system without the skills necessary for the jobs available today and in the near future.

Employers find themselves needing to provide basic skills (reading, writing, and math) instruction in order to get their employees in position to learn from training for a particular job. The one bright spot on the education front is the community colleges: they seem more in tune with current labor market needs by providing more business and vocational training related to those needs.

Demographics

Most of the data in this section comes from the Fall 1993 *Occupational Outlook Quarterly* and the November 1993 issue of the *Monthly Labor Review*. These and other related resources are listed at the end of the book.

Women.   During the 1990s over 52 percent of labor force entrants will be women, compared to 36 percent in 1966 and 42 percent in 1979. By the year 2005, 72 million women will represent 48 percent of the work force and 64 percent of new entrants to the labor force. That 72 million also represents over 63 percent of all adult women and 83 percent of women between the ages of 25 and 54.

Women are now the main breadwinner for 20 percent of the nation's families. Sixty-six percent of married women with children are now in the labor market. In 27 percent of households, the wife now makes 80 percent of the husband's salary. There are now 26 million, two-income, baby-boomer households.

African-Americans, Hispanics, and Asians.   By the year 2005, African-Americans, Hispanics, Asians, and other minorities will represent 27 percent of the work force, up from 22 percent in 1992. They will also represent 35 percent of new labor force entrants between 1992 and 2005. Also by the year 2005, minorities and immigrants will fill 69 percent of the new jobs, while women, minorities, and immigrants will together make up 75 percent of the U.S. work force.

We can also expect by the year 2005, a work force of 150.5 million workers (compared to 127 million in 1992), with an additional 3.5 million African-

Americans, 6.5 million Hispanics, and 3.7 million Asian-Americans. These statistics predict the following minority representation in the work force: 16.6 million (11 percent) African-American (a 25 percent increase), 16.5 million (11 percent) Hispanics (a 64 percent increase), and 7.5 million (5 percent) Asian-Americans (an 81 percent increase, including Native Americans, Alaskan Natives, and Pacific Islanders). The white, non-Hispanic work force representation will be 109.7 million (73 percent), an 11 percent increase.

Unfortunately, African-Americans and Hispanics are overrepresented in occupations expected to have the slowest rates of growth and underrepresented in occupations projected to have faster growth rates. African-Americans and Hispanics have lower high school completion rates as well.

Aging of the Population.   By 1995, there will be 12.7 million Americans over age 65. By the year 2005, 13 percent of the population will be over age 65, twice that of 1940. Between 1992 and 2005, the number of older workers will grow twice as fast as the labor force as a whole. The largest group of workers will be those between age 35 and 54. One of every three persons will be over age 50 by the year 2005, with an average age of 40.5, compared to 1992's average of 37.2.

Only 9.8 percent of the population will be in the 18–24 age group by the year 2005 (known as the "birth dearth"). This figure is down from 13.2 percent in 1980. As a result, fewer young people are filling entry-level jobs, leaving a shortage of workers for entry-level jobs.

Because of this, older workers are being pursued by employers, and not just for entry-level positions. Their strong work ethic and special skills are highly valued by employers. Even after downsizing, companies still need workers. They might tap into those they had let go (if they're still available) or keep retirees active (most on a part-time basis).

Technology

The emerging high-tech and service society will require highly specialized and skilled workers who are prepared to make job and career changes. One can't be too specialized, however, or risk becoming obsolete. Advances in computers, robotics, fiber optics, biotechnology, and genetic engineering have generated new businesses and shut down others. If not retrained, workers in declining industries fall into lower-paying, unskilled service jobs. The emphasis on high-tech machinery and computers is a challenge for employers and employees alike. Technology has allowed an increasing number of workers to work at home. It's estimated that by 2005, 15–25 million jobs will be performed partially or entirely at home.

Forecasting Occupational Trends

The Shortcomings.   Occupational forecasts for the future can be helpful but must not be taken too seriously for a variety of reasons. By "too seriously," we mean not to plan your career decisions on future trends alone. In
forecasting occupational trends, the statistical applications used assume that
there will be a steady rate of growth. At times, these forecasts represent "best
guesses" of what might be. The forecasting has no way to account for unanticipated events such as the following:

- Shifts in population

- Political decisions regarding international crises and domestic
  economic failures

- Technological advances

- Economic cycles of prosperity and recession

In addition, the forecasts are usually presented on a national basis and are
not localized to your particular geographic area. For example, if paralegal
work is identified as a fast growing occupation, it could still represent a very
tight job market in your area. And the opposite could be true as well. Forecasts related to the agriculture, forestry, and fishing industries have been declining for years, yet there is some growth in the agricultural services industry,
which includes landscape and horticultural services. Therefore, this one aspect of an overall declining industry is generally still strong and might be so
in your geographic area as well.

We suggest that you contact the professional associations related to your
career interests. They might have projections for their particular field on a
geographical basis. In other words, they might be able to tell you where in
the United States the demand is highest for the career you're interested in.

The *Occupational Outlook Handbook* also gives some general job outlook
information, though only on a national basis and somewhat briefly. For a
more in-depth occupational outlook including fastest-growing areas in a
particular career field, best bets in that career, and future trends, read *Jobs '94*,
by Kathryn Petras and Ross Petras.

Keeping these potential shortcomings in mind, let's examine some major
forecasted industry and occupational trends. We'll start with some general
industrial trends and then turn to some specific occupational trends.

General Occupational Trends.   Overall, there will be more jobs
in knowledge-based industries and fewer in production-based industries. By
the year 2005, and 80/20 percentage breakdown is predicted. Service indus-

tries now employ three times the number that are in manufacturing, construction, and mining industries. These service industries include health care, business services (advertising, marketing, accounting, public relations, computer and data processing, etc.), retail, wholesale trade, food, transportation, communication, education, and finance.

Two-thirds of all workers currently provide a service rather than produce a material good, yet there's a wide range of services and related pay, from fast food to managerial, legal, communications, and computers.

Specific Occupational Trends.   Let's take a look at two specific sets of occupational forecasts for 1992–2005 from the *Occupational Outlook Quarterly*, Fall 1993. Figure 8.1 shows occupations with the fastest projected

---

FIGURE 8.1

Fastest-Growing Occupations, Projected for 1992–2005

	(percentage growth)
Home health aides	138
Human services workers	136
Personal and home care aides	130
Computer engineers and scientists	112
Systems analysts	110
Physical and corrective therapy assistants and aides	93
Physical therapists	88
Paralegals	86
Teachers, special education	74
Medical assistants	71
Corrections officers	70
Detectives, except public	70
Travel agents	66
Childcare workers	66
Radiologic technologists and technicians	63
Nursery workers	62
Medical records technicians	61
Operations research analysts	61
Occupational therapists	60
Legal secretaries	57
Manicurists	54

"continued"

Producers, directors, actors, and entertainers 54
Teachers, preschool and kindergarten 54
Flight attendants 51
Speech-language pathologists and audiologists 51
Guards 51
Insurance adjusters, examiners, and investigators 49
Respiratory therapists 48
Psychologists 48
Paving, surfacing, and tamping equipment operators 48

growth, and Figure 8.2 shows occupations that will have the largest numerical increases. One-third of the occupations with the fastest projected growth for 1992–2005 are in health services. Other major occupational categories represented include computer technology and personal services. In addition, one-third of the fastest-growing occupations are professional and technical occupations that require substantial postsecondary education (a bachelor's degree or more).

FIGURE 8.2

Occupations with the Largest Numerical Increases, Projected for 1992–2005 (thousands)

Salespersons, retail 786
Registered nurses 765
Cashiers 670
General office clerks 654
Truck drivers, light and heavy 648
Waiters and waitresses 637
Nursing aides, orderlies, and attendants 594
Janitors/cleaners, including maids/house cleaners 548
Food preparation workers 524
Systems analysts 501
Home health aides 479
Teachers, secondary schools 462
Childcare workers 450
Guards 408
Marketing and sales worker supervisors 407

"continued"

Teacher aides and educational assistants 381
General managers and top executives 380
Maintenance repairers, general utility 319
Gardeners and groundskeepers, except farm 311
Teachers, elementary 311
Food counter, fountain, and related workers 308
Receptionists and information clerks 305
Accountants and auditors 304
Clerical supervisors and managers 301
Cooks, restaurant 276
Teachers, special education 267
Licensed practical nurses 261
Blue-collar worker supervisors 257
Human service workers 256
Computer engineers and scientists 236

These 30 occupations are estimated to account for more than half of the total employment growth of the 500 jobs for which projections were developed for the period of 1992–2005. Among the occupational groups represented are retail, health services, education/social services, office/clerical, and computer technology.

Occupations appearing on the fastest-growing occupation lists for both percentage and numbers include home health aides, human service workers, computer engineers and scientists, systems analysts, special education teachers, childcare workers, and guards. Some of these occupations with high replacement needs also have low average income (e.g., childcare workers and home health aides).

It doesn't take long to see that the "hot" careers for the 1990s center around health care, retail sales, and high-tech occupations. Remember that these represent the highlights of occupation trends forecasted and are in no way meant to be complete (especially with regard to geographic areas).

So what do you do if the career you're thinking of isn't on these top 30 lists? Don't give up. Do the research, find out the status of your career choice via published and people resources. If you can identify a geographic region where you would have a better chance for such a career, then consider whether you are willing to relocate. Additional suggestions follow on how to best prepare yourself for the occupational trends of the 1990s.

Preparing Yourself for the Job Market of the 1990s

Skills, Skills, Skills!   It is vital to develop new specific content/special knowledge skills that are responsive to a changing job market. For example, a writer having difficulty finding a suitable position might do some research and discover that he or she would be much more competitive in today's high-tech, service-oriented job market with desktop publishing skills. The key word here is *flexibility:* the ability to accept new ways of doing things and attempting to acquire the new skills being required of your profession.

Considering that most career areas are highly competitive, the following strategy is crucial to your success. In Chapter 3, we reviewed the first three points:

- Identify what you most want to do, your purpose or mission in life.

- Develop an expertise, become the best you can be in the career you most want.

- Learn how to effectively job search.

Now, let's add the final two pieces of advice:

- Learn new specific content/special knowledge skills to be more competitive in your career field of choice.

- Be willing to consider relocation.

If you can follow these suggestions, your chances of success are greatly enhanced.

The following list of suggestions includes a combination of personal development goals and job search strategies for you to consider in attempting to make yourself more competitive in the job market of the 1990s and beyond:

- Follow through on a thorough self-assessment process involving the identification of your interests, skills, values, personality traits.

- Combine your self-assessment information with job market demand and demographic information to identify career fields of interest to you.

- Stay open to the possibility of relocating.

- Research employers and target small and medium-sized, growth companies that are adapting to new information technologies.

- Become computer literate.

- Learn a second language.

- Develop a global perspective, especially in management, marketing, and finance.

- Consider working for a foreign company.

- Be realistic about salary expectations.

- Be flexible enough to change industries if necessary.

- Consider nontraditional approaches to employment (e.g., combine a part-time job with consulting, open your own business).

With regard to personal development, we recommend increasing your self-esteem, becoming as adept as possible at oral and written communication, and developing your interpersonal skills. Work at strengthening personal attributes such as enthusiasm, dedication, and innovation. We're confident that if you work on these types of goals, you will be making yourself more competitive for the job market of the 1990s. Now we turn to an often neglected option, that of changing careers with the same employer.

Researching an Internal Career Change

Rather than waiting around for someone to offer you a promotion, consider initiating an internal campaign to seek a change with your present employer. For an internal campaign, you will still need to set an objective, prepare a presentation, and establish contact with those who can help you reach your goal. However, it's easier to conduct an internal campaign, because the information and contacts you need are more readily available to you.

Basic Steps for an Internal Campaign

Richard Germann and Peter Arnold outlined some suggestions for an internal career change campaign:

1. All communication, oral and written, should be positive. Focus on your strengths and accomplishments.

2. Have a realistic objective that benefits both yourself and your company.

3. Timing is important. Always move from a position of strength. Don't undertake an internal campaign if you're behind in your work or have other related problems. Do your best to correct the situation and then proceed.

4. Stay with your campaign through to its resolution. Pursue the negotiation process if and when it comes about.

As with any decision, the better the information you have, the better your position for making a sound decision. This certainly holds true for career decision making. Therefore, in order to set a meaningful and realistic objective, you need to do some research:

1. Become very familiar with what your company does, its goals and methods for reaching them. This could be available in the company's brochures, public relations materials, or annual report, as well as from other employees.

2. Get familiar with the organizational structure, formal and informal, and reporting lines. Develop an organizational chart.

3. Identify key people related to your objective and learn about their professional and avocational interests in order to make it easier to talk with them.

4. Find information about formal and informal policies and procedures for seeking an internal change.

5. Broaden your scope of knowledge about developments in business, labor, economics, and related areas by reading newspapers and news magazines. These are time-consuming activities, but they can provide you with insights into current trends which in the end could more than make up for the 1–2 hours a day that you invest in them.

6. Stay abreast with what's happening in your industry or professional field by joining professional organizations, reading their publications, and attending workshops and conferences. This is also a valuable source of insight into the latest developments in your specific career field, as well as making potentially helpful contacts.

This general and career-specific information will enable you to better assess your situation and plan your future goals, including whether you should undertake an internal campaign in the first place, and if you do, what your objective might be.

Internal Campaign Objectives

Figure 8.3 will help you take the information you gathered and set an objective for yourself. Objective possibilities are listed on the Internal Campaign Objective Analysis Chart. To the left of each objective possibility are the corresponding work value categories, with space to the right of each value category to record your average satisfaction and satisfaction percentage scores from the Work Values Satisfaction Self-Assessment in Chapter 3.

In other words, if you pick one or more of the possible objectives, the work value categories to the left marked with an *X* are affected. Those marked with a question mark (?) might also be affected, but it would depend on the specific circumstances in your individual situation. You'll notice a line through

---

FIGURE 8.3

Internal Campaign Objective Analysis Chart

Work Values Categories	A. Company/Organization (/)	B. Work Environment (/)	C. Supervisor Relations (/)	D. The Job Itself (/)	E. Rewards/Benefits (/)	F. Professional Growth Opportunities (/)	G. Personal Development Goals (/)	Internal Campaign Objectives
			?	X		?	?	1. Revised job description
			?		X	?		2. New job title
				X	?	X	?	3. Increase in responsibilty/authority
		?	?	X		?	?	4. Transfer to different department
					X			5. Salary increase
		?	?	?	X	?	?	6. Promotion
		?	?	X	?	?	?	7. Newly created position

---

the work value category A. Company/Organization. If you have considerable dissatisfaction with the company/organization you're currently with, then an internal campaign is most likely not a viable goal for you.

If you know that certain work values are not in doubt and will be positively impacted by a certain objective in your current employment situation, then write in an X over the related ?. Circle those X's and ?'s that interest you and apply to your situation, thus signifying potential objectives and goals for you to pursue in an internal campaign. In addition, if you decide not to seek a change within your current employment setting, but rather externally, this analysis chart can help you focus on goals and objectives for that search as well.

Steps to Take in an Internal Campaign

First, prepare a positive, strongly written presentation in letter form about why your employer should accept your objective and how the organization will benefit from it. For a detailed description of how to prepare the presentation letter, consult Germann and Arnold. If you address your letter to someone senior to your current supervisor, consider the following suggestions:

- Ask for the person's permission to make your presentation to the decision maker.

- Send a copy of your presentation letter to your supervisor.

- If you expect a negative reaction from your supervisor to your request, address the presentation letter to both the decision maker and your supervisor simultaneously. This will make it difficult for your supervisor to obstruct your presentation.

If you're having difficulty with your current supervisor, it's best to first try to resolve that situation before pursuing your internal campaign. It could take one or two months of concentrated effort to remove this obstacle, if it's possible at all.

A few days after you send the letter, call to request a meeting with the decision maker. At this meeting, different reactions are possible. If you sense there's some interest in your proposal, you might be able to negotiate a compromise, or the decision maker might agree right up front. In any case, you don't need to reach a final decision yet; arrange for a follow-up meeting. This will give you time to think things over.

If you get a negative response, ask for the reasons why. There are at least two possibilities:

1.   You need to do something before resubmitting your proposal at a later date.

2.   You will not be able to accomplish your career goals with your current employer and therefore need to make a change.

Even the second outcome is positive; at least you know where you stand and now can proceed accordingly. If all in-house options fail or you've chosen not to try them, then the next step would be to prepare for an external job search. It is helpful at this point to talk with people who are working in positions like those you're interested in, in as many different work settings as they may be found. This process, known as networking, is the focus of the following section.

Networking

There's nothing complicated about networking, although many are confused by it, misuse it, or fear it. Networking is simply the development of mutually beneficial relationships. The key word here is *mutually*. Both you and your contacts will benefit from your networking efforts, as we'll explain as we progress with this chapter.

The Purpose of Networking

The purpose of networking is the exchange of information, advice, and referrals, via the information interview process, to assist in attaining your goal of changing careers. As competition becomes fierce in some fields and there are fewer qualified candidates available in other fields, both employers and career changers rely on networking to identify qualified candidates and to communicate professional and personal skills to employers, respectively. Employers hire those they like personally and professionally. The information interview, the vehicle for networking, gives them an opportunity to informally get acquainted with potential candidates.

The Formal and Informal Job Market

To gain a better understanding of how networking fits into the overall scheme of the job search process, you must first be aware of both the formal and informal job markets. The need to network exists because the structure of the job market is disorganized, fragmented, and not centralized in any recognizable form.

The jobs listed in newspapers, trade journals, and employment offices, which comprise the formal job market, represent only about 25 percent of the total jobs available at any given time. The ads in the newspapers tend to be either low-end or high-end jobs in terms of skills. Want ads work for some career fields better than others; you'll need to find out what works best in your field of interest. Most jobs, therefore, are part of the informal job market. They are not advertised or listed at agencies.

Therefore, you must rely on yourself to make sense of the whole process and identify available jobs. During your job search, divide your time up by the percentage of time a particular job search method works. For a general example, take networking (informal job market) and ads and agencies (formal job market). Because approximately 75 percent of the jobs are found via the informal job market through networking, that's where you should spend 75 percent of your time. However, people still get jobs via the formal job market, so you should spend the other 25 percent of your time there.

Employers Prefer Networking

This might come as a surprise, but employers would rather use informal networks also. They know if they advertise a position they could be overwhelmed with resumes, phone calls, and visits. They have a need—a position to fill—and they want the quickest way to find a qualified applicant. Many can't afford to hire through an employment agency, which charges 15–25 percent of the position's annual salary as a fee. In addition, they would rather go with a known quantity (via networking with friends, family, or business associates) than an unknown quantity (an applicant responding to an ad). Unknown applicants represent a greater risk in terms of time, money, and training to employers.

The Challenge of Networking

Be honest during an information interview—just request information, don't ask for a job. However, the networking process is indeed a good way to find a job. This sometimes seems like a contradiction. As a career changer, you probably do have many questions and could use the information. Even when you're experienced (or further along in the career planning process), there's always more to learn. Nonetheless, at this point your main objective is to get that targeted job.

So how can you be honest, in this case, without ruining your chance of gaining that new contact? The dilemma is that if you say you just want information and it becomes clear you actually want a job, you are likely to ruin your new contact. We suggest that you be specific about what type of information you want. Let your contact know, from your initial request for an information interview and thereafter, that you're interested in the following, or a similar request:

- Advice on opportunities in that particular field

- Discussing strategies for gaining employment

- Feedback on how realistic your career goals are as you research your ideal job

This approach is more straightforward about your intentions. However, whether asking in writing or on the phone, be sure to state that you do not expect a job to be offered or referred to during your information interview. This helps put the potential interviewee at ease and removes pressure because of certain expectations they think you have. If, during the course of your information interview, something in terms of a possible job comes up, great—but don't expect it. You're seeking more than general information at this point; you have decided on a career field, and it's acceptable to say so.

In regard to finding the people with the power to hire, don't go after them unless your contacts lead the way. Attempt to get to them via contacts and networking your way up. Hiring professionals are usually the busiest, and they don't usually have a lot of time for networking. Therefore, they'll be more inclined to make time if you're a known quantity with a mutually known contact person.

Although some experts will tell you not to waste your time with people who do not have the power to hire, we believe they are mistaken. This person could have insights about the career field, companies, or that particular organization. Also, many will have contacts that lead to persons with the power to hire. You will never find out unless you take the time to check it out.

What People Fear the Most about Networking

Many mature and capable adults fear picking up the phone and calling someone they don't know, even when the name is given to them by a mutual contact. After all, they wonder, who would want to talk to them. That's not a complicated question to answer. Those who have 15–20 minutes to spare and like their jobs will usually talk with you in an information interview. If you get turned down, it's likely that they're just too busy or simply don't like their job and don't want to talk about it. In this case, try not to take it personally and ask whether they can recommend someone else for you to talk with, thereby continuing to build your network. If you're hesitant about this process, start with people you know and those they refer you to. It's easier with that intermediary contact person.

Your Goal: GET HIRED

It's best to be candid with yourself about the long-range, overall goal of networking—to get hired. The networking process can be described as follows:

- Generate meaningful career options.
- Empower yourself.
- Tell everyone you know.

- Honesty
- Information
- Referrals
- Exchange
- Develop

Generating Meaningful Career Goals.

Most career planning experts advocate, as a first step in the process, the establishment of a meaningful career goal. By establishing a goal that relates to your major interests, skills, values, and personality traits, you give your career change a meaningful focus and direction. Because the job market reality is out there, and you'll have to deal with it when your search is underway, it helps to be focused. If you're not focused, at least generally in a direction that has personal meaning for you, you'll end up being scattered in approaching your job search and will increase the possibility of gaining a job you are not satisfied with. It's a matter of doing your homework (on yourself) and research (on related careers).

Empower Yourself.

Take control of your job search. Learn how to tap into the informal job market via the networking process. Networking involves connecting and interacting with other individuals who can be helpful to you during your job search. Perhaps you can be helpful to them as well, presently or in the future. However, some people think they need to be aggressive to be successful at networking.

This is not so. What is needed is the ability to establish warm, productive human relationships. You need to be purposeful, not aggressive. In addition, it helps to be patient and persistent to give the process a chance to work for you. Your attitude and how you handle yourself is of utmost importance. You will need to be honest, sincere, enthusiastic, and to dress appropriately as you seek career information, advice, and referrals from your network of contacts.

So now you might be saying, "All this networking stuff is fine and dandy, but what's a shy person supposed to do?" Networking might sound overwhelming or even unattainable for someone who is shy. However, even shy people can be successful at networking, they just have to work harder at it. You can practice networking with people you already know and feel comfortable with (family, friends, co-workers). You can call these practice information interviews. Pick three or four people who you know well and ask them if they would be willing to take part in your practice information interview.

Then set up a time and a place—on the job, at home, at a restaurant—wherever you're most comfortable, for starters. Make a list of questions you would like your interviewee to answer about his or her job. Some examples follow:

- How did you get started in this career field?

- What are the education or training requirements for your job?

- Describe a typical day on your job. What activities do you participate in?

- What do you consider to be the benefits or highlights of your job?

- What challenges (problems) are you faced with?

- How's the future outlook in this career field?

These are just meant to get you started. Of course, feel free to add other questions you think are important to ask.

After a number of practice information interviews, you should feel more comfortable branching out to talk with individuals working in jobs you're interested in.

Richard Bolles also has a suggestion to help shy people overcome their hesitancy in networking. He suggests you pick an interest, something you're enthusiastic about, and find someone else who shares that interest. For some, just finding someone else who shares an interest is challenging enough, but it is well worth the effort. It's a way to get yourself moving, to refuse to fall victim to your shyness.

When one of your contacts offers you a referral to someone, send the person an approach letter. Your letter should be typed and have a businesslike appearance. You might even create your own letterhead using a word processor and a high-quality printer, or have it created at a print shop. Include your name, address, and phone number.

Your approach letter should include the following content:

- Who referred you to the person you're addressing

- Who you are, your current employment situation, what specific information you want, and how much time you need (15–20 minutes)

- Why you picked them to speak to and how you hope they can help you

- When you'll call to set up an appointment (a specific day, within one week)

Your approach letter could also have some information about the person's employer that you have found as part of your research. You might even add some ideas related to the career field that you've been thinking about and would like the person's opinion on. This says something about your interest and commitment level and might lead your referral to be more inclined to respond positively. You need to make yourself sound worth meeting.

No resume is sent, just the approach letter. When you tell your referral what you would like to discuss, be sure to assure the person that you are not looking for a job or expecting a job to come as a result of your information interview with them. It is acceptable, however, to bring your resume along to the information interview to get feedback on it and perhaps to leave it with your contact person on your way out, if you feel the situation is right for doing so. If you feel you established good rapport and received good information, then the situation could be right for asking your referral to take a look at your resume for possible suggestions. You could either leave one with the person or mention you'll incorporate his or her suggestions and send a revised one in case he or she hears of something that might be of interest to you.

Be sure to call your referral person on the date you state in your approach letter. Be prepared prior to your call. Have a copy of the letter in front of you, along with your calendar (remember, be organized). Jot down any key points you want to state, but keep it brief, just a few minutes. You want to try for a friendly exchange with the goal of establishing rapport. Once you're connected, ask whether the person had a chance to read your letter. Be ready to suggest possible appointment times. Don't explain on the phone what is written in the letter, unless the person hasn't read it yet and asks you to summarize its content. Try not to conduct the interview on the phone. You'll need face-to-face contact to gain the best possible rapport with regard to establishing a new contact.

Sometimes you may be dealing with a secretary or receptionist on the phone, and you'll want to treat this person in a professional manner as well. The secretary will most likely ask who you are and the purpose of your call. You can then state your name and suggest that the party you're calling is expecting your call. (Remember, in your approach letter you stated specifically what day you'd be calling.)

If the person you're calling isn't there, you have a choice of leaving a message or calling back. If you leave a message, you might not get a return call. You don't want to call back too many times, you might alienate yourself. Two possible solutions are to ask for a good time to call back or to call when the secretary is not likely to be around (before or after regular business hours or during lunch).

Remember, in the scenario we're depicting here, you were referred by a mutual contact person. This should enhance the likelihood of everything working out. As you get more experienced with the process, you can also try contacting people cold (without the mutual contact person). That's when more of the potential problems might arise. Either way, with or without the mutual contact person, try not to take it personally if your calls are not returned. It's difficult for you to know why your call is not returned, and it's a terrible energy drain to worry about it. You'd be better off channeling the energy in a more productive direction.

A variety of scenarios and interactions are possible between you and a secretary or the referral person you're trying to reach. If you're interested in sample scripts for responding to these various situations, ranging from "I'm busy" to "Let me connect you to personnel," consult *Information Interviewing*, by Martha Stoodley.

As you get more familiar with the networking process, you'll soon realize the importance of being organized. Keep an index card file on each contact, including each one's name, address, and phone; who referred you to the person (and his or her name, address, and phone); a record of all contacts made by phone, in writing, or in person; your next steps related to each contact. File the cards alphabetically or chronologically using a master calendar.

Tell Everyone You Know What Your Goal Is and What You Need.

That's right, "everyone," assuming of course that they are positive relationships. Did you know that each adult has an average of 250–300 contacts? Therefore, each new contact you meet leads to another 250–300 people. It is estimated that each of us is only 6 or 7 steps away from reaching anyone else in the world. Start with those you're closest to: family, friends, and relatives. Also include past and present employers, past and present co-workers, classmates, teachers/professors, and member of organizations you belong to. Then check your personal phone book and your Christmas card list for some you might have forgotten.

Next, identify everyone you know whose business is to know others. This includes a wide range of people as shown here:

- Bartender
- Waiter/waitress
- Hair stylist
- Secretary/receptionist
- Librarian
- Stock broker
- Banker
- Accountant
- Clergy member/rabbi
- Mail carrier
- Parcel post delivery driver
- Printer
- Grocer
- Travel agent
- Mechanic
- Plumber

- Doctor
- Lawyer
- Dentist
- Pharmacist

- Car salesperson
- Gas station owner
- Real estate agent

There it is—your army of helpers, all with hundreds of their own contacts. To help your army help you, you'll need to tell them, as specifically as possible, what you need. The only way to do this is to have a focused field of interest. You will reach each of your contacts and say something like the following:

> "Hello, Joe, this is David Helfand. I'm in the midst of considering a career change into the field of health care services. I'm not sure if you can help directly, but I thought maybe you might know someone in some aspect of the health care services field who might be willing to sit down and talk about it with me for 15–20 minutes."

Joe might or might not be of assistance, but if you call everyone you know, you'll be surprised at how fast you get results. In this case of health care services, good contacts to start with would be your doctor, dentist, and pharmacist.

Once you have a firm handle on your target career, you can join a professional association. Student memberships are usually available at lower rates. To identify associations related to the fields of interest to you, consult the *Encyclopedia of Associations*. Once you join, participating on committees and related activities will afford you a better opportunity to demonstrate your abilities and skills and become known to others. Other benefits of association membership include the following:

- Membership directories are a source of additional contacts.

- Publications will keep you up to date with events and developments in the field and possibly job listings as well.

- Career information is available, such as job descriptions, information on graduate programs, professional licensing/certification, etc.

- Associations publish lists of employers in the field.

- Conferences/conventions/workshops are offered on a national, state, or local level.

- Annual national conventions will have a placement service that brings together employers and job candidates from all over the country.

••

Larry knew that a major professional training organization was holding a national conference in his area. Even though the cost was high, and at a time when he had himself on a tight budget in general, Larry requested access to the exhibit area—the best place to network and meet potential employers.

He was allowed to do so and negotiated a discounted fee. Once there, Larry visited with numerous vendors of the type of equipment he has worked with. Upon his return, he contacted three people he had met whose companies were located in his area. They all became potential employers.

Vincent took advantage of a three-day workshop offered by a national bookseller association on starting one's own business, at a modest fee. The information gained was most helpful to him as he readied himself for opening his specialty bookstore.

••

Trade publications (magazines, journals, or newsletters) in your field of interest can also contain information for generating possible contacts. A useful directory that some might overlook is the Yellow Pages. You can use this resource to identify related organizations and companies that can lead to new contacts as you build your network. Local newspapers and business magazines are also excellent sources to consult on a regular basis. They will keep you up to date with business news, activities, and events in your area and names of people you might be interested in meeting.

Another method for generating contacts is to work in the field as a field experience from school, an internship, a temporary or part-time job, or by volunteering. Not only will you get more familiar with the career field and related organizations, but you'll be able to continue to build your network of contacts as well.

Notice that we have moved from your first level of contacts (friends, family, service providers) to situations that involve more difficult contact making and situations in which you do not have the benefit of a mutually known intermediary person. You'll find that as you work with your first level of contacts and gain experience with the networking and information interviewing process, you'll feel capable of taking steps to reach out and contact people on your own. This is sometimes referred to as *cold* contacts.

We believe that cold contacts are a good idea, so as not to rely too heavily on referrals. You can always say to someone, "As a result of researching my ideal job, your company was mentioned as a place to contact." Then you can proceed to ask whether you can schedule an information interview. However, if you're still on the shy side, you might want to stay with the referral approach until you're more comfortable making cold calls.

Honesty.   Be sincere and honest in all your dealings with contacts. You know that an important part of any good relationship is being honest with yourself and others. Don't deceive others by saying you need information when you're really trying to get a job interview. In the initial stages of the career planning process, it's fairly easy to state the type of information you're seeking about a career area of interest. There's a lot to explore with someone already working in the field.

If you're at the point of looking for a job, just be more specific about the type of information you need. Using networking and information interviewing as a ploy for a job and not for information, advice, or referral will appear insincere and untrustworthy. Others will recognize that you're trying to use them for your personal gain. You will not gain, and you'll probably hurt the chance of others who follow, genuinely seeking information.

Information.   Your stage in the career planning process will determine what kind and how much information you need. Even in the advanced stages, there's still more to learn. You must communicate your purpose, do the related research, and have questions prepared. Here are some guidelines to keep in mind for carrying out your information interview and networking efforts.

1. *Develop a positive relationship:* Establish rapport by asking the interviewee about his or her background. Take a genuine interest in the person. Use tact and diplomacy, don't be pushy or overly assertive.

2. *Obtain information:* Do your research and have your questions ready. Try not to be sidetracked with taking notes. Use note taking for specific information only (names of people, organizations, etc.) and summarize responses afterward. Ask for the person's reaction to your idea and plans. Are you making sense? Toward the end, if it feels right (and you have one ready), get feedback on your resume.

3. *Continue building your network:* Add to your network of contacts by asking for a referral at the end of your information interview.

4. *Show your appreciation:* Let your interviewee know how he or she has helped you at the conclusion of your interview, as well as afterward with a thank-you note.

5. *Keep your contacts informed:* Let your interviewees know that you'll keep them informed of your progress. This step has two purposes: they'll appreciate knowing that they played a role in your success, and you'll want them to remember who you are. You never know what might come up on the very day your note or call comes in.

6. *Be flexible about who you'll talk with:* If you're unable to talk with the person you targeted, be prepared and willing to talk to someone else (if not, you could make such a request).

7. *Don't interview just a few people:* Do as many information interviews as possible, with as many different people as you can who are doing the job you're interested in, in as many different types of work settings as you can find them. This is the only way to get the clear and complete picture of your ideal job.

8. *Research the field first:* Never go on an information interview without at least reading up on the basics of that particular job. Your questions reflect what you know. Don't waste your contacts' time by asking questions that they know you can read about in a book.

Reading in preparation for your information interviews will lead you to ask your contacts more in-depth questions, such as the following:

1. What is a typical day on the job like for you? If there's no typical day, ask them to describe the variety of activities they perform and an estimated breakdown of time spent with each (on a day or overall).

2. Which of these activities do you enjoy the most?

3. What skills and qualities would you say are the most important for your type of job? You might add that your search pointed out that skills *A, B,* and *C* and qualities *X, Y,* and *Z* are the most important in this type of job and ask whether that's true for them.

4. What's the best education or training to prepare for this type of job? Any exceptions? Again, indicate what information you gained from your research and find out how that fits for your interviewee's situation and experience.

5. What would you recommend to someone with my background and experience? Would they suggest any additional training or experience?

6. What professional organizations would you recommend that I join (on a national, state, or local level)? Name two or three you've already identified.

7. Would you consider this a growth field? A growth company? You could add here, as well, what your research suggested.

8. Considering future trends predicted and developments anticipated, what aspects of this field would you say are more up and coming? Where will jobs be generated with regard to both the career field itself and geographically?

9. Is there opportunity for advancement in a position like yours? Where to? How does one qualify? Keep in mind that one reason why adults become dissatisfied with their jobs is a lack of upward mobility.

10. What do you consider your greatest challenges on this job? Do you believe they are characteristic of this career field in general or particular to this organization?

11. If you had a chance to do it all over again, would you do anything different? Here's where you might benefit from their years of experience.

12. How do people usually obtain jobs in this field? What would you suggest are the best job search methods to employ? Again, you might share some insight you already have with different job search methods, so as not to appear as a blank slate.

13. Who could you recommend that I might talk with next? May I mention your name, or would you prefer to call ahead and let them know I'll be contacting them?

●●

Larry followed a particular manufacturer for a few years by the ads it ran in the newspaper for training positions. He used library resources to further research this particular company. Once he was able to identify the person he wanted to interview with, he contacted that person and arranged an appointment for an information interview.

The interview went well. Larry and his interviewee hit it off and began a professional friendship. Larry received far more information than he contemplated, including job descriptions, desired skills and experience for new hires, and even an organizational chart.

Larry was eventually hired by the very same company for an entry-level training position, once he completed the additional education that was required.

●●

Referrals. The three major purposes of networking and information interviewing are to gain information, advice, and additional referrals related to your career area of interest. Whenever an information interview has gone well, in your estimation, you should ask your interviewee if he or she knows anyone else who would be beneficial for you to speak with. It's important not to expect a referral. Allow your information interview to progress at its own natural pace. If, by the end of the interview, you sense that rapport has been developed, then chances are that your interviewee will offer a referral. If he or she does, consider it something very personal and special. Appreciate it as a gift; it's not owed or expected, but an individual might respond to your request.

Exchange.   Offering your help, in any way possible, to your interviewee is symbolic of the exchange factor of the information interview/networking process. Your interviewee might thank you for your offer but have no request of you at that time. The person might get back to you in the future, however, if the occasion arises. In the meantime, if you think the person is competent and that people you know could benefit from his or her services, then you might consider making referrals of new clients to them.

Develop.   Developing yourself, increasing your skills, is another goal of the networking approach to job searching. The information interviewing process affords you an opportunity to develop your communication skills, as well as your ability at establishing rapport and positive interpersonal relationships. As a result, your self-confidence and self-esteem are certain to increase. However, to benefit you have to be willing to risk.

In addition to interpersonal and communication skills, you will also have the opportunity to further develop your job search skills. You'll become more familiar with a variety of job search techniques (in addition to networking), get feedback in improving your resume, enhance your interviewing skills (even if you are the one doing the interviewing), and gain invaluable insight and advice pertaining to your career field of interest.

Keep your network active by staying in touch, even while employed. It will help you stay abreast of the latest developments. Also, relating with others who have similar interests enriches your life. Finally, there's no telling when you'll be job searching next and need a solid network of contacts.

Let's assume you've contacted the person you were referred to and held a successful information interview. You need to send two thank-you letters within two days. One is to the person who referred you to the interviewee, simply letting him or her know the information interview took place and went well, and the other to the person you interviewed.

The thank-you note to the person you interviewed should include the following:

- Confirm how he or she was of help to you (be specific).

- Reinforce the person's knowledge and expertise.

- Be positive about your strengths and demonstrate a grasp of the topics discussed.

- Thank the person for any additional referrals and state approximately when you'll contact the new referrals. The person will want to pass the word along to the new contact person. State that you'll let the person know about the results.

Researching Employers*

Gathering available information about an organization or an employer will help you throughout the career change process. Your cover letter can be individualized for the specific employer. Your resume might emphasize skills and experience in the corporation's line of business. During an interview you can show knowledge, interest, and enthusiasm about specific events that have happened to the company. As a prospective employee, you can choose to accept a job offer knowing the actual strengths or weaknesses of the organization.

Gather Useful Information

Information that can always be useful includes the following subjects.

The Organization's History and Age. Significant events, founders of the organization, major changes that have occurred, and patterns of growth reveal the corporate culture and can give you an indication of what kind of company it is to work for.

Products and Services. Long-established products or services, new ones, and proposed or developing ones reveal the direction the organization is heading. Find information about the organization's industry or providers of similar services or products. Find out the strength or weakness of the industry as a whole. Uncover strategies and goals by examining products or services.

Financial Information. Examine the financial condition of the organization. Gather information on sales, profits, costs, liabilities, and assets for profit-making corporations by looking at financial statements and balance sheets. Look at the annual budget and annual reports for nonprofit organizations.

Personnel Issues. Find out about benefits and training available to employees, staff morale, and employee satisfaction. Find out about salaries. Compare the size to similar organizations and their competitors. Find out if the work force is unionized and the history of labor negotiations.

••••••••••

*Contributed by Mary Jane Hilburger, Business and Reference Librarian, Northeastern Illinois University.

Divisions, Subsidiaries (in For-Profit Companies), and Branches (in Not-for-Profit Organizations).
Chart the patterns of growth, the various divisions of the organization, and location of the divisions. Find out about the physical condition of the organization's buildings.

Management Style and Reputation.
Gather information on the corporate culture, an organization chart, and decision-making processes, if possible. Find out how it handles public relations during a crisis to judge its reputation.

Most of this information can be found in libraries. Large public libraries or academic libraries will have many sources, but even small public libraries can be used to gather some information. Because no library is likely to have every source listed below, using several libraries is recommended. You might not be able to uncover every bit of information you would like.

••

Three of our career changers benefited from their library research. Before his information interview, Larry did a search of periodicals in the library and came up with 4–5 articles about the company he was interested in. That might not sound like many, but they provided Larry with names of people in the organization, the corporate philosophy, and help in further understanding the company in general. This allowed him to ask more informed questions during the information interview.

Martha regularly does library research to keep up to date on products related to her restaurant business. Vincent even used library circulation data in researching which books were most taken out in the area where he intended to have his specialty bookstore, the fields of history and mystery.

••

Questions to Answer about the Company

Ask the following series of questions about your organization and then search out the sources mentioned at libraries. Ask for help from a reference librarian if you need suggestions for how to begin or continue searching.

Is the Employer For-Profit Or Not-for-Profit? If it is a for-profit corporation, is it public, private, or a subsidiary or division?

Public corporations have raised funds to establish, operate or expand their business by selling stocks, or equity, in their company. They sell their stock on stock exchanges: the New York Stock Exchange, the American Stock Exchange, some regional stock exchanges, or the NASDAQ computerized trading system for over-the-counter (and usually smaller) corporations. Publicly owned corporations must file reports with the U.S. Securities and Exchange Commission (SEC) and must make their financial standing available to their stockholders and prospective stockholders. Many libraries have sources that provide access to this financial information also. Because of this, it is easier to get information on a public corporation than on the other kinds of organizations.

Private corporations do not sell stocks on stock exchanges and do not have to report their financial status to the SEC. Private companies usually are smaller than public companies. But sometimes large private companies remain private to avoid revealing sensitive and highly valuable information to their competitors.

Subsidiaries and divisions of companies are owned by a parent company. Finding information about them can be difficult, because information is combined with all other subsidiaries or divisions of the parent company. Subsidiaries have their own officers and boards of directors, and divisions are an organizational unit of the firm. The parent company can be either public or private.

Check directories of businesses as a first step. Business directories give short factual information such as the address, telephone, Telex, and fax numbers; products and Standard Industrial Classification (SIC) codes; annual sales; number of employees; stock exchange (if public); and names of top executives. Usually there are several indexes: an alphabetical section by company, a geographical index, and a product or industry index. Because currency is essential, most directories are published on a regular basis, many annually or semi-annually. Several of the most useful are the following:

- *Ward's Business Directory of U.S. Private and Public Companies.* Gale Research, Inc. Annual.
  Provides directory information on 135,000 companies and identifies them as public, private, subsidiary, or division. In includes ranks by sales within industries so that chief competitors can be identified.

- *The Directory of Corporate Affiliations.* National Register Publishing Co. Annual.
  Provides information on who owns whom for U.S. subsidiaries, divisions, and affiliates. A parent company list is the main list, which provides a hierarchical order for all the "children" for both public

and private corporations. It provides headquarter addresses and names of executives, and, if available, sales and employee numbers for each.

- *Standard & Poor's Register of Corporations, Directors, and Executives.* Standard & Poor's Corp. Annual.
  Lists over 55,000 public and private corporations. Its second volume includes biographical information on executives, and its third volume contains indexes by industry, geographical location, and ultimate parent index.

- *The Million Dollar Directory: America's Leading Public and Private Companies.* Dun and Bradstreet Information Services. Annual.
  This directory includes 160,000 public and private companies with a net worth of over $500,000, a sales volume of over $25 million, and 250 or more employees.

- *Thomas Register of American Manufacturers.* Thomas Publishing Co. Annual.
  This emphasizes the products that 150,000 public and private companies produce. The 26-volume set resembles the telephone Yellow Pages. It includes products and services (v. 1–16), company profiles and trademarks (v. 17–18), and company catalog volumes (v. 19–26), which can suggest marketing strategies and identify competitors.

- *America's Corporate Families* and *America's Corporate Families and International Affiliates.* Dun's Marketing Services. Annual.
  Lists 2,400 U.S. parent companies with over 19,000 foreign affiliates and over 3,000 foreign parent companies with 11,000 U.S. affiliates.

- *Who Owns Whom.* Dun & Bradstreet Information Services. Annual.
  Traces international ownerships and relationships for North America, the United Kingdom and the Republic of Ireland, Continental Europe, Australia, and the Far East.

- *Corporate Technology Directory.* Corporate Technology Information Services, Inc. Annual.
  Contains more than 35,000 profiles of corporations producing high-technology products. It includes location, key personnel, sales, average revenues, and products.

- *Dun's Business Identification Service.* Dun & Bradstreet Information Services. Semiannual. Microfiche.
  This microfiche set provides listings of more than 10 million U.S. business establishments, both public and private. Because of the

expense of a subscription, only the largest business library can afford to own this.

Is the Corporation Public?

After you have looked at directories to identify the corporation and you have determined that it is public, you can gather a significant amount of information from its disclosure reports. Because publicly held corporations sell stock to the public, they must disclose financial information on a regular basis. This is available to the job seeker in a variety of forms. Copies of the reports are available from the corporate office. Many libraries maintain a paper copy of the larger corporations. Large libraries may maintain a microfiche copy of more of them.

The federal Securities and Exchange Commission (SEC) requires corporations to file 10-K annual and quarterly reports. Additional reports, called 8-K reports, must also be filed if the company is experiencing significant financial changes. These reports include financial statements; discuss and analyze the financial condition of the company; and disclose its subsidiaries, the properties it owns, the extent of its foreign operations, whether its sales are dependent on a few large customers, and ownership of major blocks of company stock.

The annual report is sent to stockholders and prospective stockholders shortly after the company's fiscal year ends. Annual reports depict the company to its best advantage and can have public relations purposes, but they also contain useful information for the job seeker. They contain financial and management information interspersed with expensive photographs and graphics. They contain an income statement of the company's financial activities in the last year, a balance sheet showing the company's total value or net worth, and an auditor's report certifying that the data was reported using Generally Accepted Accounting Principles (GAAP). It also contains the letter to stockholders (sometimes called the president's letter), a management discussion of the past year's activities and possible future directions of the company. It will identify specific products and how successful they are and sometimes break down a company's statistics by line of business, called segment. It might identify the location of the company's facilities. Management organization, strategies, and plans for the future are often included.

The following sources reprint information from the filings to the SEC and from annual reports, as well as providing additional information:

- *Moody's Manuals*. Moody's Investors Service. Annual.
  Summarize 300,000 corporations' and institutions' financial status and provide a brief company history, any mergers, name changes, business lines and products, location of plants and properties, and the status and rating of investment safety of its bonds. There are

seven manuals in the series, arranged by type of corporation: *Bank and Finance, Industrial, International, OTC Industrial, Public Utility, Transportation,* and *OTC Unlisted. Moody's Complete Corporate Index* identifies in which manual an entry appears. A twice-weekly *News Report* updates the hard-bound annual volume. Many libraries carry this financial service.

- *Standard & Poor's Corporation Records.* Standard & Poor's Corp. Annual.
  Lists corporations alphabetically and includes a company history and financial statements and balance sheets. It provides similar information to the *Moody's Manuals.*

- *Compact D/SEC.* Disclosure, Inc.
  This company disc business service extracts information from the SEC filings and reformats it onto one disc for over 12,000 actively traded public corporations. It includes the full text of the president's letter and management discussion from the annual report. Many large libraries subscribe to this service.

Because public corporations sell stock, there are many investment advisory services that track their status. You can evaluate the strength of the stock on the market, one measure of the strength of the corporation. Several of these services are described here:

- *Value Line Investment Service.* Value Line, Inc. Weekly business service.
  Follows the movements of more than 2,000 stocks. Arranged by industry, it measure, evaluates, and recommends specific stocks. It identifies high-growth companies and describes the well-being of the industry as a whole.

- *Standard Stock Reports.* Standard & Poor's Corp. Quarterly business service.
  Cover 4,300 public companies and provide investment advice for stocks on all three major exchanges. They include a current outlook, business summary, important developments, historical growth of earnings and dividends, net sales, per share data, income data, capitalizations, and a measure of the volatility of a stock's price.

- *Moody's Handbook of Common Stocks.* Moody's Investors Service. Quarterly.
  Covers over 900 stocks. It provides summary descriptions, advisory information, and a grading system.

Is the Corporation Private?   Most companies in the United States are not public. If you have determined from business directories that the company is private, you might have a hard time gathering additional information. *Ward's Business Directory* will provide a small amount of information. But financial data, management strategies, and annual reports will not be available. If information is not available about the specific company, gather information about the industry as a whole.

Gathering information from periodicals and business newspapers is the most likely source for additional information. Use periodical indexes to locate citations to specific articles in periodicals. Look up the company name or the industry to identify citations. You will still have to locate the periodicals that are cited. The most useful indexes follow:

- *ABI/Inform.* University Microforms Inc.
  Available in a electronic database version only, this index to over 800 periodicals provides useful abstracts (summaries) of the articles.

- *Business Index.* Information Access Co.
  Available as a compact disc product, this indexes business periodicals and covers the most recent five years.

- *Business Periodicals Index.* H.W. Wilson Co.
  Available in print and an online database version, this indexes 350 general, scholarly, business periodicals, and trade journals.

- *F & S Index United States.* Predicasts, Inc.
  Available in print and an online database version, this indexes trade journals by industry code and by name of company. Finding the journals cited might be difficult.

- *Wall Street Journal Index.* University Microfilms Inc.
  This is an index to the business newspaper, the *Wall Street Journal.*

As computer technology has developed since the 1970s, it is now possible to search the indexes listed above, the journals to which the indexes lead, and many additional sources by using automated, online database searching. Most libraries have services available to request online searching for a fee, and some have available indexes and the full-text of articles using CD-ROM technologies, or even direct online access for you, the user. If you are pressed for time and are willing to pay for information, ask a reference librarian about doing a database search or arrange to have a search performed by a commercial service. The following directory will help you identify a specific service:

- *Information Industry Directory.* Gale Research, Inc. Annual.
  Lists 5,100 organizations, systems, products, and services in the electronic information and publishing industry and provides index-

ing to locate specific services available. It can be used to identify services that will do research for you for a fee.

Most libraries carry business magazines to which these indexes and databases refer. Most are national in coverage and will only report on very large local corporations. When you find an article on a company, you can use it to make a favorable impression. Realize that most staff in the company will be very aware of the coverage, especially if it is very positive or very negative. Some of the noteworthy ones are the following:

- *Barron's National Business and Financial Weekly.* This newspaper emphasizes companies and their market conditions that affect the values of stocks, bonds, options, and other investments.

- *Business Week.* A weekly with many extensive articles on nationally famous companies. It carries many special issues on industries, executive salaries, and top public and private companies.

- *Forbes.* A general biweekly that celebrates the free enterprise system and carries articles on company activities, industry developments, and economic trends. It has a November issue listing the 200 best small companies.

- *Fortune.* A semi-monthly magazine that carries lengthy articles on national companies. An April issue identifies the *Fortune* 500, a May issue identifies the *Fortune* Service 500, and a July issue identifies the *Fortune* International 500.

- *Inc.* This monthly magazine covers small, entrepreneurial companies. It is useful because small firms are currently doing the most hiring.

- *Nation's Business.* This monthly reports on business activities, companies, and prominent business people.

- *New York Times.* This daily New York City newspaper has a useful business section.

- *The Wall Street Journal.* This business newspaper, published on weekdays, has a focus on finance, industry, and business. Its occasional feature articles on executive recruitment are useful.

There are thousands of additional magazines and newspapers that carry articles on companies that might provide job prospects. Almost all companies belong to an industry association that publishes a trade journal. Such journals provide the most recent articles on trends and new products in the industry. By reading the trade journals, you can keep informed of events in the entire industry. Ask at your library for what journal subscriptions it holds and how they might be of help to you. The *Encyclopedia of Associations* will identify what associations are relevant.

Is the Corporation a Subsidiary or Division?   A parent company might own the company in which you are interested. Finding information on the "children" of conglomerate public companies can be just as difficult as finding information on private companies. After looking in the *Directory of Corporate Affiliations, Who Owns Whom,* or *Standard & Poor's Register of Corporations, Directors, and Executives,* be sure to look for information under the parent's name in the sources listed for public companies. In addition, use the same sources listed under private companies.

Other Information about Public or Private Companies or Subsidiaries.   Information taken from directories and from reports to the SEC is not the only information available. Company histories can reveal what kind of work environment exists at a company and any corporate legends and culture the company has. By referring to such information at an interview, you can give a favorable impression. Check in your library's catalog under the name of the company to see if an entire book has been written on the company. If not, the following sources might contain information:

- *The International Directory of Company Histories*. St. James Press, 1988–.
  Arranged by industry, this profiles 1,200 major public and private companies worldwide, but with U.S. sales. Each profile has an excellent and lengthy description of its founding to its present state of activities.

- *Everybody's Business: A Field Guide to the 400 Leading Companies in America*. By Milton Moskowitz, Robert Levering, and Michael Katz. Doubleday, 1990.
  Covering both public and private companies, each two-page profile includes a company history, its products and services, brand names, work place environment, social consciousness, and information about executives and owners.

The Industry as a Whole.   Finding out about the industry as a whole and associations that serve the corporation will give you insight into the opportunities and the business climate. It might help you assess the strengths or weaknesses, even if you cannot locate information about a specific

company. There are associations and directories for every industry. Locating and reading the trade journals for the industry is helpful. The following sources are of particular additional interest:

- *Standard & Poor's Industry Surveys.* Standard & Poor's Corp. Quarterly.
  In narrative form, this describes and analyzes major industries in the United States and evaluates their status. Some financial statistics are included for the leading companies.

- *Moody's Industry Review.* Moody's Investors Service. Looseleaf service.
  This provides comparative statistics for major competitors and includes net income, profit margin, assets and returns on assets and capital, and composite stock price movements for the industry.

- *U.S. Industrial Outlook.* U.S. Department of Commerce. International Trade Administration. Annual.
  This surveys 350 industries for current trends and developments. All U.S. document depository libraries and many others will have this available.

Finding out about management and marketing practices in companies can involve careful detective work. Annual reports and 10-K reports will often carry some information on the corporate structure or an organization chart. They might mention labor negotiations that have occurred and will give salary information for its top officials. You might be able to find a job description or salary levels for specific job classifications for a metropolitan area in salary surveys. Annual reports will highlight successful products and might mention new products under development. Additional marketing information can be found in newspaper or periodical articles and trade journal articles. The following sources are useful:

- *American Almanac of Jobs and Salaries.* Avon. 1990–1991.
  This describes jobs in federal and state governments, in the arts, sciences, technology, business, service industries, and the professions. It gives salary ranges.

- *American Salaries and Wage Survey.* 2nd ed. Gale Research, Inc. Annual.
  This compilation of occupations and their corresponding salaries from over 300 federal, state, and trade associations ranges from national coverage to local city coverage. It is useful in estimating the level of salaries of an occupation.

- *Area Wage Surveys.* U.S. Bureau of Labor Statistics. Annual.
  An annual for 70 metropolitan areas includes occupations in the areas of clerical, professional, custodial work, and materials movement and maintenance and provides hourly and weekly earnings. Comparison of wages between cities is possible.

- *Dictionary of Occupational Titles.* U.S. Department of Labor, Employment and Training Administration. (See OOH.)

- *Market Share Reporter.* Gale Research, Inc. Annual.
  An annual compilation of published market share data for 5,600 companies, 2,900 products and services, and 1,500 brands. It is arranged by industry and gives proportions of sales in comparison to competitors for companies, brands, or products. It can be used to judge the strength of a company.

- *Occupational Compensation Survey.* U.S. Bureau of Labor Statistics. Annual.
  Describes level and distribution of occupational pay for many metropolitan areas and provides weekly and hourly earnings for professional, administrative, technical, clerical, maintenance and toolroom, materials movement, and custodial occupations.

- *Occupational Outlook Handbook.* U.S. Department of Labor, Bureau of Labor Statistics. Biennial.
  The OOH has job information on 250 jobs, representing 80 percent of the work force, and the *Dictionary of Occupational Titles* (DOT) has 12,000 job descriptions with references to over 20,000 job titles.

- *Organization Charts: Structures of More than 200 Businesses and Nonprofit Organizations.* Gale Research, Inc. 1992.
  Provides formal organization charts for organizations.

- *Standard Directory of Advertisers.* National Register Publishing Co. Annual.
  Lists companies with a large advertising budget and provides information about brands and the advertising agency with the account. Companion volumes are the *Standard Directory of Advertising Agencies.*

You can identify the key people in a company and gather background information about them. In an interview, knowing something about the chief executive is very impressive. *Standard & Poor's Register* and the *Million Dollar Directory* give brief background information.

- *Biography and Genealogy Master Index.* Gale Research, Inc. Annual.
  This series indexes over 95 biographical dictionaries, indexes, and sources to locate material for 450,000 citations for biographical sketches.

- *Reference Book of Corporate Managements.* Dun & Bradstreet, Inc. Annual.
  This covers 200,000 presidents, officers, and managers of 12,000 service companies and provides data on present business connections and present and former business positions.

- *Who's Who in Business and Finance.* Marquis Who's Who/Macmillan Directory Division. Biennial.
  North American and international business professionals who are of current business reference interest submit biographical data, which is reviewed and formed into a short sketch. *Who's Who in America* offers broader and more general coverage for North America.

- *Brands and Their Companies.* Gale Research, Inc. Annual.
  This and the companion volumes, *Companies and Their Brands,* gives information on 230,000 trade names, trademarks, or brand names of consumer products.

- *Dun's Consultant's Directory.* Dun's Marketing Services. Annual.
  Because this gives names and addresses for the 25,000 consulting firms listed, it is useful to locate experts in a particular field and can identify networks. The *Consultants and Consulting Organizations Directory* (Gale Research) is a similar directory.

- *Directories in Print.* Gale Research, Inc. Annual.
  Lists 14,000 rosters, guides, directory databases, and other lists available from business, industrial, entertainment, recreational, and cultural organizations, and professional and scientific rosters.

- *Dun's Employment Opportunities Directory/The Career Guide.* Dun & Bradstreet Information Services. Annual.
  Identifies employment opportunities for public, private, and not-for-profit organizations with more than 1,000 employees. It lists educational requirements and available company benefits and training opportunities.

- *Job Seekers' Guide to Private and Public Companies.* Gale Research, Inc. 1993.
  Profiles 15,000 U.S. companies and gives the address, business description, corporate officers, brief financial information, number

of employees, and human resources contact person. An index to specific skills that the industry might be seeking is included.

Is the Corporation a Small, Local, or Regional Corporation?

There are many more small for-profit companies in the United States than any other kind of company. They can range from a partnership employing five people to very large regional private companies. Gathering information on them is also difficult. Sometimes all that will be available will be listings in the telephone book or an industrial or service directory. When locating information about a specific company is not possible, gathering information about its industry can be useful. Asking for additional suggestions from a reference librarian is recommended. The following sources are some possibilities:

- *State industrial directories and state service directories.* Annual. Every state has a manufacturer's directory that lists public, private, and very small firms, their locations, products, and staff, and sometimes the computers the company uses. Most libraries own the directory for their state. Larger states will also have a services directory, which lists similar types of information for companies that sell some kind of service.

- *Local newspapers.* Often local newspapers will cover a high-profile company in the area or provide useful information about a small company. There are online databases available through large libraries that index many of the major local papers, or your library might clip articles for a newspaper file of local interest.

- *Business Dateline.* UMI/Data Courier. Online Database. There are regional business magazines or newspapers for every major U.S. city. These newspapers are indexed, and the complete articles are often available in this online database. Large libraries have access to this, usually by appointment. Ask a reference librarian.

- *Gale Directory of Publications and Broadcast Media.* Gale Research, Inc. Annual. This three-volume set lists newspapers, magazines, journals, radio stations, TV stations, and cable systems by state and by city. It includes the name, address, date founded, publishing characteristics, requirements, and ad rates. This is useful to locate newspapers and other publications in a local area. Most libraries hold this series.

- *Telephone book Yellow Pages.* The Yellow Pages are advertisements for producers, sellers, and services available in a local area. You can find locations and phone numbers of competitors to your organization.

- *Small Business Sourcebook.* Gale Research, Inc. Irregular.
  This guide to 254 small businesses includes names of primary
  associations, trade journals, educational opportunities, and supply
  sources for small businesses.

Is the Employer International?

Many companies do business throughout the world. In many cases, a well-known company is a subsidiary of a foreign company. The SEC requires some foreign parent companies that sell stock in the United States to file reports in a 20-F form, but many other companies do not have to register. Using periodical indexes to identify pertinent articles will uncover useful information also. Finally, there are many directories listing worldwide companies:

- *Directory of American Firms Operating in Foreign Countries.* 12th ed.
  World Trade Academy Press, 1991.
  Lists companies operating in foreign countries and includes officers.
  Volumes 2 and 3 list the company by country and give local
  addresses and the products the facility produces.

- *International Directory of Corporate Affiliations.* National Register
  Publishing Co. Annual.
  Provides information on who owns whom in every major international corporation and the family trees of major corporations doing
  business worldwide. It locates major facilities for companies. An
  alphabetic cross-reference index, a U.S. and non-U.S. parent company index, and a geographic index are included.

- *International Organizations.* Gale Research, Inc. Annual.
  Over 9,000 international nonprofit organizations and associations
  can be located using geographic, key word, and executive indexes.
  This formerly was included in the *Encyclopedia of Associations.*

- *Principal International Businesses.* Dun & Bradstreet International.
  Annual.
  More than 55,000 leading companies and their subsidiaries are listed
  and arranged by country. It includes approximate sales, number of
  employees, and whether the company imports or exports.

- *World Business Directory.* Gale Research, Inc. Biennial.
  Lists more than 100,000 businesses involved in international trade
  for 190 countries. Volumes 1–3 are arranged by country; volume 4
  includes product data, industry data, financial and employment data,
  and indexes.

Is the Employer a Not-for-Profit Organization?   There are
more than 300,000 employers in the United States that are not-for-profit.
They include government agencies at the federal, state, or local levels. Within
education, there are not-for-profit private schools and public schools offering
higher, secondary, or elementary education. There are social service agencies
at the national, state, and local levels. Health-related organizations often are
not-for-profit. Finding information about all of these is difficult, but information is available.

Several sources mentioned previously will be useful. A variety of organizations,
both not-for-profit and for-profit, are listed in *Dun's Employment Opportunities
Directory/The Career Guide*. Newspaper articles are written about local not-for-
profits. Local public libraries and academic libraries might be able to access these
through database searching or through a newspaper clipping file. The *Encyclopedia of Associations* will be very useful. Asking for help from a reference librarian
might uncover a surprising amount of revealing and useful information.

If the organization is a government agency or a tax-supported agency, ask
a reference librarian if there is a handbook to the metropolitan area or city.
Federal, state, and local governments publish such manuals, which describe
and summarize the activities of each department within the government.

- *U.S. Organization Manual*. Government Printing Office. Annual.
  Summarizes the activities of each federal agency. Of particular
  interest is the Office of Personnel Management, which recruits civil
  service positions throughout all agencies and maintains federal job
  information centers in major cities. Using this to research a specific
  agency will be useful.

- *State blue books*. Available from all state governments, these summarize activities of each state department. Ask at your library for your
  state's version.

- *Local governments*. Many local governments have a similar handbook
  describing activities of each department of the government. Often
  the local branch of the League of Women voters might have collected
  information about the local governments. Libraries often have a
  newspaper clipping file on local government.

If the organization is a school, there are directories of schools available at
every library. Peterson's Guides, Barron's, Lovejoy's, etc., are some of the publishers that produce such directories. Ask how to locate them at your local
library.

If the organization is a social service agency or a health organization, again
there are directories available of services. Check at your library for the subject

"social service—directories," "community health services—directories," or "health facilities—directories." Ask a reference librarian to help you find them. Check to see if there are newspaper articles on it. Many such agencies must file a report annually with a statewide regulatory agency. While these reports usually are not published, they are available for inspection at the agency. Look for the state agency that regulates corporations; often it is the Secretary of State.

Gathering information about a prospective employer will involve serious research in a library and will require a commitment of time and sometimes money. Libraries own many directories, handbooks, indexes, and histories that contain information on organizations. Asking for suggestions from a reference librarian is a worthwhile strategy. With time and energy, researchers can weave together small amounts of information from a variety of sources to produce a tapestry of information on a particular organization and enhance their chances of employment.

Job Searching Long Distance and Relocation

In today's tight job market, relocating becomes a strategy that you can employ in your job search to gain an advantage in obtaining the type of work you're most interested in. How does one go about job searching long distance?

Know Your Career Goal and City of Choice

The first task in job searching long distance may be obvious—identifying geographically where you want to live—yet many people might not be sure. You need to be specific about what city or town you wish to reside in. If you pick a general area within a state, your search will be unfocused and less effective. The same applies to your career goal. You need to be focused in order to increase the possibility of success.

If you're interested in more than one city, rather than trying to carry out more than one long distance job search, which decreases your chances for success, prioritize the cities in order of preference and begin with the most highly ranked choice. Give the process 4–6 months, and at that point you can decide whether to redirect your energies to your next city of choice.

There are a couple of ways to approach identifying your city of choice. You, or you and a significant other, might have a particular city in mind based on factors other than your career goals. Or you might know that there are better possibilities in a particular city of getting the type of job you're seeking.

Networking Long Distance

Once you've identified the city where you want to pursue your career goal, you will begin to network through the use of published and people resources:

- Subscribe to local papers and related business/industry publications.

- If you can get someone to send you a phone book (Yellow Pages), that would be helpful. Your local public library might have it, or inquire there about publications that have similar information.

- Contact officers of the Chamber of Commerce to ask for information related to the city as a place to live and any information about career fields you're interested in.

- Identify and contact civic leaders (Rotary, Kiwanis, Elks, etc.) or government office holders.

- Check for alumni of colleges you attended who live in that area.

- Ask members of your network if they know someone in your target city.

- Identify and contact officers (on a state or local level) of professional associations related to your career goal.

- Contact religious leaders (you don't necessarily have to be of the same denomination).

- Contact education leaders for information or suggestions of others to reach, such as a university placement director. Even though they're geared for helping their own graduates find jobs, they might be willing to share a name or two with you. They probably wouldn't consider you as competition for their main clientele, unless you are looking for an entry-level position.

- Contact officers of major companies for any information they might be willing to share.

Whenever possible, using names of common contacts or mutual friends will help in increasing your positive response rate.

For these initial contacts, use the telephone when requesting printed material and letters when addressing specific individuals for information or referrals to help develop your network. Start this process at least two months before making an exploratory visit to your target city. This time is to allow for responses and follow-up correspondence. The follow-up letter serves to thank the contact for any information and to state your desire to set up an information interview for the period you'll be visiting. Let the person know that you'd like to call for an appointment when you visit. Also, state that you're not expecting a job from your visit, just a chance to ask questions.

Once your preliminary research and initial letter campaign are well underway, it's time to consider when you will visit your target city. Using vacation time is a wise approach to take and perhaps your only one, if you are presently employed. Try to schedule at least one visit of at least two, and ideally three, weeks in your target city.

Upon your visit, you can treat this job search as you would where you now reside, pursuing information interviews with your contacts. However, your effort is compressed into a shorter time. With little additional time available, leave your sightseeing until after settling the employment question. You'll need to be focused, stay focused, and work hard at your networking and job search efforts.

Relocation Resources

Choosing a City to Live in.   A community's growth and decline trends should be considered as part of your criteria. Perhaps the Chamber of Commerce or a related office can send you some information. In addition, consult *Places Rated Almanac: Your Guide to Finding the Best Place to Live in America,* by Rick Boyer and David Savageau. This publication provides information for over 300 major cities by cost of living, housing, job opportunities, education facilities, climate, health care, environment, safety, transportation, the arts, recreation, and economics and provides rankings. These aspects sum up the areas to assess when considering relocation.

• •

Zephree actually visited the city of interest to her and job searched there. Upon finding a job opening in a county pre-adult probation program, she applied with the intention of moving to this city. When she returned home, she wondered why they would ever give that job to someone not yet living in that city. Worried about this possibility, especially because she felt she hadn't made clear to them her willingness to move, Zephree packed her bags and moved there.

She immediately visited the personnel office where she had her interview and let the person know that she, indeed, had moved to that city. Impressed by her desire and action, management hired her within a week. This is perhaps not the approach we'd recommend, but it was a risk, in this case, worth taking.

• •

The Expense.   Some of the major costs involved in relocation include housing, travel, child care, closing costs of old and new home, increase in mortgage payment or apartment rent, temporary living expenses, moving expenses, and a possible increase in the overall cost of living. In tax year 1994, the expenses you incur in a work-related move have become deductible only if your new job is at least 50 miles further from your old address than your past job was. The deduction will be limited to the actual cost of travel and moving household goods.

Long Distance Research.   As already mentioned, most research can take place in the library. In addition, two publishers—Bob Adams and Surrey Books—have books that identify employers and organizations (*Job Bank Guides* and *How to Get a Job in . . .,* respectively) in specific cities (or states) including the following:

- Atlanta
- Boston
- Chicago
- Dallas/Fort Worth
- Denver
- Detroit
- Florida

- Houston
- Los Angeles
- Minneapolis
- New York
- Ohio
- Philadelphia
- Phoenix

- Portland
- San Diego
- San Francisco
- Seattle
- St. Louis
- Washington, DC

Relocating Counseling Service.   Homquity Destination Service provides free information on housing and schools in any community, as well as spouse career counseling. Homquity's address is 107 Newton Road, Danbury, CT 06813. Regardless of what sources you use to research your target cities, you can evaluate them in a similar manner to that used in making a career choice. Establish and rank your particular criteria for assessing a target city and try to narrow your list down to the top two or three communities. Then, as suggested earlier, begin the long distance job search process with your top choice target city.

Part III

Strategies for Groups with Special Challenges in the Workplace

CHAPTER 9

WOMEN AT WORK

Women in the Workforce: The Numbers Keep Growing

The Statistics

In the period 1992–2005, slightly more than one-half of the labor force entrants (52 percent) will be women, compared to 42 percent in 1979. In addition, by the year 2005, there will be 72 million women in the work force representing 48 percent of the total work force and 64 percent of all new work force entrants. Women are also the major breadwinner in 20 percent of U.S. families. Sixty-six percent of women who are married with children, are working, compared to 62 percent in 1985, 57 percent in 1980, and 47 percent in 1975.

What Do These Numbers Mean?

Women are a growing force in the workplace and must be recognized. Yet certain challenges still face women on the job. We'll report on these challenges and offer suggestions on how to most effectively deal with them. On the brighter side, things are beginning to change for the better—we'll highlight where.

Corporate Culture

We can see that the corporate/business culture is an important aspect to assess as women decide on which organizations they wish to work for. How can you check out the particular culture of an organization, particularly related to how women are treated? Try to examine during your visits or research via information interviews, company literature, or library resources the following aspects: attitudes or "vibes" picked up on, whether teamwork is noticeable, how employee contributions are recognized, and any history of decision making, including the hiring and promotion of women.

If you discover a business culture that offers an atmosphere in which men and women work together and are encouraged and rewarded for their contributions and achievements rather than being caught up in vicious, unproductive office politics, then you have found what can be considered a successful culture. Essentially, you want a good match between your values and those of the organization. In the meantime, what can women do to enhance their image and power in corporate America?

Enhancing Women's Image and Power in Business

Janet Hauter offers the following suggestions.

Develop Positive, Healthy Business Relationships.   There's no better way than the networking process to build and enhance your career. Obviously, networking doesn't end with acquiring a job. A whole new focus takes place with beginning a new job, both within your organization specifically and in your career field more generally.

Women have come to realize the vitality of the "old boy network" to advance in their careers. Thus, we find that women are increasingly creating formal networks of their own. Professional relationships developed throughout one's career need to be nurtured and maintained by sharing information and offering support. Check in your geographical area for career-related women's networking groups.

Find a Mentor.   More and more large organizations are establishing formal mentoring programs as a means of speeding up the learning process for new employees. It shortens the time it takes for them to be productive and helps them to understand the big picture. The more powerful your mentor, the clearer the path to promotion. In the absence of a formal mentoring program, you might be able to identify a potential mentor in your organization. Work at establishing positive relationships with everyone possible, and perhaps a mentoring relationship will develop. It helps make life easier to have a helping hand reaching out to offer assistance and advice.

Control Information. Through your networking and research, stay up to date in your field. Many people believe that information equals power. Even if you're not all that concerned about moving up, power can help to secure where you are as well.

Control Resources. If you're responsible for a budget, then be responsible in your operation from it. Those higher up will find it difficult to promote anyone who isn't.

Tap Hidden Pockets of Power. Via your networking efforts, you will be able to establish positive, professional relationships with a variety of people, those in recognizable power positions and those not so recognizable (by title). If your goal is to move up, then these would be important people to establish positive relations with.

Protect the Power You Have. Don't abuse others by using coercion or other negative power moves (e.g., making staff do your personal chores).

Discrimination

Carol Kleiman describes discrimination as a practice that effectively keeps qualified women from rising to the top job, no matter what their education, experience, or years with the company. Kathryn Petras and Ross Petras indicate that women are likely to be found in corporate staff rather than line functions. They tend to be placed in positions in corporate communications, human resources, finance, legal, marketing research, public relations, and systems. Yet to make it into senior management, it's usually necessary to have line experience in core areas like marketing, production, and sales. Suggestions to overcome such obstacles include the following:

- Identify what experience is needed to reach your goal.

- Plan ways to get that experience.

- Ask for the type of projects and assignments you'll need.

- Seek out corporations that offer women lateral experience or those that place women in line positions.

As corporations change, becoming more flexible organizations, they'll offer cross-functional training to more of their executives.

Wages and Other Benefits.

In general, research has shown that the more women employed in a particular occupation, the lower the pay. Most low-pay, low-status, white-collar jobs are held by women in disproportionate numbers. Nearly 75 percent of working women are employed in traditionally female, low-wage jobs. One reason for this is that many employers have long viewed women as secondary earners whose families did not depend on their income. The number of working mothers who are the sole source of support for their families has steadily increased, as well as the rate of working mothers who live in poverty. Women in general earn about 67 percent of men's earnings in similar employment.

In addition, access to health insurance and other benefits is often blocked as well. Those working in traditionally female occupations have the highest uninsured rate. Sixty-two percent of minimum-wage earners are women, and one-half of all women workers earning $5 an hour or less are without health insurance. Also, over 15 million women of child-bearing age in the United States have no public or private medical coverage. One in eight births in the United States each year is not covered by any health plan. The average cost of having a baby is now $4,300.

The best suggestion for women with regard to salary and related benefits is to do the research. Know what you deserve to be paid with your particular set of skills and experience. Then prepare yourself to negotiate, as well as you can, to obtain the fairest salary possible. It's simply more difficult to do without the information. You'll be left guessing whether you're being treated fairly. With the right information, you'll be able to plant your feet solidly, stand tall, and ask for what you know you deserve.

The Glass Ceiling.

Basically, the term *glass ceiling* refers to women's difficulty in getting promoted beyond a certain point. Women have made gains. They make up 41 percent of all management positions, but less than 5 percent of top executive jobs belong to women. In fact, that percentage decreases to less than 3 percent when viewing women's representation in senior *Fortune* 500 companies' management positions.

What areas seem to offer the best chance for women interested in top-level management positions? According to Petras and Petras, financial services industries like insurance, banking, and brokerage are more likely to offer women senior management positions. In addition, high-tech jobs tend to be gender blind, because the key to success is learning how to use technology. The pay gap here is also less, with women earning 82.7 percent of male salaries.

The best bet suggested by Petras and Petras is in information systems with financial services firms or pharmaceutical companies, whereas tough barriers still exist in manufacturing and retail. In addition, we suggest that women identify corporations that sponsor corporate training for female mid-level managers for higher-level positions.

The bottom line is that companies cannot afford to eliminate what will soon be one-half of the work force from top-level management positions and expect to keep up with their competition. The good news is that businesses are now beginning to allow more local control and promotion of teamwork to ensure their place in a changing and more competitive marketplace. Those that can adjust and adapt to change will have opportunities. Diversity is more welcomed, and management styles are becoming more cooperative (an acknowledged strength of women).

Up Is Not the Only Way. With many career advancements stalled in layers of middle management, making a lateral move might be viable for both women and men. A lateral move could be used on one job as a springboard to another. Because downsizing has eliminated many positions for which the "ladder" used to be climbed, expanding oneself laterally offers greater variety and perhaps necessary experience to be competitive for those fewer, higher-level positions. It might not yield more money, but it could cure your burnout, broaden your experience, and boost your marketability both within and outside your company.

Some companies are making provisions within their newer structure for lateral moves for their employees after seeing how it helps employee motivation and productivity. The ability to transfer to a different department might become the new non-monetary reward for excellent performance. Both women and men need to rethink the nature of traditional career paths and examine how they're defining success.

Owning a Business

Many women are turning to owning a business as the path of choice for career advancement. In 1992, there were 6.5 million female-owned businesses. By the year 2005, women will own 50 percent of all businesses. Female-owned businesses are growing 50 percent faster than male-owned businesses, and their success rate is high. Perhaps the one statistic that impacts all this the most is that more Americans are employed by female-owned businesses than all *Fortune* 500 companies combined. Female-owned businesses gross $300 billion a year. Organizations you might want to contact and some useful directories follow:

- The National Association of Female Executives
  127 W. 24th Street, 4th floor
  New York, NY 10011

  Offers programs for women-owned businesses and operates a
  venture capital fund for small businesses.

- Catalyst National Network of Career Resource Centers
  250 Park Avenue
  New York, NY 10003

  Promotes changes for women in the workplace and researches and
  publishes findings on women's issues and career information.

- *A Directory of Non-Traditional Training and Employment Programs
  Serving Women.* Washington, DC: U.S. Department of Labor,
  Women's Bureau.

  Lists programs that offer apprenticeships.

- *Women Directors of Top 1,000 Corporations.* Washington, DC: National
  Women's Economic Alliance Foundation.

Sexual Harassment

Joyce Lain Kennedy describes sexual harassment as including unwelcomed
sexual advances, requests for sexual favors, or other conduct of a sexual nature,
verbal or physical. Actions can be described as sexual harassment when the
aggressor's conduct unreasonably interferes with a worker's job performance or creates an intimidating, hostile, threatening, or offensive working
environment.

What Can Be Done about It?

Sexual harassment can keep women out of certain jobs and from advancing in
the ones they have. As bad as sexual harassment is, what might be even worse
is figuring out what to do about it. Even though studies show that 45–85
percent of women have experienced some form of sexual harassment, only
about 3 percent ever complain or file a complaint.

Filing a complaint could make things rough on the job. If we take the view
of the work environment being a people environment, it's easy to recognize
the importance of maintaining good rapport with those you work with and
report to. Women are reluctant to complain for fear of being branded a

trouble-maker, becoming a victim of an unpleasant work situation, and the possibilities of future employers being reluctant to hire them.

In addition, some women are reluctant to leave a job, especially when they need the salary or lack the confidence to find another. As Richard Bolles suggests, if you think you can survive the ordeal in good shape (perhaps the harasser is disliked by many others), then seek the advice of a lawyer and consider filing a complaint.

As a beginning step, when you are harassed sexually on the job, tell the perpetrator in a cool, calm manner that the specific behavior (name it to them) bothers you and to please not repeat it. It's important to let it be known from the start that a particular behavior is disturbing to you and you want to see it ended. This will perhaps detour the aggressor from acting in such a way again and might save you the ordeal of filing a complaint. Kennedy offers some other suggestions about what to do if confronted with sexual harassment on the job.

- Don't ignore the situation; seek advice from co-workers and friends.

- Keep a log or diary noting incidents. Be sure to store it in a safe (locked) place. You will need this type of information if you decide to file a complaint with the company or a government agency.

- Carry a small microcassette (concealed) recorder to document evidence.

- Take advantage of your company's internal complaint procedures. Unfortunately, harm to you and others might never end otherwise.

- Send the offender, by certified mail, a letter outlining and stating incidents.

Will the Future Be Better?

There is some good news. As a result of the October 1991 Hill/Thomas hearings, there's been a raised consciousness across the United States with regard to sexual harassment. Many companies have developed explicit, printed policies for dealing with sexual harassment. With the increasing number of women entering the work force, a company that doesn't establish clear and effective policies in this area can leave itself open to expensive lawsuits and a negative reputation as an employer.

It is now the responsibility of every company owner and top management to create a workplace atmosphere where women can feel safe to file complaints if they feel mistreated. In researching companies, women can attempt to ascertain the company's policies toward sexual harassment.

Balancing Work and Family

More Choices

There are various options from which women can choose in pursuing work and family goals. Many positive gains have been made by women (societal, career, and family related), but these changes make decision making more confusing.

Increased Responsibility

Women (particularly those in their late twenties, thirties, and early forties) find themselves caring for both young children and aging parents while pursuing a career and holding together a marriage as well. Many women believe they have to forgo educational opportunities or postpone taking the steps necessary to advance on the job.

Let's take a look at a real problem, the lack of high-quality affordable child care and the ever-increasing need for elder care.

Child and Elder Care.   It is estimated that about 40 percent of the work force is involved with providing care for both their children and elders. As reported earlier, many mothers have lower wages and can't afford either of these alone, much less both (especially single mothers). Family care-giving roles for mothers can bring about periods of interrupted income and thus disrupt careers. Twenty-five percent of mothers of preschool children who are not in the paid work force say they would work if access to safe and affordable child care existed. It's estimated that 25 percent of a low-income working mother's earnings go to child care.

What's needed is a more comprehensive plan for subsidizing and regulating child care and elder care. With more women entering the work force and the aging of the population, eventually these types of programs will come about. In the meantime, we all need to push for it.

There Is Hope.   At least for the time being, more and more companies are offering flexible hours, job sharing, and part-time work options (some with benefits), and sometimes provisions for child care as well, to help support mothers in the workplace. These benefits have as an overall goal the balance between a good career and family life for employees. Employers' motivation is either one of benevolence or the reality that highly skilled employees are getting harder to find, and soon half of all potential employees will be women. Therefore, they do what they can to attract the most qualified women to work for them. Yet the vast majority of companies are not yet progressive enough to incorporate these improvements. Because of this and hard economic times, a tight job market, and a desire to be with their children, many women are dropping out of the work force to be full-time mothers.

Displaced Homemakers

Traditionally, the term *displaced homemakers* applied to women at mid-life whose children had grown up (or nearly so) and because of widowhood or divorce suddenly found that they could no longer continue in the role of homemaker. With the increase in divorce, women are often forced even earlier than mid-life to seek employment. Many women also decide to do so voluntarily, because they want the challenge and stimulation of a career.

Some major concerns of these career beginners or reentries are as follows:

- Can I find a job?

- Will I be able to succeed in the workplace?

- Can I do both well, work and care for children?

- Will I be able to support myself and the children?

- If I need further education or training, can I afford it?

Skill identification is a crucial part of the self-assessment process for this group. Homemakers often underestimate their skills, which usually include, for example, finance, time management, organization and planning, communication, negotiation/mediation, training, public relations, leadership, and administration/management.

Some good resources for helping women in the transition from home to the work force are as follows:

- **National Displaced Homemakers Network**
  1411 K. Street, NW
  Suite 930
  Washington, DC 20005

- **American Business Women's Association**
  9100 Ward Parkway
  P.O. Box 8728
  Kansas City, MO 64114

CHAPTER *10*

MINORITIES

African-Americans, Hispanics, and Asian-Americans: Increasing Diversity in the Workplace

The Statistics

By the year 2005, African-Americans, Hispanics, and Asian-Americans will represent about 27 percent of the work force, up from 22 percent in 1992. More than 1 in 3 (35 percent) of new work force entrants will be a minority between 1992 and 2005.

The Facts Behind the Numbers

The U.S. work force is growing in diversity. Companies are responding to shifting demographics and a shortage of highly skilled labor by actively recruiting minority workers and setting up programs to help encourage minority advancement.

Yet the percentage of minority workers who have reached management positions is still low. According to the Equal Employment Opportunity Commission (EEOC), as reported by Kathryn Petras and Ross Petras, in 1990 only 5.9 percent of all managers in the United States were African-Americans, and only 3 percent of these were in corporate management.

Richard Bolles reports that minorities are making advances in the work force. For example, African-American incomes of $50,000 or more doubled between 1982 and 1987. However, much more still needs to be accomplished, as indicated by the following facts:

- One-third of the nation's 30.2 million African-Americans live in poverty.

- African-American unemployment is twice that of the rest of the nation.

- Median incomes of African-American families is half that of white families.

What's It Like to Be a Minority?

The Label

Just being identified as a minority can have a negative impact. Some minorities wonder if they're perceived as equals by non-minorities. This in turn can cause distrust toward non-minorities. Some minorities are so sensitive about being labeled that it can cause problems ranging from poor decision making to negative self-concept, to inadequate job performance. When you add all this to the experience of possibly biased career-related testing, counseling, and placement practices, as well as workplace discrimination, one can understand how the stress can bring about a lack of confidence in ability and potential among minority workers, job seekers, and career changers.

The Role of Values

As a result of a history that includes slavery (with regard to African-Americans), disenfranchisement, discrimination, and poverty, minorities have come to value family, sharing, communication, and interdependence. This can make it tough to adjust to a work force that reflects the values of independent thinking, autonomy, and competitiveness. It's not surprising that many minorities find the white-collar work environment to be hostile and threatening.

The Pressure Is On

Unfortunately, many of the majority harbor doubts about minorities and have formulated certain stereotypes often based in ignorance and fear. Examples are that minorities are lazy, unmotivated, untrustworthy, and less intelligent.

Therefore, if a minority person gets the right kind of training and effectively competes for and gains a professional career position, Miguela Rivera believes there's even greater pressure to perform on the job than what is usually demanded of non-minorities. In other words, we all need to develop the skills in the next paragraph to succeed in our career, but Rivera asserts that minorities have to do even better to dispel the doubts.

In the workplace we need to know how to handle ourselves professionally, communicate effectively, develop positive interpersonal relations, become skillful at interoffice politics, develop expertise in our field, and basically know what and why we're doing what we're doing. Research has shown that minorities survive by overachieving, blending in, and avoiding the spotlight. Those who question, stand apart, or speak out run the risk of being further labeled as rebels, malcontents, or radicals.

Often minorities can feel torn between two worlds—their culture and that of corporate America. They can feel pulled in both directions and end up not really feeling part of either. Corporate America is also responsible for helping to eliminate stereotyped thinking and bias among its employees through multicultural education initiatives. We'll discuss ways this can be accomplished, but first, a closer look at the problem of discrimination.

Discrimination

The Law

Title VII of the Civil Rights Act of 1964 prohibits discrimination in hiring, promotion, compensation, and other conditions of employment based on race, color, creed, gender, pregnancy, or national origin.

The Challenge

The challenge is knowing how to recognize discrimination when it's occurring and how to handle it. Cydney Shields and Leslie Shields suggest going with your gut feeling for starters, then to look for disparities in treatment, wages, assignments of jobs, etc. Yet you still might have difficulty distinguishing rational opposition from racism or sexism. Listen carefully to what the person is saying and try to understand what they're objecting to. If they sound irrational, then you're probably dealing with prejudice, which literally means contempt without facts. However, if the objections seem rational, you need to be able to identify possible underlying fear and attempt to take action to allay such fears. In addition, there may be specific actions you can take about how you're going about your job that might help to remedy the situation.

Decision Time

If you do feel you're being discriminated against, you could deal with it by persevering and attempting to dispel fears through your actions. This is a slower approach, perhaps, but it can work. If the discrimination continues, then you're in a position to decide whether to proceed through the channels set up within the company (starting with your supervisor) for filing a complaint.

One tough aspect of deciding whether to file a complaint is determining whether it's worth the possible grief it might bring. You certainly could be risking possible retaliation or even losing your job. Judge your situation of discrimination on the basis of its seriousness and its effect on you. If there's a strong pattern of bias, fighting it might be advisable. However, ask yourself these questions first:

- Is it worth paying attention to?

- Can you do anything about it?

- Is it affecting your performance or place in the organization?

- Are you using this claim of discrimination as an excuse for not achieving your goals?

You need to decide whether the benefits of fighting back outweigh the potential costs. Know the consequences before taking action.

Suggested Steps to Take

Here are steps to follow and questions to answer if you think you've been discriminated against (been terminated, been passed over for a promotion, or received an unusual work assignment, etc.):

1. Stay calm, don't overreact, maintain your dignity and professionalism.

2. Find out what happened (e.g., if fired):

   Was a whole section or organization let go?

   Was your immediate supervisor fired also?

   Does the action seem to be the result of poor business conditions, slumping company sales, or loss of a contract?

3. If fired for normal changes in business and the marketplace (and it's imperative that you objectively find out), then pack your bags and move on.

4. If you're the only one fired, ask for the reason. Were any less senior or less competent staff retained? If so, you may have been a victim of discrimination.

With regard to not receiving a promotion:

1. Are you qualified in terms of education, technical expertise, communication skills, and leadership ability?

2. Had you been passed over before?

3. Did someone more qualified or with more seniority get the job?

4. Take a good look at yourself and answer the following questions:

   Are you adequately prepared?

   Has your performance been consistently good?

   Have you followed through on assignments?

   Have you been a team player?

5. Have any past difficulties between you and the company been documented in writing?

Once these questions have been answered, you're in a better position to judge whether you have a case of discrimination. Let's say you do have a case. What's next? Proving discrimination can be both difficult and upsetting. You might be stigmatized and labeled a troublemaker. Even if you gain the promotion, what will it be like for you back on the job? Your enemies can make life miserable for you and eventually drive you out anyway. Maybe so, but at least you're doing something about it. If more follow your example, it's bound to help decrease discrimination in the future, especially at your workplace. Ignoring it will not make it go away.

If you believe you have a case and want to proceed, take the following steps:

1. Go to management, starting with your immediate supervisor. Tell them how you feel and give specific reasons. Be able to show your qualifications, and state that you think the decision to fire or not to promote you was based on racial or cultural bias.

2. Talk with your company's EEO officer. Be prepared for a lukewarm response (this person might be too tied to the company) or a branch office of the EEOC (check the Yellow Pages under U.S. Government).

3. Seek the advice of a lawyer and decide whether to sue. Most cases are settled out of court but can still take 6–18 months before being finalized.

The best protection in cases of dismissal for poor performance is good record keeping, especially copies of performance evaluations. At annual reviews or evaluation time, make sure to get a copy in writing (including a summary of conversations). Make sure it's accurate and challenge anything that's not. Ask what you can do to improve and be more qualified for promotion (have this summarized in writing). In this way, you've got it in writing. This precaution can support your case or circumvent it to begin with.

Corporate America Responds

It's in Their Best Interest

With shifting demographics showing a continuous increase of minorities in our population, companies want workers that reflect their customers. Recruitment of minorities is one goal of their establishing programs to address cultural diversity, in order to attract, train, and retain minority workers. However, even with such programs, individuals still have their own biases and might view minorities as an unknown and perhaps as being somewhat threatening—that's where education efforts come into play.

Caucus Groups

Some companies have formed caucus groups in which minority workers meet to share problems and advice, as well as to offer suggestions to management on minority issues. These, however, will work only if management is serious, listens to the suggestions, and responds when appropriate.

Mentoring

It's easy for minorities in the work force to become isolated, especially if they are among the first to be integrating a particular department or business. Some businesses have established mentoring programs to help new hires learn the ropes and have a better chance to advance their careers. If none exists officially in your workplace, seek out others who can help you understand the expectations and realities of the work environment. It's also helpful if your mentor can put you in touch with the informal network that can help you attain recognition and advancement. Formal company titles might not tell you exactly where the power is.

Diversity Management

A growing trend among corporations is to have a position or office designated as diversity management to coordinate multicultural training. With the work force becoming increasingly ethnically and racially diverse, management needs to learn how to work and manage groups with a wide range of backgrounds. Some of the goals of diversity management programs include the following:

- To dispel false assumptions based on ethnic group or gender
- To enhance communication
- To work out misunderstandings that arise
- To lead to the elimination of racist and sexist discrimination

This new direction in management has led to a need for cultural diversity managers. To qualify, one needs a background consisting of human resources experience and an advanced degree in an area such as sociology or organization development.

Networking: One Key to Avoiding Racial Discrimination

Networking is perhaps the best known way to neutralize or circumvent prejudice and discrimination in the workplace for yourself. You will rarely, and probably never knowingly, be referred to someone who is likely to discriminate against persons like yourself. However, don't operate in exclusively minority networks. Tap into non-minority networks as well using any or all of the following approaches:

- Volunteering
- Community activities
- Attending career-related workshops and seminars
- Information interviews
- Connecting with non-minorities you know from school, work, etc.

Don't wait for others; reach out to them. In addition, try not to let the fact that a handful of non-minorities have an attitude problem mean that you develop one as well.

Welcoming Minorities

Look for companies that offer specific programs and recruitment drives for minority workers. A good source for doing so is the annual February issue of *Black Enterprise* covering the best places for African-Americans to work. Also, check the resources that follow, which include associations, directories, and periodicals.

Minority Trade and Professional Associations

American Association of Black Women Entrepreneurs
909 Pershing Drive, Suite 200
Silver Spring, MD 20910

Association of Black Women Entrepreneurs
P.O. Box 49368
Los Angeles, CA 90049

Coalition of Hispanic American Women
8572 SW, 8th Street
Miami, FL 33144

Hispanic Leadership Program
621 South Virgil Avenue
Los Angeles, CA 90005

Latin Business Association
5400 E. Olympic Boulevard, Suite 130
Los Angeles, CA 90022

National Hispanic Business Group
960 Southern Boulevard
New York, NY 10549

Native American Communication and Career Development
P.O. Box 1281
Scottsdale, AZ 85252

United Indian Development Association
9650 Flair Drive
El Monte, CA 91731

Resources to Organizations

Asian-American Information Directory
Black American Information Directory
Hispanic-American Information Directory

Gale Research, Inc.
835 Penobscot Building
Detroit, MI 48226

Guide to Black Organizations
Guide to Hispanic Organizations

Public Affairs Department
Philip Morris Ltd.
100 Park Avenue
New York, NY 10017

Minority Organizations: A National Directory, 4th ed., 1992, Katherine W. Cole, ed. Garrett Park, MD: Garrett Park Press, 1987.

Minority Business Periodicals

Black Careers
P.O. Box 8214
Philadelphia, PA 19101

The Black Collegian
Black Collegian Services, Inc.
1240 S. Broad Street
New Orleans, LA 70125

Black Enterprise
Subscription Service Center
P.O. Box 3011
Harlan, IA 51593

Equal Opportunity
Equal Opportunity Publications
44 Broadway
Greenlawn, NY 11740

Minority Business Entrepreneur
924 N. Market Street
Inglewood, CA 90302

CHAPTER 11

PEOPLE OVER AGE 50

The Population Is Aging

The Statistics

By the year 2005, 13 percent of the population will be over age 65, twice the number in 1940. Between 1992 and 2005, the number of older workers will grow twice as fast as the labor force as a whole. One of every three persons in the general population will be over 55 by the year 2005, with an average age of 40.5, compared to 1992's average of 37.2. About 14 percent of those over 55 will still be working by 2005 (compared to 10 percent in 1992).

The Reality

Two major trends of the 1990s are the aging of the population and the skills gap. Potential labor market entrants do not have the higher-level skills that most available jobs require. This can be an incentive for the older worker who wants to continue employment or resume it after an absence from the work force. Yet they might have some barriers in their way, the biggest being age discrimination.

Dispelling Myths

Older adults interested in remaining in or returning to the work force must fight the impression some people have that age is linked with decreasing capability for work and training. However, studies have shown that chronological age has nothing to do with one's functional capacity.

Intellectual capacity does not begin to diminish until well into the seventies, if at all. Age does not affect speed, attentiveness to detail, stamina, or accuracy. Older workers have fewer accidents and fewer sick days than younger workers. They still have the ability to learn new things, and their basic personality stays the same. Research has also shown that workers over age 50 have a stronger work ethic, higher productivity, less alcoholism and drug use, more patience, longer tenures, more willingness to learn, and better attitudes than their younger associates. The fact is most over age 65 today are vigorous, healthy, mentally alert, and still young in outlook.

Reasons Why Older Adults Choose to Stay in the Work Force

Many Still Need the Money

Many older workers were victims of downsizings, encouraged to take early retirement (or were let go) while lower-paid, younger workers took over their responsibilities. The fact is that many still need the money to pay bills or care for a loved one who is ill. Many need to supplement their social security income. (There are limits on earnings in addition to Social Security; call the Social Security Administration if you have questions.)

Other Reasons

Some choose to work because it's good for their mental and physical health. Others do it so as not to be around their spouse all day. Yet others choose to work so they can be with their spouse all day, working together. It all depends on the individuals involved and the nature of their relationships with their significant others.

Choices for the Older Worker

If an older worker can afford to do so financially, the following choices for how to return to the work force are possible.

Work Part Time

This would enable one to spend more time on leisure pursuits and hobbies. Samuel Ray states that the number of part-time jobs has increased 21 percent since 1980. Twenty percent of women and 6 percent of men are working, by choice, in permanent part-time jobs. Twenty percent of the part-time jobs require a college degree.

Employers are becoming more flexible in both offering part-time jobs and hiring older adults, in an effort to lessen the skills gap mentioned earlier. The type of jobs that offer the best possibilities for part-time work are those that can be independently completed or are project oriented. The skills looked for the most are probably writing and computer programming. We'll discuss further the skills employers are most interested in.

The organizations in which you would most likely find part-time work include the following:

- High-growth, high-tech companies in the earlier stages of growth, when there's more opportunity

- Nonprofit organizations, such as libraries, museums, universities, and human services organizations

- Small businesses, which are less bogged down in bureaucratic hiring policies and need experienced workers

- Federal, state and local government

Few *Fortune* 500 companies are recruiting; they're still downsizing. However, some have found themselves short-staffed. Therefore, possibilities might exist as a consultant or contractor. In general, though, older workers are recommended to seek out newer, smaller businesses. They're hiring more and offer better access to the person doing the hiring. Many low-pressure, low-paying part-time jobs exist as well, in fast food, retail, day care, etc. These might not sound appealing, but they might serve as a good option for the older worker without the experience or skills required by other part-time jobs.

Self-Employment

Self-employment usually involves work as a consultant or subcontractor providing services to companies and even your former employers, but now you're setting your own fees and hours. A couple of key references to check are *Starting a Mini-Business: A Guidebook for Seniors,* by Nancy Olsen, and *Going into Business for Yourself: New Beginnings after 50,* by Ina Lee Selden.

Volunteer Work

Volunteering can be done full time or part time. It's unpaid, but you have a purpose—to help create, in some way, a better world. Volunteering offers a good way to make contacts and gain valuable experience. It's a good way to test out an area of interest or to break into the nonprofit arena. The hours are usually flexible and need not be long. Some places would be willing to have you for only a few hours a week. Of course, this is all possible only if you can afford to do it financially.

Executive and Professional Temporary Work

Ninety percent of all companies now use temporary workers, and executive placement is its fastest-growing segment. Executive placements average about 3–9 months. You will usually be hired on a project basis, filling in during a search, or working in companies left too lean after downsizing. The executive/professional placement is good for people who enjoy putting out fires but get bored afterward.

If you're not at the professional or management level, a good organization to check out for temporary work is Kelly Services, the oldest and largest temporary agency. Areas of placement include accounting, clerical, light industry jobs, marketing, sales, records management, technical support, and home health aid jobs.

Other choices for how one could return to the work force are starting a business in a field unrelated to your first career, turning former hobbies into sources of income, relocating and starting all over, and returning to school to learn new skills.

What Employers Look for in Older Workers

The skills identified by companies that hire workers over 50 are the following:

- Communication
- Problem solving
- Technical skills
- Experience in industry (any industry)
- Computer related (engineering, designing, manufacturing or peripheral)
- Sales, customer service

- Banking

- Scientific

- Accounting, accuracy

- Sales experience

- Finance, mathematics

- Hospitality

- Marketing

In addition, the following qualities were most sought after by companies hiring workers over 50:

- Positive attitude

- Steady personality

- Ability to learn

- High energy

- Intelligence

- Good work ethic

- Experience

- Judgment/common sense

Suggested Responses to the Question of Age

The question of age is perhaps the most important question of all. If it's raised during your job search, in whatever disguise they try to give it, your response should be something like "It's not a problem. I have the necessary experience, education, training, and skills to perform quite well in this job." You could also highlight recent achievements and how you've kept your skills and knowledge current (which we urge you to do if you haven't been already).

If your interviewers think you are overqualified, you could respond by saying your skill level allows you to walk right in and function right away. If they press further, you can be more direct and say, "It sounds like you're concerned about my age." Stress that you are in excellent health, are in the prime of your career, are knowledgeable and skilled, and can be a valued asset to that company. If they're worried about how long you will be around, tell them five years for sure—and ask how many of their younger workers can guarantee that.

Advice for Staying, Looking, and Feeling Young

Appearance and Attitude

Because older workers' appearance and attitude play such an important role, Ray offers the following suggestions:

- Don't give away clues to your age with phrases such as, "back in the days when," "way back when," "when I was younger."

- Stay up to date with business practice and technology.

- Be aware of market forces affecting a particular industry.

- Keep on learning in your field.

- Become computer literate if you're not already.

- Stay fit and healthy. People admire older adults who have energy, vitality, and confidence.

- Keep your wardrobe current, but conservative.

We all know how important it is to feel good about who we are and how we look. If age is an issue for us, chances are that it shows and then becomes an issue with others as well. We need to do everything in our power to take care of ourselves emotionally, physically, intellectually, spiritually, and socially. First for ourselves and loved ones, and secondly for others we come in contact with, who can influence our lives for better or worse, such as employers. Most important, however, is to remember that we have the power within us to change in any of these areas.

Sources of Job Search Help

Job Fairs

Look for those targeted for mature workers age 50 and over. Representatives from a wide range of career fields usually attend. Keep an eye on the business section of your daily newspaper and local business weeklies as well.

Operation Able

Founded in Chicago, Able (Ability Based on Long Experience) helps those over age 40 by providing executive, managerial, technical, secretarial, and blue-collar temporary help. Those from a lower economic/disadvantaged background can also receive help with the assistance of some government programs.

Forty Plus Clubs

Created in the late 1930s, Forty Plus Clubs are a nonprofit nationwide network now in over 25 cities. The clubs are staffed by volunteers and dedicated to helping unemployed managers, executives, and professionals 40 or over in their job search. It assists career changers, retirees, and reentries as well.

Other Support Groups

Look for those offered through local churches and synagogues, social services agencies (e.g., Jewish Vocational Service, mental health clinics, etc.), as well as by private career counselors.

Age Discrimination

The Law

In 1967, the U.S. government passed the Age Discrimination in Employment Act (ADEA), which covered workers 40 and over from possible abuses in hiring, promotion, and compensation policies. The ADEA is administered through EEOC offices nationwide. Despite 25 years since its enactment, discrimination still occurs. Discrimination in hiring is the most difficult to detect and prove. Some may wonder if its even worth it to point it out. Those who do find out quickly that pointing out age discrimination in hiring rarely leads to getting the job. Maybe the best way to fight discrimination before being hired is to avoid it and look elsewhere.

Filing a complaint can be psychologically and financially draining and very time-consuming when what you need most is a job. However, age discrimination on the job with regard to promotion, wages, and layoffs/discharges might be easier to prove and thus perhaps worth the fight.

Be prepared and don't get caught off guard. A few things to keep in mind with regard to the ADEA follow. The law requires that layoffs be based on seniority or merit (e.g., total sale figures). Holding older workers alone to a certain standard with regard to discharges is against the law. Pressuring older workers to quit is a possible violation of the law. Employers must provide the same types of overall benefits to workers of all ages, although in some cases it might be of a lower amount. For example, an employer might spend the same amount on health insurance for older workers, but it buys less coverage.

Filing an Age Discrimination Complaint

You Must Prove

1. You're in the age group protected by the ADEA (40–70).

2. The employer is subject to the ADEA provisions (has more than 20 employees).

3. You were adversely affected by some employment action.

4. Age was an issue in the decision made.

Follow These Steps

1. File a complaint with your employer following your company's established procedures. (Check with your human resources department.) In addition, if applicable, file a grievance with your union.

2. If the discrimination practice hasn't ceased, contact the nearest EEOC office. (Check the Yellow Pages under U.S. Government.) Also contact your state government agency that handles age discrimination complaints in your state. If the rules and procedures of your state law seem more favorable to you than the ADEA provision, or if the state agency informs you that they will prosecute your case faster than the EEOC, then go ahead and file with the state just before filing with the EEOC. Usually, the one that receives it first is most likely the one to handle it. You'll probably want to meet with representatives from each office first. For guidance you can consult the American Association of Retired Persons (AARP), Worker Equity Department, 601 E. Street NW, Washington, DC 20049.

3.   You must file with both your state and federal offices to be able to bring a suit at a later time—the ADEA requires this. You have six months from the occurrence of the alleged discrimination to file with the EEOC.

4.   Once you've filed with the EEOC, you will receive a written reply to schedule an interview with an investigator.

5.   The agency will investigate the charge. If it finds evidence of age discrimination, it will attempt to negotiate a settlement. If the EEOC is unable to negotiate a settlement, it might file a lawsuit.

What's more likely is that you would decide to file your own lawsuit through your private attorney or public legal assistance agency. The EEOC track record is not good. In the past, many (900) age discrimination complaints were left sitting with no action taken, until it was beyond the statute of limitation. Therefore, be sure to select a lawyer with experience in age discrimination cases.

The Good News

Many companies have developed special programs for hiring older workers. Among these are Kelly Services, the Travelers Co., Control Data, and McDonald's. The AARP offers a variety of education and advocacy programs for older workers. Its Worker Equity Department offers resources and technical assistance to employers interested in hiring older workers.

CHAPTER 12

PEOPLE WITH DISABILITIES

Nearly 1 in 5 Americans Has a Disability

According to an August 1989 government census, there were 13.4 million working-age people (16–64) in the United States with some type of disability. In addition, about 36 percent of the men with disabilities who are of working age are in the labor force or actively seeking employment. The percentage of working-age women with disabilities in the labor force or seeking employment is 28 percent. Thus, 64 percent of men and 72 percent of women with disabilities are not in the labor force. People with disabilities are the highest unemployed group in the United States.

An additional figure of interest is that 5 of every 6 people with a disability were not born with that disability, but acquired it later in life. That statistic could be a flashing neon sign to those of us fortunate enough not to be a person with a disability that we're all just one incident away from becoming one.

The Law

President George Bush signed into law, on July 26, 1990, the Americans with Disability Act (ADA), which makes it illegal to discriminate against disabled individuals in employment, public accommodations, public service, and telecommunications. The employment provision (Title I of ADA) went into effect on July 26, 1992, for employers with 25 or more employees and as of July 26, 1994, for employers with 15–24 employees. It states that neither an employer nor an employment agency shall discriminate against a qualified individual with a disability in job application procedures, hiring, promotion, dismissal, compensation or benefits, job assignment, job training, or social/recreational programs.

Disability Defined

A disability under the ADA is a physical or mental impairment that substantially limits an individual's major life activities. If you can answer yes to any one of the following three items, then you are a person with a disability covered by the ADA:

1. Do you have a physical or mental impairment that substantially limits one or more major life activities?

2. Do you have a record of such an impairment (past illness or misclassified as having one)?

3. Are you regarded as having such an impairment? Wrongly regarded? Rumors of an impairment though there is none?

Some individuals are exempt from being covered by Title I of the ADA. These include federal government agency employers (generally covered by Section 501 of the Rehabilitation Act of 1973), Indian tribes, and tax-exempt private membership clubs. Religious organizations can give preference to individuals of their faith.

Disabilities Can Be Visible and Not Visible

Disabilities can include the more obvious—impaired sight or hearing, stuttering, or muscular or neurological disorders—and less obvious ones—cancer, emotional disturbance, epilepsy, or multiple chemical sensitivity (more commonly known as environmental illness), which is one of the fastest-growing disabilities today. Disabilities can also include individuals with AIDS or HIV and recovering alcoholics and drug addicts. Occasional or chronic alcoholics and illegal drug users are not covered.

One potential problem does exist when it comes to identifying disabilities. Over 1,000 possible disabilities could be covered, yet the ADA itself provides no listing. Therefore, court cases will determine the identification of certain conditions as being disabilities.

Attitude and Adjustment

Attitude

Anyone would probably agree that a person with a disability has a right to feel angry about his or her circumstances. It's easy to fall victim to blaming your problems on your disability. However, as unfortunate as it might be, a negative attitude will hurt you when it comes to finding a job. Employers want to hire enthusiastic and confident employees with good interpersonal and basic skills (e.g., writing and computer literate). You might feel powerless over your situation, but remember that only you can choose your attitude.

It's a fact that to get a job you must go face to face and meet with employers. Then you must convince them that you have the skills they need to get the job done right. Richard Bolles suggests focusing on what you and the employer have in common (where you're from, schools attended, or interests), rather than on differences (having a disability or not). This is called establishing rapport and becoming a known, rather than an unknown, quantity.

This might seem overwhelming at this point—researching, networking, and meeting with employers. You can work your way up to it. Set daily goals (risks/challenges), starting small and gradually working your way up to being able to hold good discussions with someone new to you (potential contact or employers). If you're having a confidence problem, then you might want to consider personal counseling. A good resource to consult with regard to the topic of attitude is *Flying Without Wings: Personal Reflections on Being Disabled,* by Arnold R. Beisser.

Adjustment

To adjust to your disability means to come to terms with it, accepting it and even with its problems going on to lead a satisfying life. Once you've accepted your disability, you finally become comfortable with yourself. This, in turn, will help others (including potential employers) to be more inclined to be accepting toward you and comfortable with you as well.

There's no denying the reality that certain challenges exist that can affect your attitude and adjustment. The major ones are the ignorance and fear of others toward persons with disabilities. You'll need to be prepared so that when the opportunity comes along, you'll be ready to educate the employer about your abilities and skills in a positive and constructive manner.

What Employers Can and Cannot Do

Melanie Witt specified what employers can and cannot do under the ADA.

Employers Cannot

- Use qualification standards, employment tests, or other selection criteria that would screen out persons with disabilities, unless the criteria are job related.

- Use employment tests without providing necessary assistance to people with disabilities (e.g., sensory, manual, or speaking problems).

- Offer tests that don't accurately reflect skills and aptitudes of individuals rather than their disabilities.

- Ask a job applicant during the pre-employment process whether he or she is disabled or not, or the nature and extent of the disability. (We'll return to this point later.)

Employers Can

- Ask the applicant about his or her ability to perform the job.

- Require a medical examination, but only after the position is offered.

- Require a pre-employment physical if all other applicants are required to have one.

Reasonable Accommodation

Reasonable accommodation means that an employer might be required to modify a task or workplace to accommodate a job-related functional limitation. Reasonable accommodation can apply to new employees, those promoted or transferred, and those with a new or progressive disability that has resulted in a functional limitation.

When seeking accommodation because of a functional limitation, Witt suggests not to speak generally about your disability (e.g., spinal cord injury), but rather describe your specific limitation (e.g., can't use left arm) and to what degree. An employer might be confused by general terms. He or she needs to know specifically how your disability pertains to the job.

Types of Accommodations

Accommodations can include any of the following, according to the ADA:

- Making workplace facilities accessible

- Modifying work schedule

- Restructuring the job

- Acquiring or modifying equipment or devices
- Changing job location
- Retraining or reassigning employees to vacant positions

Witt's book, *Job Strategies for People with Disabilities,* provides an in-depth description of many job-related functional limitations and types of accommodating solutions that can be developed, as well as related costs. For more information, you can contact the Job Accommodation Network (JAN), West Virginia University, P.O. Box 6122, Morgantown, WV 25606.

What You Can Do

Bolles stresses the importance of knowing specifically how and what needs to be redesigned. Once you've identified your career goal, talk with people doing that job who are disabled. This would be part of the networking/information interviewing process. Once you're clear on related job responsibilities, you'll have a better idea about what you're able to handle and what you might need an accommodation for. If your contacts are unable to advise you on necessary accommodations, then contact the Job Accommodation Network (JAN) for information in this area. In this way you'll be prepared, on top of the situation, and ready to advise employers on what would need to be done.

To Disclose or Not to Disclose?

When deciding whether to disclose your disability to an employer, take into account the visibility of your disability and the timing of your disclosure, if you decide to. In addition, Witt suggests using the answer to the following question as a guideline: "Does disclosure of my disability at this time and in this way support my objective of getting hired?"

If Your Disability Is Visible

When you're called for an interview, if you're talking with the person who will interview you, then this is a good time to disclose, once the interview has been set up. In this way you'll avoid surprising your interviewer when you arrive for the interview. If you don't disclose, the surprise could be followed by a feeling of mistrust, that you're trying to hide something, that you weren't being straight with the person.

On the other hand, some people with visible disabilities prefer to wait for the interview to disclose, in order to prevent the interviewer from forming negative stereotypes. However, this is a risky approach. To pull this off one would need to be strong and confident. You might have to overcome the interviewer's discomfort, silence, possible embarrassment, and even hostility. Generally speaking, in these situations employers don't like surprises.

An employer might have a difficult enough time with your disability, even when you disclose ahead of the interview. Remember, many people are ignorant about the capabilities of people with disabilities. Your task will be to educate the person and to put him or her at ease with regard to your disability.

If Your Disability Is Not Visible

You might have a disability that is not visible but would affect your performance on the job. In these situations, it's suggested that during the interview you disclose, to avoid having the interviewer feeling they've been misled. Here's where doing your homework can pay off. If you are aware of the job duties beforehand, you can come prepared to tell the employer exactly how your job performance might be affected and what accommodation would take care of the situation. Usually, without knowing, the employer's fears will lead them to think that the accommodations are worse than they actually are. In fact, most accommodations are not complicated or expensive to incorporate.

Not disclosing is an acceptable choice for you if you have a record of disability but no longer have that disability, or if your disability is invisible and won't affect your job performance or require any accommodation.

How You Disclose Is Important

The two methods suggested for disclosure related to job interviews so far are before (visible disability) or during (not visible, but affects job performance). You should be up front about who you are and what you can or cannot do, at the right time. Avoiding or denying will eventually make the situation worse.

However, it's not just the matter of disclosing that's important, it's how you do it. If you have come to accept yourself, that will allow you to present yourself in a positive manner that will help others to accept you as well. If you were able to do the research, convey exactly how your job performance might be affected, and offer suggestions about accommodations this will put the employer at ease. You could also help to educate the employer about the fact that nearly all employees with disabilities do their jobs as well as or better than other employees in similar jobs and are as reliable and punctual or more so.

Yet reality suggests that no matter how confident you might be, or how well you present yourself, there are still employers who discriminate against people with disabilities. Therefore, rejection is even more of a possibility for people with disabilities than it is for those without (and they receive their share of rejections as well). Bolles estimates that if disabled, you can expect up to 20–30 rejections before you finally hear a job being offered. (Of course, a lot depends on you, your career field and geographic location, and the economy.) With that number in mind, as discouraging as it sounds, you know that you cannot quit after only a few rejections, which is true for all job searchers.

However, if you find you're being rejected because of a lack of experience, you might consider volunteering as a way of gaining needed experience and proving to employers what you can do.

Networking Is the Key

As you work at developing your network of contacts, we suggest spreading your networking efforts beyond the disabled community. If you are referred to an employer via that network, there's a good chance that your contact person will disclose your disability for you, as a natural part of telling an employer about you, but at the same time portraying it in a positive light. Employers briefed by your mutual contact will not have a problem with your disability because the contact has already educated the person that is will not interfere with your job performance. In cases where it does interfere with job performance, you might want to target employers with a record of hiring people with disabilities.

A Final Thought

The law states that before making an offer of employment, an employer's questions about your disability must relate to essential functions of the job and determining whether you are qualified to perform them. Yet, out of genuine interest, your interviewer might ask questions about your disability because he or she is legitimately concerned about you and how you're handling everything. If you feel they're being sincere, consider pushing aside the ADA employer restriction on questions and offer a brief response that addresses the interviewer's concerns.

If the employer has concerns about your disability and doesn't ask questions, chances are that you won't get the job. Therefore, if you sense discomfort, you can attempt to address it in a calm, mature, and confident manner. By discussing your interviewer's questions you'll be doing much more for people with disabilities than by refusing to discuss them. It can go a long way to educating your interviewer and helping him or her to become more aware.

Usually, what's operating is an employer's lack of information about the capabilities of people with disabilities. Perhaps they're also acting out of stereotypes ranging from the idea that it costs more to employ people with disabilities (they assume insurance will increase, but it rarely does), to the fear that people with disabilities won't fit in with other workers. Witt's book, *Job Strategies for People with Disabilities,* provides an excellent discussion of these myths and facts you can use to help dispel them. It's smart to arm yourself with as much related information as possible.

What to Do If You Experience Discrimination

Discrimination against people with disabilities is hard to prove when it's related to the hiring process. However, once on the job, it is easier to gather information about discrimination related to promotion, compensation/benefits, job assignment, job training, or dismissal. You're in a position to compare the treatment offered to you with that of other employees.

If you believe you were discriminated against with regard to your disability, you can file a charge with your local Equal Employment Opportunity Commission (EEOC) office, found in the Yellow Pages under U.S. Government. Charges must be filed within 180 days of a discriminatory event that occurred after the related ADA section is in effect, 1992 or 1994. If you or the EEOC wins, you might expect, if applicable, a job offer, reasonable accommodation, promotion, retroactive seniority, restored benefits, reinstatement, or back pay for loss wages.

Is There a Brighter Side?

With a shrinking labor force of skilled workers, a worker shortage has been created, and people with disabilities have become a sought-after group. Petras and Petras report that new technology is making it easier for employers to hire people with disabilities. Among the products developed to help people with disabilities in the workplace are the following:

- A computer system to help deaf people communicate by telephone, developed by IBM

- Telesensory System's VersaBraille II Plus, which converts letters on a computer screen to Braille

- Telesensory System's Optiscan, a non-Braille reader

- Computer Conversation's Verbal Operating System (VOS), an electronic voice that reads what's on a screen

- IBM's PS/2 Screen Reader, also a computer with a voice

These and other computer devices are making it possible for people with disabilities to work in a wide range of occupations.

In addition, today's generation of young people have a greater awareness and appreciation for diversity. They've grown up with greater diversity in their lives, which leads to greater tolerance for differences and understanding of those differences. Eventually, myths and fears harbored by older workers (and others) will be replaced with facts and acceptance toward employees with disabilities. This is a goal that all of us can work toward, whether or not we have a disability.

Employment Recommendations

Petras and Petras recommend certain career areas for consideration by people with disabilities:

- The federal government, which since 1986 required all equipment purchased to be adaptable for people with disabilities

- Computer and other high-tech positions, like desktop publishing, because computer equipment is adaptable

For people with disabilities who would prefer to work at home, businesses like banking, insurance, publishing, and software development are heavy information businesses that rely on computers and thus are good work-at-home business possibilities. For additional information on the ADA contact the Office on the Americans with Disabilities Act, Civil Rights Division, U.S. Department of Justice, P.O. Box 66118, Washington, DC 20035.

CHAPTER 13

DUAL-CAREER COUPLES AND SINGLE PARENTS

Dual-Career Couples

The term *dual-career couple* denotes two people in an ongoing, committed relationship in which both partners are working and view their work as an important part of their identities. There might or might not be children. Many decisions are influenced by each partner's work situation, thus symbolizing its importance to them. The term *dual-earner couple* represents other motives for working, such as monetary or material possessions. Currently, more than 3 million dual-career couples are employed, which represents about 20 percent of employed couples. The majority, therefore, are dual-earner couples. Or perhaps one partner is an earner and the other is more serious about pursuing a career.

The Statistics

The following are the percentages of American households with both partners working: 1980, 45 percent; 1990, 65 percent; and predicted for 2000, 75 percent. In the last ten years, the number of working wives has doubled. More than half of mothers with children under age six are now working. What these numbers add up to is one fact: one income is simply not enough for many couples, and especially for families with children.

Balancing a Variety of Roles

In the process of managing your roles as spouse, parent, career professional, and perhaps the caretaker of aging parents, you might find it difficult to reach a workable balance between your career, relationship, and family in the time available to you. The result of this role overload can be feelings of frustration, guilt, and even remorse over the fear that you haven't fulfilled your career and family responsibilities. This, in turn, creates stress.

Coping: Communicating and Doing Your Share

Stress can be managed by both you and your partner by being sensitive and supportive, both by physically helping to get things done (e.g., meals, laundry, transportation, grocery shopping, cleaning, taking care of sick children) and providing emotional comfort. In addition, some role redefinition might be needed, especially when it comes to those (likely more men than women) who are not used to sharing household chores and child care–related duties. If the husband/father follows more traditional gender roles, then an unfair amount of responsibility falls on the wife/mother. Suggestions for helping to divide chores up include the following:

- Enlist the help of family members.
- Make use of good time management, organization, scheduling, and planning (dividing up tasks).
- Try to take advantage of any workplace flexibility.

If an imbalance of home responsibilities exists between partners, whether there are children involved or not, then roles should be redefined so that all involved feel they're being treated fairly and justly. This requires good communication. Each partner needs to understand what's happening with the other. Good communication requires both listening to your partner and talking things over.

Responsibilities can be divided according to skills, talents, and preferences. You and your partner will need to be flexible with both roles and tasks in order to manage daily life. If there are children, give them responsibilities as well that fit their age, physical condition, and other personal activities.

Handling Conflict With Your Partner

When there is conflict between you and your partner, negotiation becomes a key element of effective communication toward a solution that's acceptable to each of you—a win-win situation. Marian Stoltz-Loike identifies five typical responses couples use to resolve conflict.

Avoidance. Using avoidance is denying that a problem exists or can be resolved, which might be fine for small issues. However, when more meaningful issues need to be resolved, using avoidance only makes the situation worse.

Accommodation. As in the case of avoidance, accommodation also neglects the problem solving needed, though it does not deny its existence. Accepting that the conflict exists, partners decide not to deal with it, or one goes along with the other just to keep the peace. However, there are likely to still be underlying problems, especially with the partner doing the accommodating.

Confrontation. In confrontation, partners attack each other. This is a poor way to communicate and represents a lack of respect. Even if the issue is resolved, it won't help the relationship, the bigger picture.

Compromise. This is an acceptable solution, but one might be left with a lingering resentment and frustration, especially if they're compromising, in their opinion, to an unfair degree.

Collaboration or Problem Solving. Collaboration involves both partners working together to solve the problem at hand, with the goal of each feeling a "win" with the solution.

Areas of conflict for dual-career couples usually center around time—at work, with children, and with each other—chores, finances, and amount of business travel.

Raising Children

There's no question about it, adding children to a dual-career couple's household lends great stress to an already limited amount of available time. The amount of household tasks increases dramatically. If the relationship has gone smoothly up to this time, here's where a real test comes for how a couple communicates, solves problems, and assumes responsibility for what needs to get done.

The ages of the children seem to be more significant than the number of children, as far as impact on a couple's time. Infants obviously require more time and are more often sick. Also, sleeping and eating habits are irregular. In addition, usually parents just want to be around more for that special, new addition—the beginning of a family. Soon the importance of child care becomes a major issue. There seems to be a lack of space in quality programs, in addition to high costs. Eighty percent of working parents rely on services other than licensed day care centers, including friends, relatives, neighbors, or paid sitters either at their home or that of the sitter's.

The importance of good child care actually has some parents leaving the work force to be at home. Some parents might risk career advancement by choosing to be at home. At the same time, others will say not to underestimate the satisfaction of being with children. Clearly, child care is a critical issue for employees and employers alike. More needs to be done both in the workplace and in child care to give people, especially single parents, more options before having to leave work to care for children. Companies are coming around and offering more flexible programs for employees, including parental leave, part-time work, and flex-time.

How It's Going Could Depend on Your Relationship

An ongoing issue for dual-career couples is, how are the careers going? Career choices of both partners significantly affect the life, and thus career, of the other. How they resolve their career choices will affect work schedules, relocation possibilities, career development, development as a couple, and relationship to their children. Early in the partnership is a good time to discuss priorities with regard to family and career in each one's life.

Career competitiveness or jealousy between partners can hamper the providing of support, which is critical. This competitiveness sometimes focuses on who's doing better. For one to do better, he or she might need the other to assume more than a fair share of chores. Resolving such issues takes real working together. Some people resolve these issues by considering one partner to have the "lead" career and the other a secondary career. This can be determined by skills, talents, fields of expertise (one is more employable than the other), and earning potential.

Relocation

An employee's availability to relocate is considered an essential part of a progressive career in many companies. Obviously, in a dual-career couple the possibility of relocating is doubled. This could be the toughest career problem a dual-career couple faces. Whose career gets priority? If moves are infrequent, it might not be a problem. However, if one is continuously uprooted, the partner's career will suffer. If both partners' careers require frequent relocating, then they have a major problem. Sometimes employees have some influence with their employer about the timing of the relocation. Perhaps you can wait for your partner to find a job in the new locale, or for your child to grow to six months or older.

Corporate America Responds

The 1970s saw the entry of women into the labor force in greater numbers, preparing for careers traditionally held by men. During the 1980s, women worked hard, especially those with families, basically doing what they were supposed to do. Now, during the 1990s, women believe that not enough has changed to support them, and they're getting discouraged.

Corporate America's Realization.   Increasing numbers of U.S. corporations are recognizing that for employees to function in the workplace, they need to be able to reach a balance between their family and career concerns. Once viewed as a women's issue, family concerns are now viewed as an issue for both sexes. In addition, corporations realize that the labor force of skilled workers is shrinking. In order to hold on to their quality workers, female and male, they must offer a competitive array of benefits.

In many corporations, 60–70 percent of employees are part of a dual-career couple. The major concerns of corporations are recruitment, retention, productivity, and absenteeism. Many employees have family-related concerns. Corporate managers need to become more sensitive to the needs of the changing work force and to understand how these needs impact their business. They'll need to adapt in order to have a loyal and productive work force. A step in the right direction is the manner in which employees are evaluated. There should be more emphasis on the quality of work and less on the number of hours in the office.

Work/Family Programs Offered.   Child care services can be on-site, corporate-sponsored child care; a local child care center supported by the company; assisting employees with fees at an off-site child care center; or acting as a resource and referral service. In this last capacity, companies assist employees by contracting with local or nationwide consultants who help locate day care (including home-based child care in their community).

Some companies have a sick child policy, under which they contract with a sitter service to provide in-home care (or with a local hospital or sick care center), run an on-site sick care facility, subsidize the cost of sick care, or allow parents paid time off to care for a sick child.

Flex-time programs consist of nontraditional work hours. Flex-time can be in the form of a four-day work week (10 hours each day), a different sequence of hours worked (e.g., 7 a.m. to 3 p.m.), or other variations of the traditional work week. One potential problem in this area is who gets the benefit and who doesn't. At any particular corporation it's probably determined by a combination of policy and one's relationship with management.

Part-time work is set up so that hours can be reduced on a weekly basis, seasonally, or project-related. As corporations downsized, some found themselves too lean. They've turned to temporary and part-time help in many cases. This way they can keep their overall payroll down, as well as not providing benefits in some cases. Those companies that do provide benefits for part-time employees most likely do so for their most valued people, as a result of their skills and the role they play in the company.

In **job sharing,** two individuals share the responsibilities of one job, usually working two and a half days each. It's most important that the two employees are compatible, for they'll have to communicate well in order to promote the smooth transition of responsibilities. Job sharing is not usually in the form of a written policy. It seems to be more independently negotiated and specially arranged for particular employees. Again, as in the case of flextime (and even part-time work with benefits), a potential problem could arise related to who gets it and who doesn't.

A **flexible workplace** allows employees to work from home, either regularly or occasionally (e.g., when a crisis occurs at home). This possibility is greatly enhanced with telecommuting equipment, including the telephone, computers, modems, and fax machines.

With **flexible benefits,** employees can select the benefits best for them, cafeteria style. This allows a dual-career couple to avoid repetition in their combined benefits. In this way, they can attempt to cover their basic health, education, and child care needs more effectively.

The federal *Family and Medical Leave* Act (FMLA) of 1993 took effect August 5, 1993. The FMLA requires employers with 50 or more workers to provide unpaid leave to eligible employees who will be providing care to a newborn or newly adopted child or seriously ill family member or to take care of the employee's own serious illness.

The Act provides for up to 12 weeks of unpaid leave during any 12-month period and the employee is entitled to be restored to the same or an equivalent position on return from the leave. Studies have shown new mothers to be physically ready to return to work in three months, but not emotionally ready until six months after a birth. A part-time return option is often desirable. Therefore, a feasible program for corporations to offer could be 8–12 weeks of paid leave and an option to return part-time for several months thereafter.

Employee Assistance Programs (EAPs) offer one-on-one counseling for a wide range of personal problems. This type of program has the potential to be of great help to employees both emotionally and financially, with the high cost of these services outside of the workplace. However, to be successful it's vital to have qualified counseling professionals as well as total client (employee) confidentiality.

Can Work/Family Program Participation Hurt Your Career Advancement?

The major question about flexible work/family programs is whether they can hurt participants' career progress. Often, these programs are only offered to begin with to the more highly valued employees. Obviously, in these cases it probably won't interfere with career advancement. In major corporations, according to Susan Dynerman and Lynn Hayes, it's known that the surest route to promotion is to be willing to relocate, travel for business, and spend long hours at the office. Unfortunately, flex-time programs tend to slow participants' career development. Nontraditional hours are perceived, at times, to reflect a lesser degree of dedication, and time off might cause career goals to suffer. However, if one must take advantage of flex-time programs, part-time work seems to be considered a better option than job sharing if you have a concern about upper-level management goals.

All this adds up to a newer type of discrimination. One can be unfairly judged by focusing in on the number of hours present, rather than on the quality of work. Management attitudes need to change so that valuable part-time employees are perceived as serious, motivated workers with a professional commitment along with career goals and promotion potential.

Develop a Plan

Know Your Financial Needs. The first step is to identify specifically what your financial needs are. Then try to answer the following questions:

- What balance do you desire between work and relationships?
- How many hours are you willing to work per week?
- Which aspects of your job are most important to you?
- Can you develop a strategy to help management to see the benefits of work/family programs for the company?
- How might your career be affected?
- Could you combine flex-time with working at home as well?

Sell Your Idea. In developing your work/family plan to promote to your company, Dynerman and Hayes suggest considering the following points:

- **Demographics:** There is a shortage of skilled workers.

- **Replacement costs:** As the labor pool shrinks, replacement costs increase.

- **Productivity:** Workers will be more satisfied with the balance in their lives and are thus likely to be more productive.

- **Loyalty:** Workers stick with employers who offer flex-time programs.

- **Absenteeism:** Absences decrease because many causes of it are taken care of through flex-time programs.

- **Reduced turnover:** Employees can return to work full time as family demands decrease.

- **Recruiting power:** Employers will be able to attract the best employees.

- **Improved morale:** Employees feel that the company cares about them.

- **Turning innovation into income:** Corporations that have been innovative in these areas have shown better sales in some studies.

The bottom line is that flexible work/family benefits might cost employers more, but they gain it back (and perhaps more) in quality work by productive employees.

How to Identify Companies with Flex-Time Opportunities

If work/family benefits are important to you, then you can research in the library whether certain companies have these benefits. In addition, you can inquire about these benefits during the information interview stage of your job search process. If you're interested in part-time work, apply your networking efforts toward smaller companies, which are often in need of senior-level talent but can't afford it. In part-time arrangements, they can have it at half the cost. Your current employer is probably your best bet for possible flex-time benefits. Flex-time seems to go first to those already on the payroll.

Single Parents

Although many single parents do well in this most demanding environment, the single-parent family can also be the source of multiple stressors for both parent and children. The main cause for the recent surge in the number of single-parent homes in the United States is the increased divorce rate. It's predicted that 40–50 percent of U.S. children born after 1980 will experience a divorce in the family. Divorce forces many parents and children to move away from extended families and often results in financial hardships as well.

The Statistics

Of all mothers in the U.S. labor force, one-fourth are single with children under age 18. It's estimated that one in every four American children lives in a single-parent home. Of those living in a single-parent home, 9 of 10 children reside in a household headed by the mother. Two-thirds of all people heading households with children under 18 are in the labor force, and over half of them are full-time.

Responsibility Times Two

All of the same responsibilities attached to a dual-career couple (work, housing, child care arrangements, household chores, and relationships) also exist for the single parent. However, the impact is doubled because single parents are on their own. Therefore, time management, organization, planning, and communication (with children, former spouse, and significant other) take on an even greater emphasis for the single parent.

Finding time for children is difficult enough for a dual-career couple, but it's even more difficult for a single parent. This can be a source of discouragement for many single parents, who are not able to spend the amount of time they would like with their children. Major adjustments must be made to balance your time. Once divorced, a single parent finds him or herself more dependent on a large number of people than they were when married. A single parent's needs might include day care, an after-school program to take care of children until their work day ends, and babysitters (when needed in the evenings). Finding quality programs and personnel are always an issue.

Child Care.   The lack of affordable, reliable, and quality child care is a problem for all working parents and is an acute concern for single parents. As a result of being on their own, it's even more important for single parents to have some form of flexible hours at work in order to deal with child care arrangements and the child's school attendance schedule. This forces many single parents into hourly wage jobs because of more flexibility in hours. This type of job includes waiting tables, domestic help, secretarial, and clerical. Entry into better paying jobs with benefits depends on the key issue of child care.

Lower Socioeconomic Level.   All levels of income are represented by single parents, but a disproportionate number are of a lower socioeconomic level. Approximately 40 percent are near the poverty line. Even among wealthier families, upon a marital breakup women's earnings, plus support, usually only add up to about 50 percent of their former income.

On the Job.   Work schedules might need to be changed to handle one's role as a single parent. Life is certainly simpler if you work for an understanding employer who offers some form of flex-time and other work/family benefit programs. If not, there's always the possibility that you will be able to negotiate something for yourself. Your negotiation position with employers will be stronger if you review the selling points outlined in the previous section, dual-career couples. These points will aid you in convincing your employer of the benefits they stand to gain by offering work/family programs.

Single Fathers

Recent Increases.   About 10 percent of single-parent households are headed by fathers. For men, perhaps a bit more than for women, one issue is that they need to adopt new ways of measuring success. Career advancement might not have the emphasis it once did. Now success can be looked on as how you are doing as a parent, as well. However, it's hard to do both, career and child rearing, well. One usually suffers. The following career areas can be affected by the responsibilities of being a single parent: job mobility, earning power, freedom to work late, job performance, and job advancement. When it comes to single parenting, it's the role of being the parent and the tasks involved, not the gender of the parent, that makes single parenting difficult.

Suggestions for Single Parents

The best advice is not to try to do it on your own; get involved with a single-parent support group. Parents Without Partners, founded in 1957, is the largest self-help group for single parents in the United States. Any custodial or non-custodial parent, whether single, divorced, widowed, or never married, can join. Social activities are included in which single parents and their children can meet others like themselves. Meeting others involved with the same life issues can be a great source of emotional support as well as new friendships. When you're connected to others in the same situation as yourself, there's also the possibility of helping each other out. For example, you can trade off watching the children with someone, which enables each of you to run errands that otherwise would be difficult to accomplish.

We would also suggest soliciting help from your other friends and family members. Sometimes they will be able to run an errand for you, watch the children, or just be a good listener. Through careful planning and use of all available resources, single parents will be able to maintain some balance between work and family and come through it in good shape. Yet, at times it might all seem to be too much, resulting in excessive suffering for you or your children. If you think that personal counseling would be helpful, consider seeking professional counseling.

CHAPTER 14

Ex-Military Personnel

The Transition from Military to Civilian Life

With respect to career possibilities, ex-military personnel will find that military expertise, tactical skills, and wartime experience are not usually marketable. However, leadership and management skills are always in demand. Consider the experience you have gained in such areas as encounters with different cultures and ideas through world travel; management of materials, resources, and equipment; being part of a team effort; or the operation and maintenance of high-tech systems. Maybe you even learned a foreign language, which can open a door for you in today's global marketplace.

Employers are always looking for proven achievers and leaders. There is a high demand for most technically trained professionals. Caution is advised with regard to the defense industry, where jobs, if available, might not be stable.

The biggest challenge for ex-military personnel is in identifying skills used in the military and then translating them into language (and related job titles) that will be understood in the general marketplace. Some sources to help you do this are covered here. Using the *Guide for Occupational Exploration* (GOE), you can translate your higher General Occupational Theme scores from the Strong Interest Inventory into related Work Group numbers. Then look up specific job titles with *Dictionary of Occupational Titles* (DOT) numbers. The GOE includes a section titled: "Military Occupational Specialties with Corresponding Subgroups," which lists occupational specialties for each of the five branches of the armed forces and identifies the subgroups of related Work Groups in which comparable civilian jobs can be located. Another option is to check the personnel manual for your branch of the services, which links military jobs and tasks to the civilian DOT job titles. Finally, the two-volume *Military Occupation Training Data Series* is available from Defense Manpower Data Center, 1600 Wilson Boulevard, Suite 400, Arlington, VA 22209.

Consider Civil Service

W. Dean Lee points out that civil service is often a natural next step for military personnel. However, mid-level and senior-level jobs are very competitive, due in part to salaries and benefits approaching those of similar civilian positions. In other words, more workers from the private sector are attracted to jobs here as well.

To learn more about civil-service opportunities, contact the Federal Job Information Center located in major cities for available jobs in your region and a Federal Job Opportunities list. Also, check with your state employment office. It receives position announcements, though some will not be current. If you are interested in specific federal agencies, you can contact them directly. Their local field offices might have information about upcoming openings and future possibilities as well. Finally, request *Federal Career Opportunities* from the Federal Research Service, P.O. Box 1059, Vienna, VA 22180.

In the U.S. territories and at U.S. installations in foreign countries, most positions are offered to locally eligible Americans, their dependents, or foreign nationals. These positions are usually not published outside the local area. For information about overseas opportunities, write to the Federal Job Information Center at the following addresses:

- **Atlantic Region** (Puerto Rico, Panama, Europe)
  Office of Personnel Management
  1900 E. Street, NW
  Washington, DC 20415

- **Pacific Region** (Alaska, Hawaii, U.S. Territories, and Asia)
  Office of Personnel Management
  Federal Building, Room 1310
  300 Ala Moana Boulevard
  Honolulu, HI 96850

- **Saudi Arabia**
  Department of the Army
  Saudi Arabia Consolidated Civilian Personnel Office
  Riyadh, Saudi Arabia
  APO NY 09038

Department of Defense and Other Federal Agencies

The Department of Defense (DOD) is still the top employer of U.S. personnel overseas and the agency with the most vacancies. Other federal agencies worth checking into are the Foreign Agriculture Service, DOD Dependent Schools, National Oceanic and Atmospheric Administration, State Department, U.S. Information Agency, Army Corps of Engineers, Agency for International Development, and the Peace Corps.

You might want to increase your options by checking for positions with city, county, and state government offices. If you're a retiring, regular commissioned or warrant officer, you would benefit by obtaining a non-federal job, because it will not affect your retirement pay. Federal employment will cause a reduction in retirement pay, except for enlisted personnel and reserve officers.

The SF-171 form begins your federal employment application process. This form is available at any local Office of Personnel Management (OPM). Also, request the publication, *Veteran's Preference in Federal Employment,* from the OPM. It contains general information about determining a veteran's status, preference in examination, credit for time of service, and retirement pay regulations. You will complete a separate SF-171 form for each position you're interested in. Be sure to include detailed listings of your accomplishments in the space provided. This information will help you to receive the highest possible merit rating from the examiner. Many veterans are eligible for additional credit on their federal tests (5–10 points). If no test is required, your rating will be based on your education and experience, which you will also list on the SF-171 form.

The Corporate World

Lee reports that ex-military personnel are actively recruited by corporate America. Business managers and owners see ex-military personnel as follows:

- Highly motivated, dependable, and disciplined

- Technically trained, with many transferable skills

- Team players that strive for excellence

- Strong leaders, able to adapt to crisis and work under pressure

- Mature and responsible with a strong work ethic

Nonetheless, your resume is even more important than for other career changers. It's the medium for translating military experience and accomplishments into language that the business world can understand and appreciate. Avoid using military terminology, unless you're sending your resume to military contractors and you're sure they'll understand it. One resource that can help in this task is "Marketing Yourself for a Second Career," which has examples of "civilianized" resumes. It is available for a small fee from the Retired Officers Association, 201 North Washington Street, Alexandria, VA 22314.

Of particular importance are the transferable/functional skills that you gained from the military. Some common transferable/functional skills that many ex-military personnel can document are as follows:

- Communication (oral/written, public speaking, promoting events/ projects)

- Management (personnel, project, facility)

- Planning (strategic, cost cutting)

- Security operations

- Training

If you need to develop additional skills, check your military benefits for available training programs. You can use your VA benefits to obtain many types of education, including college, refresher courses, night classes, apprenticeships, correspondence schools, language training, and specialized programs.

It's in your best interest to at least know your comparable value. If you do and you are ever offered a salary below it, you'll be prepared to make your case for a fairer compensation package. When figuring your comparable value, look at your total compensation figure, which includes all benefits. Review your Personal Statement of Military Compensation, released each February.

Owning Your Own Business

The Federal government publishes a free book for veterans interested in starting, financing, and managing a small business:

- *Veterans Handbook* (Washington, DC: Small Business Administration, 1989).

The Small Business Administration gives preference to veterans in obtaining assistance and can guarantee loans made to veterans by banks and savings and loan associations.

Sources of Additional Help

If you are or were an officer, contact The Retired Officer Association (TROA), 201 North Washington Street, Alexandria, VA 22314. TROA has an Officer Placement Service from which you can receive a monthly magazine, job referral notices, resume preparation assistance, career counseling, and access to the TROA Career Research Center (most useful for those in the Virginia area).

Also consult the following organizations for job counseling, referrals, placement assistance, job fairs, and related services:

- Air Force Association
  1501 Lee Highway
  Arlington, VA 22209

- Association of the United States Army
  Career Assistance Service
  2425 Wilson Boulevard
  Arlington, VA 22201

- National Association for Uniformed Services
  5535 Hempstead Way
  Springfield, VA 22151

- Navy League of the United States
  2300 Wilson Boulevard
  Arlington, VA 22201

- The Non-Commissioned Officer Association
  225 North Washington Street
  Alexandria, VA 22314

- Marine Corps Association
  P.O. Box 1775
  Quantico, VA 22134

CHAPTER 15

MID-LEVEL MANAGERS

Will You Be a Victim of Corporate Restructuring?

The Statistics

Nearly half of all large U.S. corporations were restructured in the 1980s. It is estimated that during the same period, *Fortune* 500 companies eliminated 3.6 million workers. This trend has continued into the 1990s. Mid-level managers account for 5–8 percent of all workers, but 17 percent of the layoffs. Overall, some estimates have the number of mid-level executives victimized by downsizing to be around 10–12 million.

Christopher Kirkwood discusses two major reasons leading to layoffs from downsizing. The first employees targeted in downsizing are usually those who debate everything the boss says, make the boss look bad in public, joke around about the company, and tend to be uncooperative. Another type of employee at risk is those who fail to keep up with changing technology or develop new skills as the times demand.

Outplacement Counseling

If you are or will be a victim of downsizing, your company might provide some form of outplacement services. Outplacement services usually include the following:

- Career counseling, including assessment and/or testing to help you identify career options
- Resume and cover letter preparation
- Interviewing techniques
- Job search methods, including networking, want ads, employment agencies, executive recruiters, telephone techniques, and industry directories and trade journals
- Researching employers
- The emotional side of losing a job, specifically stress, anxiety, and depression

Where Can You Go?

Many downsized mid-level managers left fields like marketing, management, sales, and finance to move into franchising, consulting, and family firms or new businesses. Franchising has experienced more than 33 percent growth since 1986. Those choosing consulting have helped its overall growth since 1988 to be more than 200,000. Newer consultants were often retained on short-term contracts by organizations that let them go. One of every six mid-level managers and executives who lost their jobs due to corporate downsizing and restructuring during the late 1980s went on to create their own small business. They were either unable or unwilling to relocate to another large company. It's estimated that by the year 2005, 11.5 million workers will be self-employed (a 15 percent increase from 1992), more than twice the number it was in 1970. Developing a new business is often made possible by a second income in the family, which helps to pay the general living expenses during the important and costly start-up period.

Corporations of the Future: What Will They Be Like?

Outsourcing Is Here

When downsizing finally comes to an end, the larger corporations will not begin to rehire in large numbers. They will probably realize cost savings and efficiency by contracting goods and services from smaller companies, where many of their former employees will be working. This method of doing business is known as outsourcing.

Outsourcing occurs when upper managers realize that they do not have to employ all the people, all the time, to get the work done. The larger corporation of the future will have a small core of central employees and many smaller businesses working under contract. The core workers will be professional staff essential to the organization. A great deal of work will be contracted out to other organizations as needed. Finally, there will be a flexible labor force made up of part-time and temporary workers to be called in when customer demands present themselves. Even the core employees will be moved around due to hiring for specific, temporary assignments.

Contracting

Contracting is a joint venture with an employer to develop strategies to solve pressing company problems. To make a living from contracting, one needs to be always working on a project or getting recruited for future projects. Contracting is another situation in which networking takes on added importance. You will need word-of-mouth credibility via your contacts to get hired for new projects. Careers now and in the future might include some time spent in the core, some in outsourcing jobs, and perhaps some in part-time work as well.

Some Suggestions

Stay Abreast of Your Field.   More than ever before, you need to be on top of what's happening (and will happen) in your career field. Then, as you see the need and importance of sharpening and expanding your skills, take the necessary action and follow through. Three common ways to gain new skills are on-the-job training, courses offered through your company, and college courses.

Identify Growth Companies.   Instead of attempting to identify growth industries (or in addition to it), you might consider looking for a growth company, one in an existing industry that has adapted well to the new information technology.

Is Non-profit a Viable Alternative for You?

There is often a shift in values at mid-life toward a desire to give something back to society. If you are victim of a corporate restructuring, you might consider directing your efforts toward employment with a nonprofit organization. Mid-level managers can find worthwhile ways to apply their leadership skills in the nonprofit sector. Non-profits are entered by former corporate types via a variety of career fields, including public relations, law, government, education, social services, retail, and banking.

They sometimes find non-profits just as stressful as their former corporate management positions, but often much more meaningful. If this sounds appealing, what cause or organization might you want to help out? What types of problems would you most like to work on solving? How do your interests relate? Consider what you want your purpose or mission to be at this point in life.

What Kind of Salary Can You Expect?

In general, career changers take a salary cut when moving to the nonprofit area and hope to catch up and even surpass it in the near future. One question that usually comes up about employment with nonprofit organizations is that they might not pay much. Just because they're non-profit doesn't necessarily mean they don't pay their top executives a decent salary (especially the larger non-profits). Nevertheless, a cut in salary is likely and might be as high as 20–30 percent. This, of course, depends on what your former salary was. For information on salaries in non-profits, contact Abbott, Langer & Associates, 548 First Street, Crete, IL 60417, for its surveys on compensation in non-profit organizations. It is true that most nonprofits are constantly struggling to raise enough funds. Therefore, if you have grant writing or fund raising skills, you become even more valuable.

Resources for Researching Non-profits

- ACCESS
  Networking in the Public Interest
  50 Beacon Street, 4th Floor
  Boston, MA 02108
     Publishes *Community Jobs: The Employment Newspaper for the Non-Profit Sector.*

- *ReCareering*
  Publications Plus, Inc.
  801 Skokie Boulevard, Suite 221
  Northbrook, IL 60062
     A newsletter designed for downsized managers, early retirees, and career changers.

- Planning Communications
  7515 Oak Avenue
  River Forest, IL 60305
    Publishes *Non-Profits Job Finder, Great Careers: The Fourth of July Guide to Careers, Internships and Volunteer Opportunities in the Non-Profit Sector,* and *Good Works: A Guide to Careers in Social Change.*

- Check local libraries to identify which branches receive information on non-profits from the Foundation Center in New York.

Dealing with Executive Recruiters

Despite a percentage of head hunters that will not have your best interests at heart, there's no single action you can take that will do more to expedite your job search than to contact a good head hunter. To increase the possibility of good results in working with head hunters, be flexible, view most things as negotiable, and be realistic about yourself and your skills.

Two Types of Head Hunters

The contingency head hunter firm learns of a vacancy and contacts the person responsible for filling it. This person agrees to pay the head hunting firm a commission only if one of its candidates is selected for the position. Therefore, if you're not an exact match, don't expect much in the way of results from this method. The retainer head hunting firm is selected by a company with a vacancy to be its agent in identifying and presenting candidates to fill the vacant position. The head hunting firm gets paid whether or not a candidate is selected. Therefore, a head hunting firm that consistently fails to fill vacant positions will not be in business for long.

Kirkwood suggests spending most of your time with contingency firms. However, this can be risky if you're currently employed. Word could get out that you're looking, especially if the head hunting firm spreads your resume around more than you're aware of.

Strategies for Dealing with Head Hunters

Good head hunters will call their contacts right away. For a candidate who fits a position, the firm might be able to schedule an interview within 7–10 days. In general, give a head hunting firm up to 45 days to get you an interview. If a firm can't get you interviewing in 45 days, then try another.

If you're contacted by a retainer firm that states it has a position of interest to you, get the details: who referred them to you, the job description, experience requirements, salary range, and possible need to relocate. The key issue when dealing with head hunters is control. The idea is to establish a good relationship with a reputable firm so that you can arrange for them to inform you of each opening that is worth submitting your resume for and even seek your permission first. Head hunters should be just part of your job search strategy. Use networking most of the time and include head hunters if your background and experience fit with the type of professionals they seek to work with.

APPENDIX A:
•••••••••••••••••••••

REFERENCES

American Psychiatric Association. (1994) *Diagnostic and Statistical Manual of Mental Disorders: DSM-IV.* 4th ed. Washington, DC.

Baker, B.E., and B.B. Millsaps, eds. (1991) *The National Directory of Internships.* 8th ed. Raleigh, NC: National Society for Internships and Experiential Education.

Bear, J. (1993) *Bear's Guide to Earning College Degrees Non-Traditionally.* 11th ed. Benicia, CA: C & B Publishing.

Beisser, A.R. (1989) *Flying Without Wings: Personal Reflections on Being Disabled.* New York: Doubleday.

Bolles, R.N. *What Color Is Your Parachute? A Practical Manual for Job Hunters and Career Changers.* Annual. Berkeley, CA: Ten Speed Press.

_____. (1991) *How to Create a Picture of Your Ideal Job or Next Career: The Quick Job-Hunting (and Career-Changing) Map.* Berkeley, CA: Ten Speed Press.

Boyer, R., and D. Savageau. (1989) *Places Rated Almanac: Your Guide to Finding the Best Places to Live in America.* New York: Prentice Hall.

Bradley, L.J. (1990) *Counseling Midlife Career Changers.* Garrett Park, MD: Garrett Park Press.

Branden, N. (1988) *How to Raise Your Self-Esteem.* New York: Bantam Books.

Bridges, W. (1980) *Transitions: Making Sense of Life's Changes.* Reading, MA: Addison-Wesley.

Burka, J.B., and L.M. Yuen. (1983) *Procrastination: Why You Do It, What to Do about It.* Reading, MA: Addison-Wesley.

Burton, M.L., and R.A. Wedemeyer. (1991) *In Transition: From the Harvard Business School Club of New York Personal Seminar in Career Management.* New York: HarperBusiness.

Dynerman, S.B., and L.O. Hayes. (1991) *The Best Jobs in America for Parents Who Want Careers and Time for Children, Too.* New York: Rawson Associates.

Ellis, A. (1977) *How to Live With and Without Anger.* New York: Reader's Digest Press.

Erikson, E. (1950) *Childhood and Society.* New York: Norton.

Field, S. (1992) *100 Best Careers for the Year 2000.* New York: Prentice Hall/Arco.

Germann, R., and P. Arnold. (1980) *Job and Career Building.* Berkeley, CA: Ten Speed Press.

Gilligan, C. (1982) *In a Different Voice.* Cambridge, MA: Harvard University Press.

Haldane, B. (1988) *Career Satisfaction and Success.* Rev. ed. New York: AMACOM.

Hansen, J.C. (1992) *User's Guide for the Strong Interest Inventory.* Rev. ed. Palo Alto, CA: Consulting Psychologists Press.

Harrington, T.F., and A.J. O'Shea, Eds. (1984) *Guide for Occupational Exploration.* 2nd ed. Circle Pines, MN: American Guidance Service.

Hauter, J. (1993) *The Smart Woman's Guide to Career Success.* Hawthorne, NJ: Career Press.

Hewitt, J. (1977) *The Complete Yoga Book.* New York: Schocken Books.

Holland, J.L. (1985) *Making Vocational Choices: A Theory of Vocational Personalities and Work Environments.* 2nd ed. Englewood Cliffs, NJ: Prentice Hall.

Jung, C.G. (1971) *Psychological Types.* Palo Alto, CA: Consulting Psychologists Press.

Kennedy, J.L., and D. Laramore. (1992) *Joyce Lain Kennedy's Career Book.* Lincolnwood, IL: VGM Career Horizons.

Kirkwood, C. (1993) *Your Services Are No Longer Required: The Complete Job-Loss Recovery Book.* New York: Plume.

Kleiman, C. (1994) *The 100 Best Jobs for the 1990s and Beyond.* Chicago: Dearborn Financial.

Lee, W.D. (1991) *Beyond the Uniform: A Career Transition Guide for Veterans and Federal Employees.* New York: Wiley.

Levinson, D.J., et al. (1978) *The Seasons of a Man's Life.* New York: Ballantine Books.

Lock, R.D. (1992) *Taking Charge of Your Career Direction: Career Planning Guide, Book I.* Pacific Grove, CA: Brooks/Cole.

_____. (1992) *Job Search: Career Planning Guide Book II.* Pacific Grove, CA: Brooks/Cole.

Macdaid, G.P., M.H. McCaulley, and R.I. Kainz. (1986) *Myers-Briggs Type Indicator Atlas of Type Tables.* Gainesville, FL: Center for Applications of Psychological Type.

Maze, M., and D. Mayall, eds. (1991) *The Enhanced Guide for Occupational Exploration.* Indianapolis, IN: JIST Works.

McHolland, J. (1987) *A Positive Approach to Self-Development.* Evanston, IL: National Center for Human Potential Seminars.

Mills, C.W. (1951) *White Collar: The American Middle Class.* New York: Oxford University Press.

Moskowitz, M.,R. Levering, and M. Katz. (1990) *Everybody's Business: A Field Guide to the 400 Leading Companies in America.* New York: Doubleday.

Myers, I.B. (1987) *Introduction to Type.* Palo Alto, CA: Consulting Psychologists Press.

_____, and M.H. McCaulley. (1985) *Manual: A Guide to the Development and the Use of the Myers-Briggs Type Indicator.* Palo Alto, CA: Consulting Psychologists Press.

_____. (1991) *MBTI Type Booklets.* Palo Alto, CA: Consulting Psychologists Press.

Olson, N. (1988) *Starting a Mini-Business: A Guidebook for Seniors.* Sunnyvale, CA: Four Oaks Publishing.

Parker, Y. (1989) *The Damn Good Resume Guide.* Berkeley, CA: Ten Speed Press.

Petras, K., and R. Petras. (1993) *Jobs '94.* New York: Simon & Schuster.

Rathus, S.A., and J.S. Nevid. (1977) *BT: Behavior Therapy: Strategies for Solving Problems in Living.* Garden City, NY: Doubleday.

Ray, S.N. (1991) *Job Hunting after 50: Strategies for Success.* New York: Wiley.

Riehle, K.A. (1991) *What Smart People Do When Losing Their Jobs.* New York: Wiley.

Rivera, M. (1991) *The Minority Career Book.* Holbrook, MA: Bob Adams.

Robbins, P.I. (1978) *Successful Midlife Career Change: Self-Understanding and Strategies for Action.* New York: AMACOM.

Schlossberg, N.K. (1989) *Overwhelmed: Coping with Life's Ups and Downs.* Lexington, MA: Lexington Books.

Selden, I.L. (1988) *Going into Business for Yourself: New Beginnings after 50.* Washington, DC: American Association of Retired Persons and Glenview, IL: Scott, Foresman.

Seligman, M.E.P. (1990) *Learned Optimism: How to Change Your Mind and Your Life.* New York: Pocket Books.

Sheehy, G. (1976) *Passages: Predictable Crises of Adult Life.* New York: Bantam Books.

Shields, C., and L.C. Shields. (1993) *Work, Sister, Work: Why Black Women Can't Get Ahead and What They Can Do About It.* Secaucus, NJ: Carol Publishing Group.

Simon, S. B. (1988) *Getting Unstuck: Breaking Through Your Barriers to Change.* New York: Warner Books.

_____, L.W. Howe, and H. Kirschenbaum. (1972) *Values Clarification: A Handbook of Practical Strategies for Teachers and Students.* New York: Hart Publishing.

Simosko, S. (1985) *Earn College Credit for What You Know.* Washington, DC: Acropolis Books.

Smith, A.W. (1990) *Overcoming Perfectionism: The Super Human Syndrome.* Deerfield Beach, FL: Health Communications.

Stoltz-Loike, M. (1992) *Dual Career Couples: New Perspectives in Counseling.* Alexandria, VA: American Counseling Association.

Stoodley, M. (1990) *Information Interviewing: What It Is and How to Use It.* Garrett Park, MD: Garrett Park Press.

U.S. Department of Commerce. *Franchise Opportunities Handbook.* Annual. Washington, DC: Government Printing Office.

U.S. Department of Education. (1988) *The Student Guide: Five Federal Financial Aid Programs, 88–89.* Washington, DC.

U.S. Department of Labor. (1991) *The Dictionary of Occupational Titles.* 4th ed., rev. Indianapolis, IN: JIST Works.

_____. *Monthly Labor Review.* Monthly. Washington, DC.

_____. *Occupational Outlook Handbook.* (1994–95) Lincolnwood, IL: VGM Career Horizons.

_____. *Occupational Outlook Quarterly.* Quarterly. Washington, DC.

Witt, M.A. (1992) *Job Strategies for People with Disabilities.* Princeton, NJ: Peterson's Guides.

APPENDIX B:
••••••••••••••••••••••

RECOMMENDED READINGS

Being Fired

Dubin, J.A., and M.R. Keveles. (1990) *Fired for Success: How to Turn Losing Your Job into the Opportunity of a Lifetime.* New York: Warner Books.

Koltnow, E., and L.S. Dumas. (1990) *Congratulations! You've Been Fired: Sound Advice for Women Who've Been Terminated, Pink Slipped, Downsized, or Otherwise Unemployed.* New York: Fawcett Columbine.

Morin, W.J., and J.C. Cabrera. (1991) *Parting Company: How to Survive the Loss of a Job and Find Another Successfully.* San Diego: Harcourt Brace Jovanovich.

Career Change

Banning, K., and A. Friday. (1991) *How to Change Your Career.* Lincolnwood, IL: VGM Career Horizons.

Boldt, L.G. (1993) *Zen and the Art of Making a Living.* New York: Arkana.

Brans, J. (1989) *Take Two: True Stories of Real People Who Dared to Change Their Lives.* New York: Doubleday.

Danna, J. (1960) *Starting Over: You in the New Workplace.* Briarwood, NY: Palomino Press.

Kanchier, C. (1991) *Dare to Change Your Job and Your Life.* New York: Master Media.

Moreau, D. (1990) *Take Charge of Your Career: How to Survive and Profit from a Mid-Career Change.* Washington, DC: Kiplinger Books.

Dress and Appearance

Molloy, John T. (1988) *John Molloy's New Dress for Success.* New York: Warner.

_____. (1977) *The Woman's Dress for Success Book.* New York: Warner.

Nicholson, J., and J. Lewis-Crum. (1986) *Color Wonderful.* New York: Bantam.

Ex-Military Personnel

Betterton, D.M. (1990) *How the Military Will Help You Pay for College: The High School Student's Guide to ROTC, the Academies, and Special Programs.* 2nd ed. Princeton, NJ: Peterson's Guides.

Drier, H.N., Jr. (1994) *Out of Uniform: A Career Transition Guide for Ex-Military Personnel.* Lincolnwood, IL: VGM Career Horizons.

Reardon, D.F. (1993) *In or Out of the Military: How to Make Your Own Best Decision.* Oak Harbor, WA: Pepper Press.

Roberts, R. (1989) *The Veteran's Guide to Benefits.* New York: Signet Books.

Schlachter, G.A., and D.R. Weber. (1990) *Financial Aid for Veteran's, Military Personnel, and Their Dependents, 1990–91.* San Carlos, CA: Reference Service Press.

Small Business Administration. (1989) *Veteran's Handbook.* Washington, DC.

Financial Aid for Additional Education and Training

College Board Publications. *Meeting College Costs.* New York.

College Scholarship Service. (1994) *The College Costs and Financial Aid Handbook.* 14th ed. New York: College Entrance Examination Board.

Dilts, S.W., D.L. Martin, and M.A. Zidrik, eds. (1989) *Peterson's College Money Handbook, 1990: The Only Complete Guide to Scholarships, Costs, and Financial Aid at U.S. Colleges.* 7th ed. Princeton, NJ: Peterson's Guides.

Federal Student Aid Program. *The Student Guide to Federal Financial Aid Programs.* Washington, DC.

Macmillan. (1987) *The College Blue Book: Scholarships, Fellowships, Grants, and Loans.* New York.

Peterson's Guides. *Peterson's Financial Aid Service.* Princeton, NJ.

Women's Equity Action League. *Better Late Than Never: Financial Aid for Re-Entry Women Seeking Education and Training.* Washington, DC.

Future Trends

Aburdene, P., and J. Naisbitt. (1992) *Megatrends for Women.* New York: Villard Books.

Basta, N. (1989) *Top Professions: The 100 Most Popular, Dynamic and Profitable Careers in America Today.* Princeton, NJ: Peterson's Guides.

Boyett, J.H. and H.P. Conn. (1992) *Workplace 2000: The Revolution Reshaping American Business.* New York: Plume.

Cetron, M., and O. Davies. (1991) *Crystal Globe! The Have and Have Nots of the New World Order.* New York: St. Martin's Press.

Feingold, S.N., and M.H. Atwater. (1989) *New Emerging Careers.* Garrett Park, MD: Garrett Park Press.

Harkavy, M.D. (1990) *101 Careers: A Guide to the Fastest Growing Opportunities.* New York: Wiley.

Krannich, R.L., and C.R. Krannich. (1993) *The Best Jobs for the 1990s and Into the 21st Century.* Manassas Park, VA: Impact Publications.

Naisbitt, J. and P. Aburdene. (1990) *Megatrends 2000: Ten New Directions for the 1990s.* New York: Morrow.

Satterfield, A. (1992) *Where the Jobs Are: The Hottest Careers for the '90s.* Hawthorne, NJ: Career Press.

U.S. Department of Labor. (April 1990) *Outlook 2000: Occupational Projections and Training Data Bulletin 2351.* Washington, DC.

Interviewing Skills

Medley, H.A. (1984) *Sweaty Palms: The Neglected Art of Being Interviewed.* Berkeley, CA: Ten Speed Press.

Yate, M. (1993) *Knock'em Dead: The Ultimate Job Seeker's Handbook.* Holbrook, MA: Bob Adams.

Job Search Strategies

Bruce, Robert B. (1994) *Executive Job Search Strategies: The Guide for Career Transitions.* Lincolnwood, IL: VGM Career Horizons.

Figler, H. (1988) *The Complete Job Search Handbook: All the Skills You Need to Get Any Job and Have a Good Time Doing It.* New York: Henry Holt.

Jackson, T. (1991) *Guerrilla Tactics in the New Job Market.* New York: Bantam Books.

Krannich, R.L. (1993) *Careering and Re-Careering for the '90s: Skills and Strategies for Shaping Your Future.* San Luis Obispo, CA: Impact Publications.

Wendleton, K. (1992) *Through the Brick Wall: How to Job Hunt in a Tight Market.* New York: Villard.

Managers

Bruce, R.C. (1994) *Executive Job Search Strategies: The Guide for Career Transition.* Lincolnwood, IL: VGM Career Horizons.

Minorities

Educational Facilitators. (1990) *Dollars for College: A Handbook of Financial Aid Sources for Minority Students: An Easy-to-Use Resources Matching Your College Major with Private Scholarship Dollars.* Chicago, IL.

Garrett Park Press. (1992) *Minority Organizations: A National Directory.* 4th ed. Garrett Park, MD.

Johnson, W.L., ed. (1986) *Directory of Special Programs for Minority Group Members: Career Information Services, Employment Skills Banks, Financial Aid Sources.* 4th ed. Garrett Park, MD: Garrett Park Press.

Kastre, M.F., N. Rodriquez and A.G. Edwards. (1993) *The Minority Career Guide.* Princeton, NJ: Peterson's Guides.

Swan, R.V., ed. (1993) *Financial Aid for Minority Students.* Garrett Park, MD: Garrett Park Press.

Need for Additional Experience or Education

National Society for Internships and Experiential Education. *The National Directory of Internships.* Raleigh, NC.

Peterson Guides. *Internships.* Princeton, NJ.

U.S. Department of Education. *Higher Education Opportunities for Minorities and Women.* Washington, DC.

Networking

Boe, A. and B. Younger. (1989) *Is Your Net Working? A Complete Guide to Building Contacts and Career Visibility.* New York: Wiley.

Krannich, R.L., and C.R. Krannich. (1993) *The New Network Your Way to Job and Career Success.* 2nd ed. Manassas Park, VA: Impact Publications.

Roane, S. (1988) *How to Work a Room.* New York: Warner Books.

Vila, D., and S. Vila. (1992) *Power Networking: 55 Secrets for Personal and Professional Success.* Austin, TX: Mountain Harbor Publications.

Non-Profits

Cowan, J. (1991) *Good Works: A Guide to Careers in Social Change.* River Forest, IL: Planning/Communications.

Eberts, Marjorie and Margaret Gisler (1991) *Careers for Good Samaritans and Other Humanitarian Types.* Lincolnwood, IL: VGM Career Horizons.

Lauber, D. (1993) *Non-Profits Job Finder.* River Forest, IL: Planning/ Communications.

Paradis, Adrian (1994) *Opportunities in Nonprofit Careers.* Lincolnwood, IL: VGM Career Horizons.

Smith, D.C., ed. (1990) *Great Careers: The Fourth of July Guide to Careers, Internships, and Volunteer Opportunities in the Non-Profit Sector.* River Forest, IL: Planning/ Communications.

Office Politics

Durbin, A. (1990) *Winning Office Politics.* Englewood Cliffs, NJ: Prentice Hall.

McDermott, L. (1993) *Caught in the Middle: How to Survive and Thrive in Today's Management Squeeze.* Englewood Cliffs, NJ: Prentice Hall.

People Over Age 50

Anthony R.J., and G. Roe. (1991) *Over 40 and Looking for Work? A Guide for the Unemployed, Underemployed, and Unhappily Employed.* Holbrook, MA: Bob Adams.

Bird, C. (1992) *Second Careers: New Ways to Work After 50.* Boston: Little, Brown.

Brown, Duane (1994) *How to Find Your New Career Upon Retirement.* Lincolnwood, IL: VGM Career Horizons.

Connor, R. (1992) *Cracking the Over 50 Job Market.* New York: Plume.

Goldstein, R., and D. Landau. (1990) *Fortysomething: Claiming the Power and the Passion of Your Mid-Life Years.* Los Angeles: Tarcher.

Jones, R. (1980) *The Big Switch: New Careers, New Lives After 35.* New York: McGraw-Hill.

People with Disabilities

Allen, J.G. (1994) *Successful Job Search Strategies for the Disabled: Understanding the ADA*. New York: Wiley.
Bolles, R.N. (1991) *Job Hunting Tips for the So Called "Handicapped" or People Who Have Disabilities*. Berkeley, CA: Ten Speed Press.

Personal Growth

Burns, D.D. (1981) *Feeling Good: The New Mood Therapy*. New York: Signet.
Hyatt, C. and L. Gottlieb. (1988) *When Smart People Fail: Rebuilding Yourself for Success*. New York: Penguin Books.
Ilardo, J. (1992) *Risk Taking for Personal Growth*. Oakland, CA: New Harbinger.
Jeffers, S. (1987) *Feel the Fear and Do It Anyway*. New York: Pocket Books.
Preston, J. (1992) *You Can Beat Depression: A Guide to Recovery*. San Luis Obispo, CA: Impact Publishers.
Viscott, D. (1977) *Risking*. New York: Pocket Books.

Relocating

Bastress, F. (1993) *The New Relocating Spouse's Guide to Employment*. Chevy Chase, MD: Woodley Publications.
Saari, P., and D.L. Dupuis, eds. (1989) *Cities of the United States: A Compilation of Current Information on Economic, Cultural, Geographic, and Social Conditions*. 1st ed. Detroit, MI: Gale Research, Inc. Vol. 1, The South; Vol. 2, The West; Vol. 3, The Midwest; Vol. 4, The Northeast.
Thomas, G.S. (1990) *The Rating Guide to Life in America's Small Cities*. New York: Prometheus Books.
Worldwide Chamber of Commerce Directory. Annual. Loveland, CO.

Researching Career Fields and Employers

Crowther, Karmen N.T. (1993) *Researching Your Way to a Good Job*. New York: Wiley.
Daniells, L.M. (1993) *Business Information Sources*. 3rd ed. Berkeley, CA: University of California Press.
Gale Research. (1993–94) *Encyclopedia of Business Information Sources*. 9th ed. Detroit.
Harkavy, M.D., and the Philip Lief Group. (1989) *The 100 Best Companies to Work for in America*. New York: Doubleday.
Krantz, L. (1992) *The Jobs Rated Almanac*. New York: Pharos Books.
Lavin, M.R. (1992) *Business Information: How to Find It, How to Use It*. 2nd ed. Phoenix, AZ: Oryx Press.
Lombardo, J., and A. Lombardo. (1986) *The Job Belt: The Fifty Best Places in America for High Quality Employment, Today and in the Future*. New York: Penguin Books.
Most, J.A. (1993) *The Job Seeker's Guide to Top 100 Employers*. Detroit: Visible Ink Press.
U.S. Department of Commerce. *U.S. Industrial Outlook*. Annual. Indianapolis, IN: JIST Works.

Resumes and Cover Letters

Beatty, R.H. (1989) *The Perfect Cover Letter.* New York: Wiley.

Block, Deborah Perlmutter. (1993) *How to Write a Winning Resume.* 3rd ed. Lincolnwood, IL: VGM Career Horizons.

Jackson, T. (1991) *The Perfect Resume.* Garden City, NY: Anchor Press/Doubleday.

Krannich, R.L., and C.R. Krannich. (1992) *High Impact Resumes and Cover Letters.* Manassas Park, VA: Impact Publications.

Langhorne, K.E., and E.R. Martin (1993) *Cover Letters They Don't Forget.* Lincolnwood, IL: VGM Career Horizons.

Parker, Y. (1988) *The Resume Catalog: 200 Damn Good Examples.* Berkeley, CA: Ten Speed Press.

Provenzano, S. (1994) *Slam Dunk Resumes.* Lincolnwood, IL: VGM Career Horizons.

Swanson, D. (1990) *The Resume Solution.* Indianapolis, IN: JIST Works.

VGM Career Horizons. *VGM Professional Resume Series.* Lincolnwood, IL.

Yate, M. (1991) *Cover Letters That Knock'em Dead.* Holbrook, MA: Bob Adams.

_____. (1988) *Resumes That Knock'em Dead.* Holbrook, MA: Bob Adams.

Salary Information

College Placement Council. *CPC Salary Survey.* Annual. Bethlehem, PA: College Placement Council.

Reddy, M.A. (1993) *American Salaries and Wages Survey; Statistical Data Derived from More Than 300 Government, Business and News Sources.* Detroit: Gale Research, Inc.

U.S. Bureau of Labor Statistics. *Area Wage Survey.* Annual. Washington, DC.

U.S. Department of Labor. *Employment and Earnings.* Monthly. Washington, DC.

_____. *Occupational Compensation Survey.* Annual. Washington, DC.

Wright, J.W. (1993) *The American Almanac of Jobs and Salaries.* New York: Avon Books.

Starting Your Own Business

Bangs, D.H. (1992) *The Business Planning Guide.* Dover, NH: Upstart.

Berle, G. (1990) *Planning and Forming Your Company.* New York: Wiley.

Davidson, J.P. (1988) *Avoiding the Pitfalls of Starting Your Own Business.* New York: Sahpolsky Books.

Kamoroff, B. (1988) *Small Time Operator.* Laytonville, CA: Bell Springs.

J.K. Lasser Tax Institute. (1994) *How to Run a Small Business.* New York: St. Martin's Press.

Matthews, John R. (1993) *The Beginning Entrepreneur.* Lincolnwood, IL: VGM Career Horizons.

Maul, L.R., and D.C. Mayfield. (1992) *The Entrepreneur's Road Map to Business Success.* Alexandria, VA: Saxton River.

Peterson, C.D. (1988) *How to Leave Your Job and Buy a Business of Your Own.* New York: McGraw-Hill.

Pollan, S., and M. Levine. (1990) *The Field Guide to Starting a Business.* New York: Simon and Schuster.

Stevens, M. (1988) *The Macmillan Small Business Handbook.* New York: MacMillan.

Franchising

Bard, R., and S. Henderson. (1987) *Own Your Own Franchise: Everything You Need to Know About the Best Opportunities in America.* Reading, MA: Addison-Wesley.

Bond, R.E. (1989) *The Sourcebook of Franchise Opportunities.* Homewood, IL: Dow Jones-Irwin.

Foste, D.L. (1994) *The Complete Franchise Book.* 2nd ed. Rocklin, CA: Prima.

Sterling. (1991) Franchise Opportunities. 22nd ed. New York.

Consulting

Brown, P.C. (1993) *Jumping the Job Track: Security, Satisfaction and Success as an Independent Consultant.* New York: Crown Trade Paperback.

Cohen, W.A. (1991) *How to Make It Big as a Consultant.* 2nd ed. New York: AMACOM.

Work from Home Business

Arden, L. (1992) *The Work at Home Sourcebook.* 4th ed. Boulder, CO: Live Oak.

Edwards, P., and S. Edwards. (1991) *Best Home Businesses of the 90's.* New York: Tarcher/Putnam.

_____. (1990) *Working from Home: Everything You Need to Know about Living and Working Under the Same Roof.* New York: Tarcher/Putnam.

Glenn, R. (1993) *The 10 Best Opportunities for Starting a Home Business Today.* Boulder, CO: New Careers Center.

Kern, C.S., and T.H. Wolfgram. (1994) *How to Run Your Own Home Business.* Lincolnwood, IL: VGM Career Horizons.

Temporary Work

Lewis, W., and N. Schuman. (1993) *The Temporary Worker's Handbook.* New York: American Management Association.

Mendenhall, K. (1993) *Making the Most of Temporary Employment.* Cincinnati, OH: Betterway Books.

O'Connell-Justice, P. (1994) *The Temp Track: Make One of the Hottest Job Trends of the '90s Work for You.* Princeton, NJ: Peterson's Guides.

Thrailkill, D. (1994) *Temporary by Choice.* Hawthorne, NJ: Career Press.

Tests and Testing Resources

Bennett, G.K., H.G. Seashore, and A.G. Wesman. *Differential Aptitude Test (DAT).* New York: The Psychological Corporation.

Cattell, R.B. *Sixteen Personality Factor (16PF) Questionnaire.* Savoy, IL: Institute for Personality and Ability Testing.

Gough, H.G. *California Psychological Inventory (CPI).* Palo Alto, CA: Consulting Psychologists Press.

Hammer, A.L., and G.P. Macdaid. (1992) *Myers-Briggs Type Indicator Career Report Manual.* Palo Also, CA: Consulting Psychologists Press.

Harrington, T.F., and A.J. O'Shea. (1988) *CDM Interpretive Folder.* Circle Pines, MN: American Guidance Service.

Holland, J.L. *The Self-Directed Search (SDS)*. Odessa, FL: Psychological Assessment Resources (PAR).

Johansson, C.B. *The Career Assessment Inventory (CAI)*. Minneapolis: NCS Professional Assessment Service.

Knapp, L.F., and R.R. Knapp. (1976) *CAPS: Career Ability Placement Survey*. San Diego, CA: Edits.

Maze, M. *Eureka Skills Inventory*. Richmond, CA: EUREKA the California Career Information System.

Myers, I.B., and K.C. Briggs. *The Myers-Briggs Type Indicator*. Palo Alto, CA: Consulting Psychologists Press.

Nelson, D.B., and G.R. Low. *Personal Skills Map (PSM)*. Oakland, CA: MMHH The Management Mentors.

Strong, Jr., E.K., J.C. Hansen, and D.P. Campbell. *The Strong Interest Inventory*. Palo Alto, CA: Consulting Psychologists Press.

Tieger, P.D., and B. Barron-Tieger. (1992) *Do What You Are: Discover the Perfect Career for You Through the Secrets of Personality Type*. Boston: Little, Brown.

United States Employment Service. *USES General Aptitude Test Battery (GATB)*. Washington, DC.

Unemployment

Beyer, C., D. Pike, and L. McGovern. (1993) *Surviving Unemployment*. New York: Henry Holt.

Jud, B. (1993) *Coping with Unemployment*. Avon, CT: Marketing Direction.

Women

Jackman, M., and S. Waggoner. (1991) *Star Teams, Key Players: Successful Career Strategies for Women in the 1990s*. New York: Ballantine Books.

Morgan, H., and K. Tucker. (1991) *Companies that Care*. New York: Simon and Schuster.

Mulroy, E.A., ed. (1988) *Women as Single Parents: Confronting Institutional Barriers in the Courts, the Workplace, and the Housing Market*. Dover, MA: Auburn House Publishing.

Nivens, B. (1989) *Careers for Women Without College Degrees*. New York: McGraw-Hill.

Olmstead, B., and S. Smith. (1989) *Creating a Flexible Workplace: How to Select and Manage Alternative Work Options*. New York: American Management Association.

White, J. (1992) *A Few Good Women: Breaking the Barriers to Top Management*. Englewood Cliffs, NJ: Prentice Hall.

Women's Equity Action League. (1987) *Better Late Than Never: Financial Aid for Re-Entry Women Seeking Education and Training*. Washington, DC: WEAL.

Zeitz, B., and L. Dusky. (1989) *The Best Companies for Women*. New York: Simon and Schuster.

APPENDIX C:

••••••••••••••••••••••

MENTAL HEALTH PROFESSIONALS

Below is a list of the titles of various mental health organizations that can provide referrals in your area. There are a number of titles mental health professionals use. Here, these titles are organized by the groups with which they're associated. For more information on specific credentials, contact the relevant association.

American Counseling Association (ACA)
5999 Stevenson Ave.
Alexandria, VA 22304
Licensed Professional Counselor (LPC)
Licensed Clinical Professional Counselor (LCPC)
Certified Professional Counselor (CPC)
National Certified Counselor (NCC)

National Board of Certified Counselors (NBCC)
3-D Terrace Way
Greensboro, NC 27403
Administers certification for National Certified Counselor and Certified Mental Health Counselor

American Mental Health Counselor Association (AMHCA)
5999 Stevenson Ave.
Alexandria, VA 22304
Certified Clinical Mental Health Counselor (CCMHC)

American Association for Marriage and Family Therapy (AAMFT)
1100 17th St. N.W. (10th fl.)
Washington, DC 20036
Clinical Member of the American Association for Marriage and Family Therapy (AAMFT)

American Association of Pastoral Counselors (AAPC)
9504A Lee Highway
Fairfax, VA 22031
Fellow of American Association of Pastoral Counselors (AAPC)

National Association of Social Workers (NASW)
750 First St. N.E., Suite 700
Washington, DC 20002

Academy of Certified Social Workers (ACSW)
Licensed Social Worker (LSW)
Licensed Clinical Social Worker (LCSW)

American Psychological Association
750 First St.
Washington, DC 20002
Counseling Psychologist
Clinical Psychologist
Registered Psychologist

American Psychiatry Association
1400 K. St., N.W.
Washington, DC 20005
Psychiatrist

All of the professionals, listed above, should be capable of dealing with issues related to fears, perfectionism, procrastination, anxiety, stress and depression that can accompany career and life transitions, as well as related relationship issues.

Certification and Licensure

Certification generally has less stringent requirements than licensing. However, not all states provide licenses. Whoever you choose to work with, be sure that they have the appropriate professional qualification. These professionals have made a commitment to continuing education and high ethical standards.

Where to Find Mental Health Professionals

These are the possible work settings of mental health professionals:

- independent private practice or group practice (group in this context indicates a partnership of more than one professional counselor)
- health maintenance organizations (HMOs)
- employee assistance programs (EAPs)
- community mental health centers
- social service agencies
- community colleges (most serve non-students)
- universities (check with regards to non-students)
- hospitals
- pastoral counseling centers and churches

Range of Fees

A typical counselor, located in a major urban setting, will have a per-hour fee ranging from $50 to $90 (averaging $70-$75).

Some of the above mental health professionals may use a sliding scale to determine their fees, especially pastoral counselors and some social workers, which is based on your income and ability to pay.

Psychologists' fees can range from $60 to $115 per hour, averaging $85-$100 per hour. Psychiatrist fees average $125 per hour.

Your HMO or related insurance may provide for counseling services.

Usually the professionals who are eligible under insurance plans are licensed clinical social workers, licensed psychologists, and psychiatrists. Check with your health insurance provider for further information.

INDEX
•••••••••••••

VGM CAREER BOOKS

CAREER DIRECTORIES
Careers Encyclopedia
Dictionary of Occupational
  Titles
Occupational Outlook
  Handbook

CAREERS FOR
Animal Lovers
Bookworms
Computer Buffs
Crafty People
Culture Lovers
Environmental Types
Film Buffs
Foreign Language
  Aficionados
Good Samaritans
Gourmets
History Buffs
Kids at Heart
Nature Lovers
Night Owls
Number Crunchers
Shutterbugs
Sports Nuts
Travel Buffs

CAREERS IN
Accounting; Advertising;
Business; Child Care;
Communications;
Computers; Education;
Engineering; Finance;
Government; Health Care;
High Tech; Journalism; Law;
Marketing; Medicine;
Science; Social &
Rehabilitation Services

CAREER PLANNING
Admissions Guide to
  Selective Business Schools
Beginning Entrepreneur
Career Planning &
  Development for College
  Students & Recent
  Graduates
Career Change

Careers Checklists
Cover Letters They Don't
  Forget
Executive Job Search
  Strategies
Guide to Basic Cover Letter
  Writing
Guide to Basic Resume
  Writing
Joyce Lain Kennedy's Career
  book
Out of Uniform
Slam Dunk Resumes
Successful Interviewing for
  College Seniors

CAREER PORTRAITS
Animals
Music
Sports
Teaching

GREAT JOBS FOR
English Majors
Foreign Language Majors
History Majors
Psychology Majors

HOW TO
Approach an Advertising
  Agency and Walk Away
  with the Job You Want
Bounce Back Quickly After
  Losing Your Job
Change Your Career
Choose the Right Career
Find Your New Career Upon
  Retirement
Get & Keep Your First Job
Get Hired Today
Get into the Right Law
  School
Have a Winning Job Interview
Hit the Ground Running in
  Your New Job
Improve Your Study Skills
Jump Start a Stalled Career
Land a Better Job

Launch Your Career in TV
  News
Make the Right Career Moves
Market Your College Degree
Move from College into a
  Secure Job
Negotiate the Raise You
  Deserve
Prepare a *Curriculum Vitae*
Prepare for College
Run Your Own Home
  Business
Succeed in College
Succeed in High School
Write a Winning Resume
Write Successful Cover
  Letters
Write Term Papers & Reports
Write Your College
  Application Essay

OPPORTUNITIES IN
This extensive series provides
detailed information on
nearly 150 individual career
fields.

RESUMES FOR
Advertising Careers
Banking and Financial
  Careers
Business Management
  Careers
College Students &
  Recent Graduates
Communications Careers
Education Careers
Engineering Careers
Environmental Careers
Health and Medical Careers
High School Graduates
High Tech Careers
Midcareer Job Changes
Sales and Marketing Careers
Scientific and Technical
  Careers
Social Service Careers
The First-Time Job Hunter

 VGM Career Horizons
a division of *NTC Publishing Group*
4255 West Touhy Avenue
Lincolnwood, Illinois 60646–1975